Higher Education and the Carceral State

Higher Education and the Carceral State: Transforming Together explores the diversity of ways in which university faculty and students are intervening in the system of mass incarceration through the development of transformative arts and educational programs for students in correctional institutions.

Demonstrating the ways that higher education can intervene in and disrupt the deeply traumatic experience of incarceration and shift the embedded social-emotional cycles that lead to recidivism, this book is both inspiration and guide for those seeking to create and sustain programs as well as to educate students about the types of programs universities bring to prisons.

From arts workshops and educational courses to degree-granting programs, individuals and communities across multiple disciplines in higher education are actively breaking the cycle of shame and division in mass incarceration through direct engagement. This book explores the inspiring, innovative, and change-making initiatives in carceral spaces—from arts workshops and educational courses to degree granting programs—through the lens of faculty, artists, scholars, students, and administrators. Readers will learn the diverse ways in which these interventions and partnerships can take shape and the life changing impacts that they have on all those involved, in particular students who are incarcerated. The book includes authors with lived experience of incarceration throughout.

Section I highlights the voices of students who are currently or formerly incarcerated, while **Section II** addresses diverse collaborations through and across systems of corrections and education. **Section III** features the voices of teaching artists, while **Section IV** includes those that start and lead these programs, offering roadmaps for others interested in engaging in this transformative work.

Annie Buckley is the founder and director of Prison Arts Collective, an internationally recognized statewide Arts in Corrections program that has brought multidisciplinary arts classes and arts facilitator trainings to over 7,000 participants in 16 state prisons across California since 2013. In addition, she is the founding director of VISTA (Valuing Incarcerated Scholars through Academia), a new BA degree-granting program at San Diego State University, where she is also a professor and associate dean. Buckley is an artist, curator, and widely published author whose work has appeared in leading international contemporary art publications, including *Artforum*, *Art in America*, the *Huffington Post*, and she is an editor at large with the *Los Angeles Review of Books*, where she also wrote the series, "Art Inside" about facilitating arts programming in correctional settings.

Higher Education and the Carceral State

Transforming Together

Edited by Annie Buckley

LONDON AND NEW YORK

Designed cover image: Cover image by Peter Merts, 2018; courtesy of the California Arts Council.

First published 2024
by Routledge
4 Park Square, Milton Park, Abingdon, Oxon OX14 4RN

and by Routledge
605 Third Avenue, New York, NY 10158

Routledge is an imprint of the Taylor & Francis Group, an informa business

© 2024 selection and editorial matter, Annie Buckley; individual chapters, the contributors

The right of Annie Buckley to be identified as the author of the editorial material, and of the authors for their individual chapters, has been asserted in accordance with sections 77 and 78 of the Copyright, Designs and Patents Act 1988.

All rights reserved. No part of this book may be reprinted or reproduced or utilised in any form or by any electronic, mechanical, or other means, now known or hereafter invented, including photocopying and recording, or in any information storage or retrieval system, without permission in writing from the publishers.

Trademark notice: Product or corporate names may be trademarks or registered trademarks, and are used only for identification and explanation without intent to infringe.

British Library Cataloguing-in-Publication Data
A catalogue record for this book is available from the British Library

Library of Congress Cataloging-in-Publication Data
Names: Buckley, Annie, editor.
Title: Higher education and the carceral state : transforming together / edited by Annie Buckley.
Description: Abingdon, Oxon ; New York, NY : Routledge, 2024. | Includes bibliographical references and index.
Identifiers: LCCN 2023044845 (print) | LCCN 2023044846 (ebook) | ISBN 9781032495620 (hardback) | ISBN 9781032495606 (paperback) | ISBN 9781003394426 (ebook)
Subjects: LCSH: Prisoners--Education (Higher)--United States--Case studies. | Education, Higher--Aims and objectives--United States.
Classification: LCC HV8883.3.U5 H53 2024 (print) | LCC HV8883.3.U5 (ebook) | DDC 365/.6660973--dc23/eng/20231228
LC record available at https://lccn.loc.gov/2023044845
LC ebook record available at https://lccn.loc.gov/2023044846

ISBN: 978-1-032-49562-0 (hbk)
ISBN: 978-1-032-49560-6 (pbk)
ISBN: 978-1-003-39442-6 (ebk)

DOI: 10.4324/9781003394426

Typeset in Sabon
by KnowledgeWorks Global Ltd.

Contents

List of Images	*viii*
List of Contributors	*xi*
Foreword	*xvii*
Introduction from Editor, Annie Buckley	*xix*
Acknowledgments	*xxii*

SECTION I
Voices of Students   1

1 Scheduled Conflict   3
   ALEXANDER BOLLING

2 Transformation and Redemption: A Personal Narrative from
   a Position of Lived Experience   12
   GINNY EMIKO OSHIRO

3 Transforming Lives Through Prison Higher Education   21
   JEFFREY STEIN

4 The Freedom & Captivity Curriculum Project   31
   LINDA SMALL

5 Humanizing the Numbers: A Photographic Collaboration   42
   JAMAL BIGGS AND ISAAC WINGFIELD

SECTION II
Collaborating in and through the System   57

6 Scaling Walls: Dismantling Asymmetries Through
   Empowering Song   59
   ANDRÉ DE QUADROS, WAYLAND "X" COLEMAN,
   AND KRYSTAL MORIN

vi   *Contents*

7 "Disappearing Acts" and Education as the Practice of
   Freedom: Feminist Pedagogy in Carceral Spaces   67
   LAURA E. CIOLKOWSKI

8 The Brutal Stories That Connect Us   76
   JOSHUA FERNANDEZ

9 Matters of Life and Death: Art, Education, and Activism on
   Death Row   85
   ROBIN PARIS, TOM WILLIAMS, AND BARBARA YONTZ

10 An Achingly Realized Sunset: The Importance of Prison
    Creative Writing   94
    JASON KAHLER

11 Transcommunal Peace, Cooperation, and Respect for
    Diversity: A University/Prison Multi-Partnership Approach   104
    JOHN BROWN CHILDS, FLORA LU, AND SARAH WOODSIDE BURY

SECTION III
Voices of Teaching Artists and Scholars   115

12 Writing About Art   117
    DUSTON SPEAR

13 Beyond This Door: Photographic Vision and Carceral Experience   123
    EVAN HUME

14 Why French?: Fear and Freedom in Stepping Outside
    Our Languages   134
    CECELIA RAMSEY

15 Pushing Back/Pushing Forward: Embracing the Margins
    to Build Non-Punitive Learning Environments in Canadian
    Correctional Facilities   144
    NICOLE PATRIE

16 Excursion and Return: Exploring Transformative Texts,
    Great Questions, and the Human Experience in the Prison
    Classroom   155
    DALE BROWN

Contents vii

SECTION IV
Changemaking and Coalition Building   167

17 The Poem. The Painting. Us   169
    KYES STEVENS

18 Building Bridges Through Prison-University Partnerships   177
    EMMA HUGHES

19 Arts Research in Carceral Settings: Prison Arts Collective   189
    BRIAN L. HEISTERKAMP, BRYANT JOACHIM JACKSON-GREEN,
      GINNY EMIKO OSHIRO, AND ANNIE BUCKLEY

20 Reimagining Our Futures: The Beginning, Middle, and End
    of the Digital Higher Education Journey for Incarcerated
    Learners   198
    HELEN FARLEY AND STEPHEN SEYMOUR

21 Structuring the Conduit: Expanding Prison-University
    Partnerships Through the Readers' Circle   207
    KEZIAH POOLE AND ROWAN A. BAYNE

22 An Octopus in the Scaffolding: Ten Years of Prison
    Arts Collective   215
    ANNIE BUCKLEY

    Index   227

List of Images

Chapter 3

3.1   Dr. Taffany Lim and cohort 1 and 2 graduates on the prison yard at Lancaster (October 5, 2021). Photo Credit: R. Husky   22

3.2   Jeffrey Stein, cohort 1 member, at master's graduation (May, 2022). Photo Credit: E. Flores   23

Chapter 5

5.1   Paint over photograph. By Jamal Biggs, 2016   43

5.2   The Creator. I came to prison with blood on my hands; I will leave with paint on them. By Johnnie Trice, 2015   44

5.3   Choices. By M, 2015   44

5.4   My children to this day do not really understand why I cannot come home. Each and every time they visit, when it's time to leave they cry, which breaks me down on the inside. My children and family no longer trust the police or the justice system, they have experienced firsthand the injustice that has been done to me. I constantly remind them that all police are not corrupted, but it's hard for them to trust police when I'm still fighting to get out of prison for a crime I am actually and factually innocent of. By LaVone, 2016   47

5.5   Being aware of how college and learning helped change my thinking, I now try to help spark that change in others by working as a tutor, helping other prisoners obtain their GED. The greatest reward is in helping individuals get their GED who didn't believe they could, for whatever reason. Working with them for weeks and months and seeing that surprised look on their face and joy in their heart when they finally get the news, "You've passed!" is priceless. By Jamal Biggs, 2016   48

List of Images ix

5.6	As I continue to make progress in life, I am determined to leave my bad choice behind me. I am now prepared to become a pillar in the community. I have truly outgrown confinement. By Corey, 2017	49
5.7	Anti-mug$hot. By Sankofa 360°, 2019	52
5.8	My father, Lensey Earl Mason, was killed on August 16, 1974. I gaze at the scene where his life was tragically taken. At 4 years old, August 16, 1974 was the day I lost it all. By Connell Howard, 2018	52
5.9	Tired of the Chaos. By DLG, 2019	53
5.10	Loss of identity. By June, 2018	54
5.11	I am not a number. My name is José Burgos, I was born in Ponce, Puerto Rico. I am a brother, an uncle, a friend, and a mentor. I am not a number. By José Burgos, 2018	54

Chapter 9

9.1	Tyrone Chalmers, self-portrait, from the series Our Town, organized by Bryce McCloud, 2014, print. Funded by the Nashville Metro Arts Commission	89
9.2	Life after death and elsewhere, Apexart, New York, NY, September 10–October 24, 2015. Courtesy of Apexart NYC © 2015	91

Chapter 11

11.1	US incarceration and imagining abolition panel at the Practical Activism Conference at UC Santa Cruz in 2023. Credit: Flora Lu	105
11.2	Santa Cruz Barrios Unidos' interactive prison cell at the 2023 UC Santa Cruz Practical Activism Conference. Credit: Flora Lu	105
11.3	UCSC students of the first transcommunal peacemaking class in 2019, in front of Soledad Correctional Training Facility. Credit: Flora Lu	111
11.4	Meeting of the joint UCSC/CTF transcommunality class in 2019. Credit: Nane Alejandrez	112

Chapter 13

13.1	Photograph by Steven Foernzler	127
13.2	Photograph by Adam Clendenning	128
13.3	Photograph by Nathaniel Dodson	129
13.4	Photograph by Conor Jackson	130
13.5	Photograph by Joshua Fisher	131
13.6	Photograph by Jarrell King	132

x *List of Images*

Chapter 22

22.1 "Redemption," a collaborative installation by artists at the California Institution for Men, photo by Ashley Woods, 2017   216

22.2 "Redemption," a collaborative performance by artists at the California Institution for Men, photo by Ashley Woods, 2017   216

22.3 Multidisciplinary arts classes are facilitated by student teachers and faculty from state universities at prisons in California, photo by Peter Merts, 2017   219

22.4 Origami art created by Lyle, artist participating in PAC programming, photo by Ashley Woods, 2017   221

22.5 Peer facilitator with PAC installation part of a collaborative artwork, photo by Peter Merts, 2017   223

22.6 Student teachers lead a workshop for participants at an Arts in Corrections conference, photo by Peter Merts, 2017   224

22.7 Author with PAC participants and student teachers with a collaborative mandala, photo by Peter Merts, 2016   225

List of Contributors

Rowan Bayne teaches in the Writing Program at the University of Southern California, where he is also Faculty Director of the Readers' Circle. He holds a PhD in English from the University of Chicago.

Jamal Biggs has been incarcerated with a Life Without Parole sentence since 1990, at the age of 19. His time in prison has been spent educating and bettering himself, working as an artist, as well as teaching and mentoring younger prisoners. He participated in *Humanize the Numbers'* 2016 cohort.

Alexander Bolling is a writer and an advocate for education in the carceral system. Born and raised in Boston, Massachusetts, he lived through the trials of poverty and the trauma of violence. Alexander has found solace in the transformative capacity of learning since being sentenced to an extended term in prison in the late 2000s. In 2022, Alexander graduated summa cum laude from Emerson College with a BA in Media, Literature and Culture. In the same year, Alexander was published in *College Behind the Wall: Why and How We Teach College in Prison*.

Dr. Larry Brewster is Professor Emeritus and former dean at the University of San Francisco. Before joining USF, he was academic dean at Menlo College, and prior to that, Dean of the School of Liberal Studies and Public Affairs at Golden Gate University, and professor and associate dean at San Jose State University. He regularly consults in public policy and program evaluation and is author of journal articles and books, including *The Public Agenda: Issues in American Politics*, 5th edition, Wadsworth & Company, 2004; *A Primer of California Politics*, 2nd edition, Wadsworth & Company, 2004; and *Paths of Discovery: Art Practice and Its Impact in California Prisons*, 2nd edition, Createspace & Company, 2015.

Dale Brown is the Manager of Humanities Outreach in the Center for the Humanities at Western Michigan University, where he is also an Interdisciplinary Studies doctoral student. He is the founder and director of WMU's Higher Education for the Justice-Involved Program, for his work on which he was named a K. Patricia Cross Future Leader by AAC&U

xii *List of Contributors*

in 2022. Dale has published in *Philosophy of Education* and the *Journal of Prison Education and Reentry*. As a first-generation college student who grew up in poverty, Dale writes about the humanizing and transformative potential of higher education for all.

Annie Buckley is a Professor of Visual Studies and the Director of the Institute for the Arts, Humanities, and Social Justice at San Diego State University (SDSU), as well as the founder/director and Principal Investigator of Prison Arts Collective (PAC).. Buckley is the author of over 200 essays and reviews on contemporary art in leading global publications and is a contributing editor to the *Los Angeles Review of Books* where she has written a series of essays about teaching art in prisons. Her cross-disciplinary research is focused on expanding access to the arts and embraces participatory art, creative and critical writing, and community-based arts. She has received numerous grants and awards at the state and federal levels for her work with Prison Arts Collective over the past 10 years. Buckley is a graduate of U.C. Berkeley with an MFA from Otis College of Art and Design.

Sarah Woodside Bury is Senior Director for College Student Life for John R. Lewis College and College Nine, University of California, Santa Cruz. She earned her BA in Sociology from the University of California, San Diego and her Masters in Student Affairs in Higher Education from Colorado State University.

John Brown Childs is a Professor Emeritus of Sociology at the University of California, Santa Cruz. He is the 2022 recipient of the Constantine Panunzio Distinguished Emeriti Award. He is an enrolled member of the Indigenous "Massachuset-Ponkapoag Tribe" on his mother's side and is of African-Madagascan descent on his father's side.

Laura Ciolkowski is Senior Lecturer in the Department of Women, Gender, Sexuality Studies at the University of Massachusetts, Amherst, and co-founder of the UMass-Amherst Prison Education Initiative. Her work lies at the intersection of feminist pedagogy, literary studies, and critical prison studies. In 2021, she was awarded the Provost's Distinguished Community Engagement Award for Teaching in recognition of her work in prison education. In 2023, she was awarded the College Outstanding Teacher Award.

Wayland "X" Coleman was born in Birmingham, Alabama, on January 18, 1978. His family was very poor. To escape the poverty of the south, they moved to Massachusetts, in 1988. At age 11, he was given a 1-year scholarship to the Worcester Art Museum, because of drawings he had created as a child. While he attended the Art Museum, he was introduced to hustling in the streets. At the time of writing, he is an incarcerated activist and organizer. He is a collaborator with Boston University's Race, Prison, Justice Arts and has appeared as a speaker with The Choral Commons.

List of Contributors xiii

André de Quadros is a professor of music at Boston University with affiliations in African, African American, Asian, Jewish, Muslim studies, Prison Education, Forced Migration, and Antiracist Research. As an artist, scholar, and human rights activist, he has worked in over 40 countries in the most diverse settings including professional ensembles, projects with prisons, psychosocial rehabilitation, refugees, and victims of sexual violence, torture, and trauma. His work crosses race and mass incarceration, peacebuilding, forced migration, LGBTQ+ folx, and Islamic culture. In 2019, he was a Distinguished Academic Visitor at the University of Cambridge.

Helen Farley is the Director of Criminal Justice at the University of Canterbury | Te Whare Wānanga o Waitaha. She is interested in prisons and corrections, with her research focussed on prison education and training, technology for learning in prisons, dynamic security, and neurodiversities in the prison population. Before coming to UC, Helen worked for Ara Poutama Aotearoa Department of Corrections, overseeing prison education across the South Island's 5 prisons. Helen is the President of the Australasian Corrections Education Association, and is part of the Expert Working Group on Technologies for Prisoner Rehabilitation for the United Nations Interregional Crime and Justice Research Institute.

Stephen Seymour's current professional role coordinates the University of Southern Queensland (UniSQ) Incarcerated Students, Military-Connected Students, and Elite Athletes. The role builds on the results from the award-winning and successful HEPPP "Making the Connection" project. Stephen is currently the secretary for the Australasian Corrections Education Association and is undertaking Doctoral studies at UniSQ. Before joining the USQ team in mid-2014, Stephen spent ten years in the Vocational Education Sector, working closely with clients and stakeholders as an acting Director for Business Development and Industry Engagement. Stephen also has professional experience in agri-business, aviation, and Not-for-Profit Sector in cross-cultural contexts, specifically in economic and community development in central and southern Africa, primarily in the Congo and Zimbabwe.

Joshua Fernandez is an anti-racist organizer, father, husband, runner, fighter, English professor, and a writer, whose stories have appeared in Spin Magazine, the Sacramento Bee, The Hard Times, and several alternative news weeklies. His memoir, *The Hands That Crafted the Bomb: The Making of a Lifelong Antifascist* is forthcoming from PM Press.

Brian L. Heisterkamp (PhD, Arizona State University) is professor in the Department of Communication Studies at California State University, San Bernardino. His research interests involve the relationship between social action and social structures and the manner in which conversation can be examined to understand mediator behavior, conflict, and interpersonal relationships, particularly gay and lesbian relationships. Currently, he is examining the role of memorable messages in managing work-life tension and the impact of arts-based programming on the well-being of those who are incarcerated.

xiv *List of Contributors*

Emma Hughes, PhD, is a Professor of Criminology at California State University, Fresno (Fresno State). Her research focuses on education programs in prisons and the role of the voluntary sector in prisons. Publications include the book *Education in Prison: Studying through Distance Learning* (2012, Routledge). She co-ordinates Fresno State's Bachelor's Degree program in two prisons in California, and serves as Executive Director of Fresno State's Project Rebound, a support program for formerly incarcerated students. She earned her PhD from Birmingham City University (UK), and her MPhil in Criminology from the University of Cambridge (UK). She has a BA from Stanford University

Evan Hume is an artist living in Ames, Iowa, where he is the Assistant Professor of Photography at Iowa State University. He was previously the Visiting Lecturer of Photography at the University of Notre Dame and an instructor for Holy Cross College's Moreau College Initiative at Westville Correctional Facility in Westville, Indiana.

Bryant Jackson-Green is a doctoral student in Social Ecology and a JD candidate at the University of California, Irvine. His research lies at the intersection of criminal justice policy and organizational theory, focusing on how organizations perceive and make decisions about social risk. Using mixed methods, his work highlights the importance of law and organizations in a larger social-ecological context. Bryant is a Robert Wood Johnson Foundation Health Policy Research Scholar.

Jason Kahler is a teacher, writer, and researcher from Southeast Michigan. He earned a PhD in Composition and Rhetoric from Wayne State University. Dr. Kahler's work has appeared in *The Columbia Journal*, *Analog*, *Seneca Review*, *College English*, the *Journal of Contemporary Criminal Justice*, the *Stonecoast Review*, and other publications.

Flora Lu is a Professor of Environmental Studies and Provost of College Nine and John R. Lewis College at the University of California, Santa Cruz. She earned her AB in Human Biology from Stanford and her PhD in Ecology from the University of North Carolina at Chapel Hill.

Krystal Morin is a New England-based conductor, singer, and educator who is passionate about leading singing experiences rooted in empowerment, co-creation, community building, and storytelling. Krystal's background includes diverse music-making experiences including 10 years as a public high school choir and music teacher, designing, and implementing music curriculums in varied settings, providing artistic development and ensemble leadership, multi-modal artistic work in incarceration settings, field leadership, and experience performing in a broad range of community and professional ensembles. Currently, Krystal is a conductor for Boston Children's Chorus, sings with VOICES 21C, and a teacher for Boston University's Prison Arts Initiative.

List of Contributors xv

Ginny Emiko Oshiro is a Robert Wood Johnson National Health Policy Research Scholar, a Women's Policy Institute and California State University, Fullerton Project Rebound Alumna, a member of the Prison Arts Collective research team, and a policy advocate in the criminal legal reform landscape. She brings lived experience as a formerly incarcerated person and works closely with organizations serving currently and formerly incarcerated populations. Ginny is working toward her doctoral degree at the University of California, Irvine, as she believes that research has often been the catalyst for meaningful reforms in the criminal justice system.

Robin Paris is an Associate Professor of Photography at Belmont University. Several of her photographic projects have addressed Tennessee's death row. Her collaborations with prisoners (alongside Williams and Yontz) have resulted in 11 exhibitions, including at Apexart in New York, and it has been featured in *The Guardian, Hyperallergic, Huffington Post*, and other publications.

Nicole Patrie is an Assistant Professor in the Department of Public Safety and Justice Studies at MacEwan University and a PhD student in the Faculty of Education at the University of Alberta, specializing in Adult Education. Her research focus is on the role of education and learning in the criminal justice system. Nicole has over a decade of experience working in Canadian prison education programs as a teacher and administrator.

Keziah Poole holds a PhD in Comparative Literature from the University of Southern California, where she taught in the USC Dornsife Prison Education Project as a graduate student and went on to found the USC PEP Readers' Circle. She is currently employed as an ACLS Fellow at the Petey Greene Program.

Cecelia Ramsey holds a master's degree from New York University in literary translation and is currently a PhD student in the Department of French and Italian at Princeton University. Her research interests range from early modern books to 20th-century francophone literature, exploring the creation and deformation of conventions in translation. As an educator, she is passionate about connecting students to stories through language instruction and has taught in diverse environments, ranging from a two-room schoolhouse to a liberal arts university to a women's prison.

Linda Small is the founder of Reentry Sisters, a support organization specializing in a gender-responsive and trauma-informed approach for women. Linda serves on the New England Commission for the Future of Higher Education in Prison and is a Columbia University Woman Transcending Fellow, focusing on the impact of the carceral state on women and girls. She is a member of the Justice Scholars Network and Colby College Think Tank, highlighting the scholarship and research of justice-impacted people. Linda is a program coordinator for Maine Prisoner Advocacy Coalition and a DJ for Justice Radio, a talk show about the carceral state.

xvi *List of Contributors*

Duston Spear's artworks have been in the collections of the Brooklyn, High and Weatherspoon Museums. She holds an MFA in writing from Vermont College of Fine Arts and an MA from New York University. She received an Art Matters Fellowship for the "3 Women in Black" project, a Creative Time award, an Opportunity Grant and three sponsorships from the New York Foundation of the Arts. Spear collaborated with Judith Clark to make an operatic video, "Red Thread: the prisoner and the painter", the film received awards from the New York State Council on the Arts in Media and The Puffin Foundation.

Jeffrey Stein was a participant in the first cohort of the Cal State LA BA Graduation Initiative at Lancaster Prison in California. Upon returning to the community, he completed his bachelor's and master's degrees on campus. Since then, he has taught at the university level, facilitated college readiness workshops at California prisons, and serves as the Project Rebound Cal State LA outreach coordinator, helping create opportunities for persons who are system-impacted statewide. Along with volunteer and advocacy work, he enjoys gardening, travel, and music.

Kyes Stevens is the founder and director of the Alabama Prison Arts + Education Project at Auburn University. She has been working as a human being among fellow human beings inside places of confinement since 2001.

Tom Williams is a lecturer in art history at Belmont University. He received his PhD in Art History and Criticism from Stony Brook University, and he is a graduate of the Whitney Independent Study Program. He has collaborated with Paris and Yontz in their work on death row in Tennessee.

Isaac Wingfield teaches photography in the Residential College at the University of Michigan. Since 2015 he has led *Humanize the Numbers*, a collaborative photography-based workshop in Michigan prisons. He received an MFA in Photography from the Rhode Island School of Design and a bachelor's degree in Technical Photography from Appalachian State University.

Barbara Yontz is an artist/educator previously Professor of Visual Art at St. Thomas Aquinas College in NY, currently teaching in the MFA program at Belmont. Her nationally and internationally exhibited conceptual artwork shifted to include collaborations, exhibitions, and topics based on relationships with men on death row (in conjunction with Paris and Williams.).

Foreword

The growth of prison-based higher education programs is a critical step in preparing incarcerated men and women for life after prison. Further, these programs in their many different configurations help to relieve tension and improve behavior of those who are incarcerated. In other words, the pursuit of a college education is one path to an understanding of self and the world returned residents will encounter on the other side of the razor wire.

When evaluating prison fine arts programs, I've asked students—many of whom enrolled in college courses—why they decided to turn the corner to travel down a different path than the one that brought them to prison. Various reasons are given—both vague and specific. Sometimes, it is a person or program that sparked the change of attitude, or more often, it is the culmination of reading, exposure to alternative ways of thinking and acting, and introspection that leads to a heightened desire to live a more fulfilling life with the hope of leaving prison never to return.

The forming of a higher education community inside the walls allows students to share their vision and work with others regardless of skin color or gang affiliation, making it possible for the entire prison population to benefit and be inspired by those who choose to use their incarceration as an opportunity for growth and change. This model for self-improvement exists in stark contrast to the lowest common denominator—tough guys, gang groupings, and an antiauthoritarian ethos that restrains personal growth.

One goal of a partnership between colleges, universities and carceral facilities is to provide intellectually stimulating educational experiences that foster human connection and resources for positive self-expression and personal growth. It is assumed that such a collaboration is an evolutionary and dynamic process fueled by a dedicated group of professors and administrators who believe that knowledge and skills development can be a life-changing experience.

A national trend is to look for public, private, and nonprofit partnerships as a possible solution for many of the intractable problems confronting the

xviii *Foreword*

country today. Community colleges, public and private universities, and prisons are one example of a partnership that can result in a more efficient and effective delivery of educational services to prisoners eager to acquire life-effectiveness skills and a college education. It is time we teach incarcerated women and men how to live in the outside world, rather than simply exist on the inside.

Introduction from the Editor

Welcome

Whatever has brought you to this particular volume, thank you for your desire to learn about the amazing collaborations happening throughout the nation, beyond, with, and through institutions—of higher education and of corrections—and *by* people: people who are teachers, people who are artists, people who are students, people who are scholars, people who are incarcerated. It is the people who cultivate relationships and drive meaningful change. And it is the people that you will hear from throughout this collection: from students juggling college classes while imprisoned, to students entering correctional sites to teach and learn; from artists cultivating connections for students across the wall, to scholars navigating often competing policies of correctional and higher education institutions to build expansive programs linking the two for the purpose of expanding access, opening minds, and cultivating collaborations.

Context

Before we dive in further, I want to take a step back to view the system in which these transformative practices take place from a wider lens. (The majority of essays in this book focus on programming in the United States, with one essay from Canada and one from New Zealand, so I will focus on the United States for this context.) The United States prides itself on being the land of the free but is also the nation that, until very recently, imprisoned more people than anywhere else on the planet, now surpassed only slightly by China. With only 5% of the world's population, 25% of the world's prisoners are held in the United States. There are approximately 1.9 million individuals in detention in the United States, a 700% increase over fifty years (https://static.prisonpolicy.org/factsheets/55facts_2023.pdf Prison Policy Initiative, 2023). Strikingly, this shift is not tied to a decrease in crime or to marked improvements in communities. In 2016, the overall crime rate in the United States was approximately half what it was in 1991, and the rate of violent crime had fallen by about 20%; during that same period, the

xx *Introduction from the Editor*

prison population doubled (The Brennan Center, 2016). Race and poverty heavily and disproportionately influence who is imprisoned in the United States. In one tragic statistic, boys from poor families are more than 40 times likely to experience incarceration than boys from families in the top 10% of income distribution (Looney, 2018). People of color are disproportionately represented in prisons. Black Americans are incarcerated at five times the rate of white Americans, and Latinx are incarcerated at 1.3 times the rate of whites (Nellis, 2021).

What is often neglected in thinking about the problem of mass incarceration is that the vast majority of those who are incarcerated are also victims, often of cyclical trauma. There is a saying in the reentry and restorative justice community that "hurt people hurt people." The Bureau of Justice Statistics shows that 36.7% of women in state prisons experienced childhood abuse, compared to 12 to 17% of all adult women in the United States (Widra, 2020). While approximately 3–6% of the general male population has experienced post-traumatic stress disorder (PTSD), a 2014 study determined that number rose to 30–60% for men in state prisons (Widra, 2020). Rates of education for those who are incarcerated are also out of sync with society at large. The United States Bureau of Justice Statistics and Census Bureau data show the median education of an incarcerated person ages 27–42 is 11 years of school completed (Rabuy and Kopf, 2015), and the average person in prison reads at an eighth-grade level (Stipek). Compounding the problem, the United States spends more than $80 billion on incarceration annually, about two-thirds more than it spends on education (The Annie E. Casey Foundation, 2016).

Community

This is the complex and deeply embedded scenario into which the authors of this book enter, and it is the site of their stories and experiences, projects, and collaborations. Reading the chapters and working with these authors was deeply moving and inspiring in ways that I hope reading them will be for you, too. I have been teaching and learning with students in prisons and universities for 10 years and set about this book with a goal of learning more about who is engaging in this work and what they are doing. I did learn that, in spades, but one of the most surprising aspects of this incredibly enriching experience was how often authors noted the utter uniqueness of their programs; though proud of the work, they also seem to feel very alone. I hope that this book shows them, and you, that we are not alone. There is a whole community invested in the project of expanding access to the arts and education to people in prison. Each of these stories is proof of the positive changes that are happening, individually and communally, as well as inspiration and fodder for continued growth, collaboration, and coalition building.

Organization

It was difficult to determine how best to organize the content for readers. You will discover themes—humanity, hope, frustration, fear, overcoming, interconnectivity, learning, and growth—as well as voices from both inside and outside of prison throughout the chapters. In the end, I aimed to organize it in a way that might be helpful to readers. It begins with the reason and purpose of education, the students, and proceeds with stories of collaborations in and across prison walls. There are stories from teaching artists and faculty, followed by chapters that share more about the development of programs and partnerships between institutions of higher education and correctional institutions. Voices of people with lived experience of the prison system are represented among the faculty, artists, scholars, and students included throughout. So, while the four sections each variously feature stories from a particular point of view or focus, most chapters could have existed comfortably in other sections. Here, mirroring the work in general, there is more overlap than separation. I invite you to read them in the way that makes the most sense to you, whether in order or out of order, whether a full section or select chapters in each section that resonate for you. I hope you will find inspiration, growth, connection, and an expanded understanding of yourself and our community.

Language

Words have the capacity to trace, erase, embrace, evolve, devolve, or cultivate meanings and understandings of identity. In this book, the authors refer to people experiencing incarceration in many ways: students, artists, inmates, prisoners, relatives, people experiencing incarceration, and more. Throughout, I have retained the words that authors chose in recognition of the broad and fluctuating understanding and preferences for how to refer to people who are incarcerated.

Content

Among these stories of transformation, you will at times encounter narratives of the covert violence of imprisonment and how it impacts a person. In addition, due to the nature of the subject matter, there are some descriptions of overt violence in a few chapters. We do not wish for this message to discourage you from engaging with these incredible stories.

Acknowledgments

I want to thank every author who reached out to be part of this project, in particular those who took this journey with me. I offer a special thanks to those authors who are currently and formerly incarcerated for their courage in sharing personal experiences, which valuably helps humanize the experience for those less familiar with it. I also thank the two authors from outside the United States for reaching out and participating to enlighten us about some of the many changes happening globally. I want to thank the team at Routledge, including Lydia de Cruz, Medha Malaviya, and Riya Bhattacharya, for their consistent support and guidance. My deepest thanks to Dr. Larry Brewster, for his encouragement and inspiration to me and others in this work and for writing the foreword. This process was a learning and growing experience. I am grateful above all for my intrepid editorial assistant, Mack Moore, who jumped at the chance to join this project and helped it go more smoothly and enjoyably along the way. Finally, I acknowledge and thank the thousands of people throughout the state of California who have taken part in programs that I have taught or developed over the past 10 years, as well as the hundreds of thousands throughout the country and world who take the brave step of entering a classroom in a prison. This work has been, and continues to be, a journey that is as inspiring as it is challenging. It has introduced me to a truly dedicated community of like-minded people here and abroad: artists, scholars, activists, and collaborators inside and out.

Annie Buckley, Editor
Professor and founding Director,
Institute for the Arts, Humanities, and Social Justice,
San Diego State University
[for full bio, see list of contributors]

Works Cited

Looney, Adam, 5 Facts About Prisoners and Work, Before and After Incarceration, Wednesday, March 14, 2018, Brookings Institute.

Nellis, Ashley, "The Color of Justice: Racial and Ethnic Disparity in State Prisons," The Sentencing Project, October 13, 2021.

Acknowledgments xxiii

Prison Policy Initiative, Criminal Justice Fact Sheet. 2020 https://www.prisonpolicy.org/reports/pie2020.html

Rabuy, Bernadette; Kopf, Daniel. "Uncovering the Pre-Incarceration Rates of the Imprisoned," Prison Policy Initiative, July 9, 2015. https://www.prisonpolicy.org/reports/income.html

Stipek, Deborah. "Schools vs. Prisons," Stanford University. 2014 https://ed.stanford.edu/in-the-media/schools-v-prisons-educations-way-cut-prison-population-op-ed-deborah-stipek

The Annie E. Casey Foundation, "Children of Incarcerated Parents, a Shared Sentence," April 19, 2016. https://www.aecf.org/resources/a-shared-sentence

The Brennan Center for Justice, Crime Trends, 1990-2016.

Widra, Emily, "No Escape, the Trauma of Witnessing Violence in Prison." The Prison Policy Initiative, December 2, 2020.

Section I

Voices of Students

1 Scheduled Conflict

Alexander Bolling

Introduction

Pursuing higher education in a carceral setting presents a number of unique challenges. When the Department of Correction (DOC) agrees to allow a college program to operate within one of its facilities, this does not mean that education is going to be prioritized. The Massachusetts Department of Correction's esteem for education is reflected in the fact that less than 1% of its payroll is dedicated to teacher salaries (Massachusetts Office of the Comptroller CTHRU – Statewide Payroll for the year 2022). Security is the DOC's governing principle. To this end, certain measures are implemented to ensure the orderly running of each prison. Head counts and movement schedules are designed to account for each inmate throughout the day. In addition to the routine shakedowns and fire drills, unanticipated fights impede the process of education. Colleges must coordinate their activities within this hyper-structured existence, fitting their programs into DOC's schedule. As a student, I lived in the nexus between these two institutions. I had to navigate through the strictures of imprisonment while bearing the strains of academia.

Time management became my governing principle. I constructed my days and my life around being a student. This process entailed several adjustments, including requesting a cell change, altering my daily routine, and learning to plan my days or sometimes weeks ahead.

Between fall 2021 and the spring of 2022, my senior year in the Emerson Prison Initiative, I had 22 schedule changes. Any reported case of Covid-19 within the prison resulted in a lockdown. These lockdowns resulted in classes being canceled and rescheduled. It was a testament to the havoc that the coronavirus wreaked on the college and the prison. Delays, cancellations, and unexpected lockdowns became regular occurrences. The ability to focus on assignments and deadlines amid these uncertain conditions became essential to my success as a student.

DOI: 10.4324/9781003394426-2

4 *Alexander Bolling*

Transitions

Prison

Prison is indoctrination. The experience of incarceration is guided by time-tested principles, a body of knowledge disseminated by the incarcerated themselves. It is a code, a set of unwritten rules meant to shepherd neophytes into a new reality. After I was convicted, I became familiar with this esoteric credo, and I learned how to do time.

The first and most frequent bit of advice I received was to set a routine. The idea was to actively structure my day, scheduling everything from workouts to what time I would shower. This advice provided the logic behind the maxim, "do the time, don't let the time do you." While I grasped the significance of utilizing this last bit of autonomy, I could not ignore the truth that I was on the state's time.

My days were fitted into the DOC's schedule. The DOC decided what time I wake in the morning for headcount. The DOC decided what time breakfast, lunch, and dinner were served. The DOC decided what time I was allowed out of my cell for recreation and programming. My personal routine was weaved in and around this existing structure. What I gained from this state of affairs was an appreciation for time.

College

Enrollment in EPI was not a given. On August 7, 2017, I attended orientation with nearly 100 college hopefuls. As we sat in a packed room, we were warned that our lives were about to change. What this warning told me was that the routine that I had put together within the DOC's schedule could soon be subordinate to the demands of college. It was a trade-off that I hoped to be lucky enough to make.

A week later, I was invited to take a written exam. I had 90 minutes to respond to one of three essay prompts. The unnerving quiet of the room amplified my anxiety, and the clock on the wall taunted me as I worked to put my essay together. Every few minutes, I looked up to gauge what I could afford to edit before I ran out of time. Satisfied with my work, I had to wait and see if I was selected for an in-person interview.

It was another long week before I heard whether or not I had made it to the next phase of application. When I got the letter in the mail informing me that I was invited for a 10-minute interview, I was again filled with excitement and nervousness. I remember sitting at a wooden desk in the hallway, waiting to be called in for the interview. The wait seemed like an eternity, but the interview was over in a flash.

In another week's time I received my acceptance letter. I rushed into this new reality without any of the trepidations that accompanied my transition into prison. The letter prepared me for what was ahead, advising, stating,

Scheduled Conflict 5

"please prepare yourself for an entirely new day-to-day routine that may conflict with some of your current commitments." The DOC, however, was not as prepared to alter its operations for the purpose of my education.

Movement

Life in prison is coordinated through adherence to schedules. Daily recreation is allocated to four time slots: 9:00–11:00 am, 1:00–2:30 pm, 3:00–4:00 pm, and 6:30–9:30 pm. This is not to be confused with the recreation schedule, which details what time each housing unit has access to the gym, the yard, the library, and other areas of the prison. There is also a daily movement schedule that alerts individual inmates to any appointments they are scheduled for each day.

College courses, like other programs, are scheduled during recreation hours. With my classes scheduled from 1:00 to 3:45, a significant portion of my afternoon was full. However, when I received my course schedule, it felt like I was holding a road map in my hand. My intuition told me that I was headed in the right direction.

As excited as I was to begin classes, the prospect of arriving to school early was voided by DOC policy. Although my classes were scheduled to begin at 1:00, I was not allowed to leave the housing unit until the movement for programs was announced. This announcement was typically made at the start of recreation but could be delayed for a number of reasons. When movement is announced, a crowd of bodies flood out of the housing unit to various destinations.

Walking to the school building, I passed officers standing at various posts, randomly choosing inmates to stop for pat-downs. I stepped briskly, hoping my journey to class would not be delayed. The environment was nearly parallel to the conditions described by Ann Arnett Ferguson in *Bad Boys: Public School in the Making of Black Masculinity*, where she says, "All movement in school is regulated, organized, and monitored by adults" (Ferguson, 2001, p. 62). Of course, the incarcerated are adults, but the level of monitoring and regulation within a prison is meant to be dehumanizing. As a part of this regulation, there is a time window for movement to and from housing units. While this window is usually 10 minutes, it can change from day to day. The time window for movement is also a period when unrelated actions can hinder the learning process.

When fights occur, the standard procedure for the prison is to "freeze" all movement. This means that inmates are to remain wherever they are at the time of the altercation. If I happened to be in the housing unit, that is where I would have to remain until there is a "return to normal operations." Depending on what time the altercation occurs and how long it takes to return to normal operations, movement may be canceled altogether.

I first experienced one of these episodes during a summer semester. As I walked with a classmate to the school building, a fight started. With one

6 *Alexander Bolling*

glimpse, we both sped up, knowing that if we remained close to the housing unit, we would be returned to our cells. We made it into the school building as officers were responding to the fight. Unfortunately, a number of our classmates did not. We met with our professor as a small group until the rest of our class was able to join us. It wasn't until the 2:30 movement that our entire cohort was able to meet. I took this as a lesson not to take any class for granted.

The moment EPI faculty enter the prison, they, like their incarcerated students, are on the state's time. The plans of EPI faculty had to be adjusted to the daily operations at Massachusetts Correctional Institution-Concord. In *Education Behind the Wall: How and Why We Teach College in Prison*, Professor Cara Moyer-Duncan details EPI's approach in adapting to DOC scheduling:

> EPI has created its own academic calendar for faculty to use when planning their course calendars. The EPI academic calendar follows DOC's calendar for its educational programs, listing dates when the prison school is closed for holidays and school vacations. This does not always align with Emerson College's academic calendar, so faculty need to be alerted to this.
>
> (2022, p. 108)

The flexibility of EPI faculty mirrored the lives of the incarcerated, finding time in the margins of the DOC policy.

The Classroom

The classroom is a cherished place. The moment I stepped into the classroom I sensed a shared reverence for what this space represented. The walls of the prison faded from consciousness as we discussed theories of power and debated the value of literature to society. I was encouraged to think critically and analyze my life as well as course material. In *Education Behind the Wall*, Professor Wendy Walters provides an aptly describes the classroom environment:

> We aim to create in our prison classrooms an insubordinate space that gives intellectual agency to our students so that they may take the tools offered them by a liberal arts education and use them as they need to. This classroom space is in direct contrast to the goal of the prison, which is ultimately to dehumanize.
>
> (2022, p. 19)

The agency that I had as a student was not paralleled by any other aspect of my incarceration. In juxtaposition with the expected relations in prison, the classroom was a space that was open to "both emotional and critical responses to the text, as well as challenges to the constructed authority of the text, the syllabus, and even the role of the professor" (Walters, 2022, p. 25). The challenges made to authority are presented on ideological grounds and require introspection to be articulated. It was a challenge that also undermined the constructed identities of many incarcerated individuals, opening the possibility for positive growth.

Many challenges of attending college in prison come down to logistics. One issue that emerged early on was access to the computer lab. EPI students used computers not only to type assignments but also to conduct research. However, access to the computer lab was hinged on a multitude of factors. First, the computer lab was also a classroom for other DOC programs. Any time scheduled for EPI students had to be coordinated in consideration of these programs. The second issue that arose when scheduling for the computer lab was related to staff schedules. DOC policy required a correctional officer as well as DOC school staff to be present while students were in the lab. Although MCI-Concord's educational staff made many sacrifices to create time for college students to access the computer lab, the uncertainty of staff availability began to crystallize.

The most pressing need for the computer lab was access to the JSTOR database. Research was a complicated process as I had to gauge the relevancy of potential research requests by perusing the abstracts. It was usually one class period of frantic scanning as I had to go through convoluted measures to get research. I had to fill out research request forms naming the desired articles and hand these to professors. In turn, the professors handed these requests to Emerson College Librarians, who filled the request. This was a complicated and time-consuming ordeal, which left little room for mistake.

Research papers required a preemptive approach. Professors typically introduced the concept of these larger assignments early in the semester, giving students time to plan ahead. I took this time to scan the syllabus and begin to formulate ideas as soon as possible. Knowing I had limited time to peruse the JSTOR, I prepared a few areas of focus to search. By the time research made it into the prison and into the hands of students, there was not much time to read, analyze, and apply them to research. When I received my research, I limited socializing, using my time to read and take notes.

Aside from the educational aspects, other security measures threatened time in the classroom. From time-to-time classes were unexpectedly cut short. I can remember the first time that a correctional officer entered our classroom and summarily informed us that we had to return to our housing units for an emergency head count. Our professor scrambled to give us instructions as we packed our things to leave. I could see the frustration and disappointment on her face as I tried to hide my own.

These interruptions are detrimental for a number of reasons. One reason is that it directly disrupts the contact hours required for college students. This began a process of rescheduling classes that would become all too familiar

8 *Alexander Bolling*

as the program progressed. In these matters, the Principal at MCI-Concord provided invaluable assistance, helping to orchestrate the rescheduling. Each time a class was interrupted, I knew that it meant I had one less day off in the future, as this time would be designated to making up class hours. These interruptions were reminders that my college campus was still, in fact, a prison. This is not to say that the classroom was a place where I practiced escapism, but the progress and growth that occurs in this space was routinely vulnerable to the demands of security.

The Cell

The cell is the definitive measure of security. When altercations threaten the orderly running of the prison, all inmates are locked in their cells. The cell is also the decisive measure of dehumanization. A two-man cell has built-in conflict. Sharing the confinement of a prison cell with another human is traumatic. Sharing this space as a student is chaotic. Living in a two-man cell means being aware and considerate of another person's schedule. There are times when each person needs privacy in the cell to use the bathroom or to get dressed after showering. There are also lifestyle differences that could lead to conflict.

I was fortunate to move in with another student during my first semester. Under this arrangement, I knew there would be understanding and less conflict. For instance, the cell has one large fluorescent light; being in college requires a lot of reading, which means leaving this light on during the late hours. For someone who is not in college and trying to sleep, this would have created enmity. I ended up sharing this cell with my classmate for the next five years, which brought advantages when it came to continuing class discussions and developing ideas for papers. Living with a member of my cohort was a key step in fortifying my student lifestyle.

Transformation

Daily Routine

Be intentional. I received this advice from Professor and EPI Director Mneesha Gellmen at the end of our first semester. I wanted to shore up my academic schedule. A part of this process was accepting that interruptions were inevitable. However, I remained determined to control what I could. My decisions throughout the day were made in accordance with my obligations as a student.

The first thing I did each morning was make sure that my school affairs were in order. I made sure all of my assignments and reading materials were together before I left my cell to proceed to my institutional job. I performed this routine as a precaution. In the event that my housing unit was scheduled for a shakedown or if I was scheduled for an appointment, I would not have to scramble to get ready for class. It was a minor, yet important step taken that would help me avoid delays on my way to school.

Each day when I returned from class, I assessed the work ahead of me and planned what I would work on that evening. Once I decided on a course of action, I devoted the remaining recreation time to decompressing. Although college was my top priority, self-care was a vital component of my routine. Regardless of what was ahead of me, I recognized when it was time to relax and take a break.

I often took time for myself ahead of my more rigorous assignments. It appeared to some that I was choosing inopportune times for leisure. However, the times that I could go out to the yard for a walk were predetermined, and I knew that combatting the stresses of incarceration eased the pressure of academia.

I formed unique study habits to accommodate my living situation. In a unit that houses roughly ninety men, it is unrealistic not to expect distractions. Designating a work study area in the limited space of a cell crowded with books, televisions, and the personal belongings of two men is a daunting task. However, I understood that working in the common area of the housing unit was an invitation for interruptions. Ultimately, my primary workspace became my bed. The top bunk in my cell, where I rested and slept doubled as a reading and writing station. I was in a place where I could not demand silence nor expect privacy. Nevertheless, I spent countless hours surrounded by course readers, books, and writing pads. With my headphones on, I tuned out the cacophony of prison and tuned in to my studies.

As unusual as it may sound, the cramped quarters of my cell became a functional work environment. Friends and acquaintances became accustomed to seeing me perched on my bunk, engrossed in my studies. At times, this work carried over into the late hours of the night. Because I had a cellmate who was engaged in the same curriculum, I was able to take advantage of this uninterrupted time block. Studying at night brought silence that I rarely experienced in the daytime, as well as the comfort of knowing that my cell door was not going to open. It was a rare part of the day when I could expect to work without any interference.

This routine was tailored to my unique tendencies. However, different lifestyles and commitments will affect how each incarcerated student creates a routine. For me, being a student had become a lifestyle. Enrolling in college did not impinge on my existing routine, it replaced it. My identity as an incarcerated scholar made it all the more difficult to bear the disruption of the coronavirus pandemic.

Pandemic

The coronavirus pandemic upended people's lives globally, but in prison it was trying in novel ways. The trauma of the cell was magnified as the lockdown commenced. After days of being locked in 24 hours of the day, I was

10 *Alexander Bolling*

relegated to 15 minutes of recreation time each day. College courses, like all DOC programs, were halted. It was a dramatic turn from trying to manage every free hour of the day to having hour upon hour of unfree time. The uncertainty of my education was only overshadowed by the shared unease brought on by the pandemic.

As EPI professors reached out to check on students, I was touched by their care and commitment. It was beneficial psychologically to maintain a connection with people outside of the prison. I received letters with tips on yoga and meditation, as well as general inquiries about my well-being. I also received enrichment lessons that were not related to our semester but provided a welcomed outlet for my anxiety.

Eventually, EPI devised a plan to complete the semester by asynchronous work. It was during these particularly trying times that the working relationship between EPI and DOC became essential. The Principal at MCI-Concord made weekly and sometimes bi-weekly rounds, delivering and picking up assignments from students. I crafted a new routine within this lockdown that mirrored my previous schedule, setting aside late-night hours for schoolwork. As I worked through this intricate network, EPI administration worked to create a realistic path to completing our BA degree.

When EPI was allowed to return to in-person classes, our cohort was split into two groups due to Covid-19 restrictions. This meant that our professors had to spend twice as much time in prison. Even after our initial return to the classroom, we experienced numerous cancellations as outbreaks occurred within the prison. Ultimately, classes were halted again, and our fall 2020 semester carried over into the spring of 2021.

Gradually, the routine in the DOC began to stabilize, and we were able to meet as a full cohort. There were still occasional lockdowns, and these lockdowns led to more cancellations and rescheduling. The survival and success of EPI was a testament to the discipline, dedication, and determination of students, EPI faculty, and DOC staff. The collaborative effort to ensure the efficient running of this program signaled the potential for change in people and institutions.

Conclusion

Upon my conviction, I received a DOC ID number. My movement throughout the DOC as well as my institutional record was tracked using this number. This number is on my ID and etched into every piece of property that I have purchased. I always viewed this number as an instrument of dehumanization, and for years I resisted what it represented. Conversely, when I received my first transcript from Emerson College, I fixed my eyes on my student ID number and felt empowered.

The ideologies of prisons and colleges may differ, but that does not preclude a meeting ground for these two institutions. Education behind the wall cultivates agency in incarcerated people. Knowing the collaborative effort to bring the college into prison introduces a new path to change and self-improvement, I wanted to live as an endorsement for its value.

I graduated from EPI in the fall of 2022. The honor of being selected as class speaker filled me with pride. I looked out from the podium at my classmates, my professors, family, friends, mentors, DOC educational staff, and other distinguished guests, and I saw hope. What I was looking at was the possibility of something better. Beyond the concept of second chances, it was the flourishing of human potential. The pride not just in accomplishment but in the confidence that the road ahead was passable. After witnessing the hard work, growth, and resiliency of my cohort, I wanted nothing more than for others to experience the same. Graduating was a dream come true, but what my experiences had taught me was that this dream could and should be tangible for others. The experience of self-actualization, which is encouraged by higher learning, is essential to rehabilitation. It is a project that enriches both institutions.

References

Ferguson, A.A. (2001) *Bad Boys: Public School in the Making of Black Masculinity.* The University of Michigan Press.

Gellman, M. (2022) *Education Behind the Wall: Why and How We Teach College in Prison.* Brandeis University Press.

Massachusetts Office of the Comptroller CTHRU – Statewide Payroll for the year 2022. Commonwealth of Massachusetts. *http://cthrupayroll.mass.gov/#!/ year/2022/full_time_employees,others/pay1,pay2,pay3,pay4/explore/0-0-1-0-0/department_division/DEPARTMENT+OF+CORRECTION+(DOC)/0-barChart-0/ position_title*

McLarin, K. and W. Walters. (2022) "Teaching Literature Inside: The Poet's Report." *Education Behind the Wall: Why and How We Teach College in Prison.* Brandeis University Press.

Moyer-Duncan, C. (2022) "The Logistics of Preparing to Teach Inside." *Education Behind the Wall: Why and How We Teach College in Prison.* Brandeis University Press.

2 Transformation and Redemption

A Personal Narrative from a Position of Lived Experience

Ginny Emiko Oshiro

In my teens and early twenties, it would have been inconceivable that I would be contributing towards anything with the word "transformation" in it, let alone a piece of literature that might be distributed broadly in institutions of higher education. While I proudly provide this piece to those who choose to read it, I encourage you to gain additional perspectives (even perhaps from this reader) as I do not speak for all formerly incarcerated people and women. I simply offer my experience in the hopes that you might gain some insight and compassion for currently and formerly incarcerated people.

In this chapter, I share briefly about my experiences with incarceration, homelessness, and addiction. I do so to more adequately contextualize how meaningful and impactful rehabilitative and transformative programming was for me. Specifically, having the opportunity to engage with a reentry program in higher education has led me to personal and professional empowerment. I was fortunate to receive reentry services, and experienced total transformation as a result of having a community of formerly incarcerated people who allowed me to shadow them closely. I provide an overview of the different areas I work in now to suggest to currently and formerly incarcerated people and allies that there is more work to be done to transform carceral systems, and we absolutely need everyone's help to do it.

I always thought I was absent from school on the day they gave out the instructions for life. I looked at other people and wondered why they weren't afraid. I lived with crippling insecurity, fear, and low self-esteem, but I didn't have the words to articulate it. I didn't feel comfortable in my skin, and I desperately wanted to escape. Initially, I used achievements and accolades as a means to prop myself up. As long as I could get other people to tell me I was wonderful, I felt worthy of taking up space on earth. I used this method of managing and controlling my feelings almost as long as I can remember. It took a lot of effort, but it kept the tortuous feelings of shame manageable.

But when presented with an alternative that is both easier and more efficient at overcoming fear and anxiety, such as drugs and alcohol, I immediately

DOI: 10.4324/9781003394426-3

Transformation and Redemption 13

recognized it as a solution to the enduring problem inherent within me. The first time I put a substance in my body, I felt instant relief. All my life, I wanted to be someone else, and now I could magically feel like someone else in my own body. I never wanted to be myself again and staying fully inebriated was the only way to accomplish that goal. I chased that feeling with great consequence. As a teenager, I ran away from home, stopped going to school, and chose homelessness. The consequences of those choices were: mental health issues, sexual exploitation, violent victimization, and incarceration.

The cycle was vicious and predictable. I would be incarcerated with little access to my family and no access to rehabilitative programming, counseling, or supportive services. I would be released (often in the middle of the night) with no identification, phone, or resources. I was vulnerable as a single female living on the streets. I did the only thing that I knew how to do at that time, I sought out drugs and continued the lifestyle that would lead me back to incarceration to continue the seemingly hopeless cycle.

Even though I was homeless, addicted, and my life was totally out of control, education was still attractive to me. I had always felt safe in the classroom and thought that if I could get an education, I wouldn't continue in the cycle of madness. I was accepted to California State University, Sacramento (CSUS) and I remember feeling proud and hopeful. However, I continued to experience stints of incarceration that prevented me from showing up for class and was academically disqualified after a year.

When my family tried to help me, I would tell them with great certainty that I was sorry, that I didn't know why I was hurting myself and hurting them, but I would die this way. At one point, I was sentenced to drug court and was given the opportunity to go to a sober living facility. I had been to detoxes and treatment before but never completed them. While I couldn't see why this would be any different, I saw it as an opportunity to get temporary rest and shelter before going back out into the streets.

By chance I landed in a sober living owned by a woman who was a formerly incarcerated heroin addict.[1] She recognized my resignation to a life of homelessness, incarceration, and addiction because she had felt that same resignation before herself. She shared her experiences of using, hustling, and prison time. When I listened to her, I couldn't help but feel hope. If she could do it, could I? Equally as important as being able to identify with her experiences with addiction and incarceration, she generously shared about her personal transformation. She was a credible messenger that had struggled with reentry and addiction herself.

Reentry journeys can look different for everyone, but generally, they share commonalities, such as difficulty finding employment, challenges navigating community supervision, and internalizing stereotypes about formerly incarcerated people. I had very little hope of navigating these barriers. I looked for

14 *Ginny Emiko Oshiro*

employment in places that did not do background checks, which oftentimes exposed me to toxic work environments. I dreaded hearing from my probation officer as I knew that any contact could quickly turn into quicksand, and I could be returned to custody. But more than anything, I battled the internal monologue about what my life was worth because of the poor choices that I had previously made. I felt as if I would never overcome my past because I was afraid to do anything that would require anyone finding out about my history. After all, I could not forget the look on the face of one of the correctional officers who was escorting me to be released when he smirked and said with such ridicule, "Have fun! See you soon."

Even though these thoughts were terrorizing me, I couldn't bring myself to verbalize them. I had learned to be "hard" and appear stoic and unbothered despite feeling insanely scared and chaotic on the inside. The beauty of shared experience is that she knew what I was feeling and also knew that I could not and would not talk about it. She told me that I could do anything I wanted. I looked up briefly and hoped she didn't see the hope in my eyes. Worried she saw my interest, I quickly rolled eyes at her and gave her what I hoped would be an angry stare to deter her. She didn't give up on me and insisted I just needed to start somewhere and suggested I try going back to school.

I enrolled in a community college but almost didn't make it to my first day of class. I felt deeply ashamed that I had previously had the opportunity to attend a state school and didn't succeed. I felt different than the students walking around the campus laughing with their friends and raising their hands freely in class. I called my mom crying and she gently encouraged me to just show up for just one day.

Once in the classroom, I remembered that academia was a setting that I could navigate, and I discovered that it had a uniquely equalizing effect. It didn't matter that I was on probation, I was traveling back and forth to court on a regular basis, I had Hepatitis C as a result of my intravenous use of drugs, or I had been disqualified from another university. What mattered was that I read the syllabus, took direction, came prepared, and most importantly, had the will and desire to learn. What a freedom! I desperately wanted to prove to myself and others that I was worth more than those tired labels. The structured environment allowed me to excel. I chose Administration of Justice as my major because it gave me words for my experiences.

As someone who had never talked about trauma, addiction, or incarceration, I felt relieved that dialogues existed, even if they were making currently and formerly incarcerated people objects of study.

Although I recognized that the environment provided a safe container for my rehabilitative and reentry efforts, I was only able to engage to a limited extent. I went to class to participate but was very careful not to engage fellow students as I was deeply afraid to be "found out" as formerly incarcerated. I worried that if professors or students knew about my experience, they would

Transformation and Redemption 15

reject me and I would lose access to the environment that was giving me structure, allowing me to make productive use of my time. I was talking to a friend about my attempts at integration through education and he told me about Project Rebound, a program that supported students with incarceration experiences.[2]

Intrigued, I mustered up the courage to call the program. The woman on the other end of line allowed me to make an in-person appointment with her at the university. Upon arrival to campus, I was shaking with anxiety. The state school had beautiful buildings, intricate walkways, and signage that encouraged students to "Reach Higher." I didn't feel like I even belonged at community college, so setting foot on a state campus again was very overwhelming. I walked directly to the Project Rebound office, avoiding eye contact with anyone along the way. I learned that the woman I had talked to on the phone was the Program Director.[3] She greeted me in a manner in which I was unaccustomed to in academia; she related to me as if I was equal, as if I already belonged.

I learned that Project Rebound was founded in 1967 by Dr. John Irwin at San Francisco State University.[4] Dr. Irwin experienced incarceration and, upon his release, pursued higher education and ultimately received his doctoral degree in Sociology. He took a faculty position at San Francisco State University and founded Project Rebound as a program for incarcerated people to matriculate into the university system upon their release. Project Rebound expanded in 2016 and I was fortunate to be located close to one of the campuses that had advocated to be a part of the expansion.[5]

Project Rebound offered wrap-around services such as meal support, book stipends, assistance with acquiring a parking pass, and academic advisement. While some may look at the services and support as financial, I saw them as affirmations that I might belong on a college campus. I desperately wanted to be a part of the program, so I did what I had not done before, I told the truth. I clumsily shared my history. Having never shared my story before, I didn't know how much or how little to tell. I offered the woman my Federal Live Scan, which could confirm my history of incarceration, and she gently declined taking it. It seemed that my ineloquent attempt at the truth was sufficient. She allowed me to fill out the application to the university and program, and I provided her with all of my transcripts. That day and opportunity changed my life.

I left the campus, now looking wistfully at my surroundings because I had just been given a mustard seed of hope that I might belong here despite my repetitive inner monologue telling me differently. I headed to the grocery store where I worked and tried not to get my hopes up. When I left my shift that night, I had a voicemail; it was the woman from Project Rebound. Her message said, "Congratulations, Ginny. Welcome to Cal State Fullerton. Welcome to the Rebound family!"

My first day of school at California State University (CSU), Fullerton was almost as difficult as my first day of community college. However, this time I

16 *Ginny Emiko Oshiro*

had a safe place to go; I walked into the Project Rebound Program Director's office on my very first day. I choked back tears because I was unwilling to be vulnerable and say I was scared. She saw right through me, and I learned that perception was due to personal identification. She told me without flinching that she had served 23 years in a California prison until her release, where she attended a private university for her bachelor's degree and later master's degree. She looked me squarely in the eyes and told me that education was her reentry practice and it could be mine too. She didn't just encourage me, she insisted that I go to class, sit up front, and participate. She said that as a criminal justice major and Project Rebound scholar, I had a responsibility to raise my hand and ask questions of common disparaging narratives about currently incarcerated people and provide commentary on alternative narratives.

I had been given many labels: addict, runaway, inmate, repeat offender... no one had ever called me a scholar. Somehow hearing it from someone who understood my experience and had gotten on the other side made all the difference. Her resolute belief in my ability to overcome adversity based on her own lived experiences gave me hope. I went to class that day, and I forever felt different because I knew that I wasn't alone. My original conception of Project Rebound was that it was a program that provided services to students. While it does do that, a more important function became obvious from the very first day. Project Rebound is a community that connects formerly incarcerated scholars to form a tightly knit group that fiercely supports each other through academic, personal, and professional hurdles. Knowing that a whole community had my back, I felt empowered.

Project Rebound has been the springboard for my growth. Whereas before I was surviving reentry, the program allowed me to thrive. I had never felt comfortable taking up space before, but with the encouragement and support of my new community, I began sitting up front in classes, showing up early and staying late, engaging with students, and going to office hours to ask questions. I had a productive outlet in my life, I had a community, and I had goals and a means of achieving them. Beyond a reentry practice, education has been my transformative practice. The nature of engaging with academic materials, asking critical questions, and interacting with my peers and professors has changed me on a cellular level. I learned that my experiences with trauma, addiction, and incarceration were connected to broader societal structures housed within historical and political contexts. I learned how to communicate my point of view and experiences, honor other peoples' perspectives, and work through conflict. I learned that failing wasn't the end, but a new opportunity to learn and sharpen my skills. The implicit lessons in higher education were and continue to be as valuable as the substance of the materials assigned to me.

Initially, Project Rebound convinced me that I was worthy of being on a college campus, and over time, it helped me to believe that I had something to offer. I began participating in student government organizations on campus. I served as the President of a student organization for formerly incarcerated and system-impacted students and on the board for a substance use awareness club and the criminal justice honor society.

Project Rebound never insisted that I share my experience, but they did give me the opportunity and support to craft my narrative in a way that felt authentic, safe, and empowering. Sharing my story felt vulnerable and scary at first, but I learned firsthand that being honest could change someone's life. It had certainly changed my life when the Program Director shared her experience with me. I began speaking at events on campus and in classrooms, not just about my experience with incarceration but about what the second chance of higher education meant to me and how it had and continued to impact my life. After we (formerly incarcerated scholars) spoke, we were met with a variety of reactions such as curiosity, care, or compassion. I learned that I could be honest without being rejected and that my ability to be honest and authentic created safe spaces for others.

It is impossible to articulate the layers that were pulled back or the seeds that were sown in my time with Project Rebound. I used to be worried about people from my past recognizing me, but I am confident that I could sit among my old acquaintances and they wouldn't recognize me. Not only have I had many of my tattoos removed, I stand taller and can look people in the eyes. This transformation, while positive overall, has also meant that I have grown out of some relationships. At one point someone told me with disgust that they didn't know me anymore. I was hurt because, if I was unrecognizable, it was because I was experiencing a positive transformation. This individual did not want to be a part of my life anymore, and today I know it is because I outgrew the relationship. I have shed many relationships since that one. At first, it was difficult to accept that I may lose my longest relationships, but if people did not share my growth mindset, it would be nearly impossible for us to continue to relate to each other.

Finding a supportive community gave me clear pathways to overcome those barriers. The wrap-around services offered by Project Rebound were affirmations from the university that I belonged, but what made all the difference were the people who had been incarcerated that could identify and share their experiences with me. In particular, two scholars were incredibly generous with their time and support. Both served lengths in prison that I could not begin to imagine and simply being a witness to their reentry and transformation fanned the flame of hope within me. They treated me as a family member and poured into me lessons big and small, coaching me on public speaking, talking about what was possible with my major, how to navigate difficult conversations with professors, and encouraging me to take on a minor in Ethnic Studies for a more well-rounded education. They, along with the Program Director, taught me through their actions that education was a pathway to liberation.[6]

18   *Ginny Emiko Oshiro*

I started to develop questions that my professors couldn't answer, sometimes because I had a different perspective, but other times because there simply wasn't research to help my understanding. With the encouragement of a professor, and my Project Rebound community, I made the decision to pursue a graduate degree. While this may seem logical to the reader, I still often felt like the girl who cried on her first day of community college, so applying to doctoral programs was terrifying. However, I had so much evidence that I could move forward despite feeling scared that I applied anyway. I was fortunate to be accepted into my top choice, and I continue to be grateful for the opportunity on a daily basis.

When I graduated with my undergraduate degree, it was so bittersweet. All of my graduation photos have some variation of me crying. Graduating was an amends to family, to my community, and to myself. I didn't dare dream of achieving this before finding Project Rebound, and I owe my transformation and continuing redemption to their program. I was so happy to graduate but was also afraid to leave the community that facilitated my transformation. Fortunately, I found that enrolling in another university did not change my relationship with my Rebound family. To this day they are my biggest cheerleaders. I lean on the woman who gave me the opportunity to join Project Rebound for mentorship. I share resources and commiserate with my two friends who are also on their doctoral journeys. The founder of CSU Fullerton's Project Rebound[7] generously spends his limited time helping me to understand punishment theory and what abolitionism might look like in practice.

I was aware that access to this program changed the trajectory of my life so completely, and I wondered what would happen if I hadn't been referred or accepted. I wondered why I didn't have access to rehabilitative resources earlier and what my life could have been like if I had gotten services during my first incarceration. Passionate about the ability to transform given the tools, I chose to study rehabilitation services in prisons and how we might conceptualize these as interventions in mass incarceration. I was very fortunate to form a relationship with a supportive advisor who continues to allow me to bring my authentic self to a graduate program while always challenging me to ask empirical questions. I came to my doctoral program with a lot of heart; my advisor teaches me how to use my head and heart to interrogate new domains in correctional rehabilitation.[8]

Identifying my research interests led me to a state-wide organizing body for community-based in-prison programs.[9] Working with over 85 community-based organizations made up of diverse practitioners, healers, and teachers has taught me that rehabilitation and transformation often happens as a result of caring individuals who recognize the humanity and dignity of incarcerated people. I used to question which programmatic offering was the most effective; today I understand that the program might be dog training, gardening, art, mediation, or restorative justice dialogues, it is the care and connection in these that facilitate healing and growth. I am fortunate to

Transformation and Redemption 19

support the organization's advocacy goals to increase access to rehabilitative programs for incarcerated people through policy and budget advocacy.

The convergence of my personal, professional, and academic interests aligned when I had the opportunity to join the research team of Prison Arts Collective (PAC).[10] PAC is an art-based in-prison program that operates throughout California by way of California State University chapters. The program believes that art is a human right and has developed three offerings for incarcerated Californians that facilitate healing, transformation, and successful reintegration. PAC has used its connection to the university system to develop a research project that measures both technique development and overall impact of arts programming on wellbeing. It is a meaningful project for a number of reasons, but it feels aligned with my integrity as PAC creates spaces where participants engaged in the research can talk with myself or other PAC researchers about the purpose and impact of the project in a collaborative and participatory process.

Recently, I had the opportunity to visit a state prison and support incarcerated people enrolling in a bachelor's degree program. It was difficult for me to articulate what higher education had given me because its impact has been so great, but I did my best to share how valuable the explicit and implicit learnings had been in altering how I viewed myself and related with others. I am not sure I was able to articulate the magnitude of the transformative power of education, but I hope sharing my experience helped encourage these scholars just as the Project Rebound Director sharing her story had encouraged me. Together with a small team of faculty and staff, I helped to answer practical questions about applications and congratulate them on their academic accomplishments and resilience. Being present with incarcerated people speaks volumes.

Some days, it is difficult to believe that I used to be accustomed to living on the streets or in a cinderblock box. Other days, especially when I go inside correctional facilities, I remember like it was yesterday. I don't expect that everyone reading this will perceive my journey sympathetically or empathetically, but my hope is that it reaches one person and encourages them to think critically about our criminal legal system and to challenge commonly held stereotypes and stigmas about incarcerated and formerly incarcerated people. And, if the reader is formerly incarcerated, I hope it will help them to consider that higher education or other healing programs may facilitate total transformation, and through that transformation, offer the ability to reach back to the next individual who is struggling with redemption and give them hope as well. For our allies, there have been people along this journey who have never experienced incarceration but have made all the difference in my feeling like I belonged. I hope you can be that person for someone.

Ending a chapter feels final, but even as you end this reading, know that my journey for transformation and redemption continues as both are essential to me. Transformation is for me and redemption is for family, friends, and community.

Author Note

I offer this chapter from a place of lived experience and acknowledge that my experience is not representative of all formerly incarcerated people. I chose higher education as a reentry practice, but there are many programs that facilitate transformation and healing.

Notes

1 Wendy Rudin fought her own harrowing battle with drugs and alcohol and got clean in 1991. She now owns and operates a sober living home for women struggling with addiction.
2 https://www.calstate.edu/impact-of-the-csu/student-success/project-rebound
3 Romarilyn Ralston is a highly decorated and celebrated black feminist prison abolitionist scholar working to interrupt criminalization at the intersections of race, gender, and education. She is now the Executive Director of CSU Fullerton's Project Rebound.
4 https://asi.sfsu.edu/project-rebound
5 https://www.calstate.edu/csu-system/news/Pages/Project-Rebound.aspx
6 Mir Aminy is now an Academic Counselor for Project Rebound after receiving his master's degree in counseling and entering a doctoral program. Mir received a formal pardon from California Governor Newsom. James Cavitt is now the Program Director of Project Rebound at CSU Fullerton after receiving his master's degree in social work and entering a doctoral program. Both scholars have continued to shape possibilities and futures for formerly incarcerated students.
7 Brady Heiner, PhD is the Founding Chair of the CSU Project Rebound Consortium, the Founder of Project Rebound at Cal State Fullerton, and a Professor of Philosophy.
8 Valerie Jenness, PhD is a Distinguished Professor in the Department of Criminology, Law and Society at the University of California, Irvine.
9 https://www.thetpw.org/
10 https://www.prisonartscollective.com/

3 Transforming Lives Through Prison Higher Education

Jeffrey Stein

A Resurgence of Prison Education and Reentry Support

Prison higher education reduces recidivism greater than any other factor. Prisoners who participated in education programs while confined experienced a 43% reduction in recidivism rates compared with prisoners who did not participate in educational opportunities. In 2016, the California State University, Los Angeles (CSULA) led the effort to create an educational opportunity for incarcerated citizens that was unique at the time in California. After the ban of the use of Pell Grant funding for the incarcerated in 1994, prison higher education was severely limited to distance learning courses from a few community colleges. Without Pell Grant funding, colleges and universities across the United States could no longer receive the tuition reimbursement that helped sustain their programs in carceral facilities. The federal Pell Grant covers a significant portion of the tuition at many public institutions of higher learning and is available to those who are income-restricted but not necessarily poor. Toward the end of President Obama's second term, Pell Grants were restored to a select number of universities (Korte, 2016). Cal State LA received generous private grants and was selected as a Second Chance Pell Pilot site in 2016, providing the university the leverage to collaborate with the California Department of Corrections and Rehabilitation (CDCR) to launch the Prison BA Graduation Initiative pilot program at California State Prison-Los Angeles County (CSP-LAC or Lancaster) Facility "A" in 2016.

As of February 2023, 37 students have earned bachelor's degrees in Communication with an emphasis in Organizational Communication—many with high honors. In 2021, graduations were held at Lancaster and on the main campus. The picture below (Image 3.1) is of the graduation ceremony held at Lancaster Prison in 2021.

Of those 37, 15 have returned to the community and are thriving. These students graduated on the main campus in May of 2021.

Of those 15, all but three were sentenced to life-without-the-possibility-of-parole (LWOP) and received sentence commutations from the Governor; the other three had life sentences. Taken altogether, the BA Program is a

DOI: 10.4324/9781003394426-4

22 Jeffrey Stein

Image 3.1 Dr. Taffany Lim and cohort 1 and 2 graduates on the prison yard at Lancaster (October 5, 2021). Photo Credit: R. Husky.

once-in-a-lifetime, destiny-altering opportunity that each student has made good on.

Once a student returns to the community, Project Rebound at CSULA takes a central role in the reentry navigation process. Project Rebound is a program designed to support students in the state California University system who are formerly incarcerated. Founder, Professor John Irwin of San Francisco State University, became an expert on Criminology after experiencing incarceration (Institute for Scientific Analysis, 2017). While confined, he took correspondence community college courses that altered the trajectory of his life. He founded Project Rebound in 1967 to provide a space, community, and resources for people like himself who experienced incarceration but sought to change their lives through higher education. For decades, Project Rebound only existed at San Francisco State University. In 2016, Project Rebound began to expand to 14 of the 23 California State University (CSU) system campuses, including Cal State LA.

My Educational Journey

I participated in the BA program as a prisoner/student from the inception of the program in 2016 until I was released in 2019 after serving ten and a half years in prison. I went on to return to the community and earn bachelor's and master's degrees on the CSULA campus while working for Project Rebound on campus at (PRLA). My firsthand experiences make me uniquely positioned to offer key insights into the BA program and PRLA. The picture

Transforming Lives Through Prison Higher Education 23

Image 3.2 Jeffrey Stein, cohort 1 member, at master's graduation (May, 2022). Photo Credit: E. Flores.

below (Image 3.2) is of me being hooded at the master's degree confirmation ceremony in 2022.

I was housed on the Progressive Programming Facility (PPF—formerly known as The Honor Yard) at Lancaster State Prison between 2009 and 2019; in 2016, I became a member of the first cohort of the CSULA BA Graduation Initiative. I returned to the community in 2019, where I immediately continued my studies on the CSULA main campus. I graduated with my bachelor's degree in December of 2019 and then went on to earn a CSULA master's degree in communication studies with honors in 2022. I currently serve as the outreach coordinator for Project Rebound Cal State LA (PRLA). Since returning to the community, I have worked for Project Rebound, was a teaching and research assistant for on-campus and prison classes, taught a university-level public speaking class on campus, and performed with the university classical guitar ensemble in addition to volunteering with social justice organizations such as Getting Out By Going In (GOGI) and at the El Sereno Community Garden near campus. In graduate school I had the added challenge of staying housed during the COVID pandemic. For most of that time, I worked three jobs—including one at Amazon unloading trucks. The work ethic, professionalism, and belief in myself that I cultivated while in the Prison BA Graduation initiative, along with university support, gave me the tools I needed to meet challenges I had never faced before.

24 *Jeffrey Stein*

The Key to Success—The Progressive Programming Facility

The underlying factor related to the unalloyed success of students from Lancaster comes from Facility "A's" unique designation as a Progressive Programming Facility (PPF). Formerly known as the Honor Yard, the PPF is wholly unlike most prisons, which are characterized by rampant drug abuse, gang activity, racial segregation, and violence. Author Ken Hartman was serving a life without parole, or LWOP, sentence in the early 2000s when he and other leaders on the yard submitted a proposal to the warden to do something innovative: change the culture and climate of Facility "A" into one that would support rehabilitation by removing residents who clung to antisocial behavior and replace them with residents who wanted to stop participating in antisocial behavior (Hartman). The Honor Yard was born of that collaboration between inmate residents and the warden. Within a year, the reduction in violence, both inmate-on-inmate and against custody staff (guards), was statistically significant to the point of reducing medical costs (paid by taxpayers) by hundreds of thousands of dollars. The value of a preexisting culture of transformation on the prison yard to the successful outcome of the BA program cannot be overstated. Simply put, the success of the Prison BA Graduation initiative would have been tenuous at best if it had been located on a typical California prison yard characterized by rampant drug use, race and/or gang violence, and lack of institutional support.

A Focus on Rehabilitation and Transformation

I arrived at the Honor Yard in late 2009. I had just left the reception center at the California Correctional Institution at Tehachapi, where I had spent 8 months on lockdown waiting to be transferred to a level four yard (maximum security). Tehachapi was always on lockdown and the tension there was palpable. I never felt safe at Tehachapi; nor did I feel like a human being at any point. There was nothing there but concrete, steel, and bad vibes. Not knowing of the existence of the Honor Yard, I arrived at Lancaster expecting more of the same or worse. When I first walked onto the yard at Facility "A," I was shocked to see people of varying races walking laps on the track together, someone doing yoga on the crabgrass, and an older fellow sunning himself. Conspicuously absent was the tension, fear, and dread. I asked the guard who was removing my handcuffs, "What is this place?" He casually replied, "The Honor Yard." Lancaster "A" yard was a level four (maximum security) facility at the time, which made this designation even more remarkable. Not to over-generalize, but typically at any prison you will observe three personality types emerge: (1) those who remain more or less the same as when they arrived; (2) those who are decidedly unrepentant and ever-worsening; and (3) those who are daring enough to begin the work of becoming the best version of themselves in the most unlikely of environments. After a few months, I got to know dozens of people at the Honor Yard who were already years into that journey of becoming their best selves. There were 600 souls on that yard in 2009, and the vast majority were peaceful people just trying to live as much like a human being as they possibly could. Nearly everyone on the Honor Yard had LWOP or a life sentence.

A Culture of Peer Support

All of the organizing of self-help classes and workshops on the yard was done by the LWOPs. It is important to understand, because at the time, no amount of rehabilitation or good deeds would earn them any sort of reprieve on their sentences. In fact, I did not meet anyone who had a release date until my final five years there. Instead, they chose to focus on their rehabilitation from an inner motivation to become the best versions of themselves. They were also supportive of anyone who wished to make the same journey. One LWOP helped me sign up for educational classes; another handed me a Bible; another saw me running the track on shredded shoes and gave me a brand-new pair; another found out I was a guitar player and lent me an acoustic guitar; and another helped me find a work assignment. This culture of support and safety not only helped me to feel like a human being again, but I could drop the hypervigilance that is necessary to survive in other prison environments. I was now in a space where I could address my defects of character safely. It is noteworthy that many of the self-help classes and workshops were peer-led with the support of the facility administration. Interestingly, studies in the field of neuroscience have validated the notion that peer support is highly effective in achieving wellness from a mental health perspective (Neuroscience Research Institute, 2022). Shortly after my arrival to the Honor Yard, the CDCR renamed it the PPF, but the transformational culture and climate persisted.

An Environment That Promotes Education and Healing

Being housed on the PPF yard changed the entire trajectory of my life and ultimately led to my being prepared for the BA Program when it arrived. Little by little, I began to feel more like a human being again. At the PPF, I could discard the survive-at-all-costs, do-or-die philosophy that presumes a hostile environment that one must navigate to make it through the day. I could concentrate on my studies instead of spending every waking minute dragged down by uncertainty. I no longer had to exist in a diminished and woeful state of fear and anger; neither did the others housed there.

A Foundation of Transformation and Change

The culture of transformation on the PPF was the bridge to success for the students in the BA program. I believe the BA program would likely have succeed even if it had been placed on a typical prison yard, but with more difficulty [or some such to explain...the logic you are presenting is that PPF was a factor in the success so if it would succeed anywhere so this needs something

26 *Jeffrey Stein*

to bridge to next]. With varying degrees of difficulty, professors and administrators would have been able to acculturate a different yard, but that would involve changing the mindset of prison bureaucrats, correctional officers, and imprisoned prospective students. Instead, CSULA benefited from an established PPF yard where all inmates–whether they were students or not–were eager to support the transformational benefits of higher education.

The PPF yard provided the culture and foundation for the Prison BA Graduation Initiative to thrive. We learned in our organizational communication courses that changing the culture of an organization is difficult if not impossible to accomplish. For the emerging BA programs at other facilities, it is more practical to have the program at facilities similar to Lancaster's "A Yard" and have prospective participants transfer there. In my analysis, this is the smartest use of resources and personnel when implementing future BA programs elsewhere. At the PPF, many of the LWOPs committed to positive transformation eventually became my classmates in cohort 1 of the Prison BA Graduation Initiative. In addition to leaning on each other as a support system while living in harsh conditions, we became a support system of university students as well. Taking in-person, upper-division college courses instead of lower-division courses through distance learning modalities was quite a leap for us. We formed study groups and tutoring sessions for anyone struggling with the material. It became increasingly necessary to rely on each other while experiencing new kinds of anxiety related to increasingly challenging assignments and the "imposter syndrome" (Weir, 2013). Like many colleges, the prison had extremely limited mental health resources, so we relied on the peer-to-peer model of support to manage and overcome anxiety and feelings of inadequacy that were school-related (Mace, 2014).

Benefits of an In-Person BA Degree Program

The Cal State LA Prison BA Graduation Initiative prides itself on offering face-to-face courses. When we took correspondence courses, we were limited to writing the professor through standard mail, which took weeks at best to get any clarification. Often, our letters to the distance learning professors went unanswered or arrived too late to make a difference. The primary benefit of an in-person bachelor's degree program is that when we needed clarification on a complex topic or assignment, we were able to access the professor face-to-face in real time. Another important difference is that my experience with the in-person classes is that the university professors were warm, accessible, and had a humanizing effect. They treated us as human beings, not as lesser others. Along with the curricula, they imparted their own decency and humanity, which importantly enabled us to manage stigma and reconstruct a positive social identity that transferred to our successful reentry. Feeling like a human being again, after years of feeling like a disposable thing, is one of the beautiful takeaways the BA Graduation Initiative still provides to the current cohort at Lancaster.

Project Rebound—The Key to Reentry and Higher Education Success

The Importance of Giving Back

Initially, my intention as I left the prison was to put on a suit and blend in with society. I was aware that returning citizens face thousands of barriers to reentry such as difficulty finding work or even renting an apartment. Nevertheless, shortly after returning home, I represented Project Rebound Los Angeles (PRLA) at a prison workshop and left with a burning desire to help our brothers and sisters who still languish in carceral facilities. Seeing them suffering yet full of hope imbued me with a sense of duty and purpose to help create access and opportunity for more people who had similar experiences as me. Knowing that I had been given much, it became important to me to get involved in this work. Like my fellow Prison BA Graduation Initiative cohort members, I wanted to give back—and Project Rebound is a great enterprise for those who wish to do so. As the official brochure states: "Project Rebound at Cal State LA supports meaningful reintegration through higher education after incarceration…our mission [is] to reduce recidivism, affirm our rights to an education, and to contribute to stronger and safer communities" (CSULA, 2022). As someone who once created chaos in the community, suddenly being able to assist others with their transformation in meaningful ways helped me to manage the stigma of being formerly incarcerated in a society that historically ostracized us. Having the opportunity to take a role in rebuilding communities went a long way toward my goal of reconstructing a positive social identity. I am a part of the solution now, rather than being a part of the problem. I could never have achieved a master's degree with honors if I was burdened with stigma and feeling like I could never contribute meaningfully to society.

Overcoming Challenges and Barriers

When I arrived on campus in January 2019, I was immediately hired by PRLA and joined the communication and outreach team. My new life as an undergrad employed by the university allowed me to overcome those two key barriers to successful reintegration: managing stigma and reconstructing a positive social identity. With that, I found it easier to find work or housing as I had a good credit score and recent job history—two factors that once severely restricted a justice-involved person's options and seriously diminished their quality of life, contributing to a high recidivism rate.

Assisting fellow persons affected by the justice system in their own transformations has been richly rewarding. The work I have been able to contribute to benefits the 80 formerly incarcerated students on campus. PRLA has a 95% graduation rate, significantly higher than the US national university rate of 64% (U.S. Department of Education, National Center for Education Statistics, 2020–2021). To that end, I worked closely with Allen Burnett,

28   Jeffrey Stein

another BA Graduate initiative alum, throughout his graduate school journey. From applying for grad school to applying for graduation two years later, I was with him every step of the way. He recently successfully defended his master's thesis and earned his graduate degree in Communication Studies. Another BA Graduate initiative alum, Tin Nguyen, completed his MBA program at CSULA this May—making a total of three former Lancaster students who have earned master's degrees since returning to the community.

Reversing the School to Prison Pipeline

A key part of the transformative work of the Prison BA Program Initiative and PRLA is to reverse the school-to-prison pipeline. Sociologists and activists have raised awareness and have shown that people of color and people from income-restricted communities are grossly overrepresented in jails and prisons and that this trajectory is evidenced as early as grade school. For example, youth of color are suspended and expelled more often than their white classmates who get into trouble at school, which severely limits their chances of success. In the past, critics dismissed the notion that a school-to-prison pipeline exists, but we now have enough statistical data to confirm its existence (Camera, 2021). I witnessed the effects of this phenomenon firsthand while incarcerated. Personally, I felt disenfranchised all of my life because of coming from a broken home, being orphaned at the age of 12, and ultimately experiencing incarceration. When a professor told me in our first BA class at the prison that only 7% of the earth's inhabitants hold BA degrees, I realized that education was a great equalizer. Although I had a less than ideal start made more difficult by years of poor choices, I realized that higher education would level the playing field for me. I no longer felt incapable of reaching my potential. On a personal level, simply hearing that I would have such an advantage was one of the most liberating events of my entire life.

In my perspective, many people who experience incarceration do not necessarily need to be "rehabilitated," but rather, they need an opportunity and support to overcome the inequities they are burdened with from birth such as growing up in an income-restricted neighborhood that experiences high rates of crime. The success of the BA Program and PRLA is proving that people who have had contact with the justice system are redeemable and that we can fully contribute to society if given the chance. Having benefitted from these opportunities, I find it deeply satisfying to be able to expand the scope and magnitude of the BA Program and PRLA's activities that create the access and opportunity needed by so many.

Hope for the Future

The impact of state and federal support for the BA Program, PRLA, and similar programs means that there are fewer barriers to reintegration to society for those coming out of prison. The first student to return to the community

Transforming Lives Through Prison Higher Education 29

from the BA Program at Lancaster, Brad "Woody" Arrowood, is an amazing success story. After earning his bachelor's degree in 2020, he went on to create his own rescue dog training business that was ranked in the top ten in the state of California in 2022. Clifton "Lee" Gibson came home in 2019, graduated in 2020, and leveraged his education and lived experience to find a remote career position with Initiate Justice. Today he lives his best life, traveling all over the world. Allen Burnett returned to the community in 2020 and earned his master's degree in May of 2023. Since coming home, he has worked with Human Rights Watch, Drop LWOP, and several justice reform efforts. He is the co-founder and Director of The Prism Way, a nonprofit serving people who are system-impacted. They, like me, work in academia and/or as professional Project Rebound staff. The impact to those still experiencing incarceration is also powerful. At work and at home, on a daily basis, I receive calls, texts, and letters from members of the BA Program's third cohort.

They often tell me that the stories of those of us who came home inspire and motivate them through the difficult times they experience on the inside. They are given hope that they can rebound from poor decisions they have made and overcome the barriers to success that they once thought to be insurmountable. They realize that there is light at the end of the tunnel and that if they keep doing the right things for the right reasons it was eventually pay off. With that hope, they are able to make choices that are in their best interest leading to the cessation of drug abuse, violence, and criminality in general.

In closing, the opportunity to belong to the inaugural cohort at Lancaster may be the greatest gift I have ever received. The BA Program is the true opportunity and unwavering support that I needed to finally begin reaching my potential. In one of our first BA Program classes, a cohort 1 member stated, "Knowing others believed in me caused me to believe in myself" (B. Arrowood, personal communication, September 21, 2017). My hope is that what has been accomplished by the BA Program on the PPF might be replicated again and again, and that a multitude of people who were previously marginalized might experience the same things I was fortunate enough to experience.

References

American Civil Liberties Union. (2011). *School to prison pipeline.* School-to-Prison Pipeline | American Civil Liberties Union (aclu.org)

California State University, Los Angeles. (2022). *Project rebound.* https://www. calstatela.edu/engagement/project-rebound

Camera, L. (2021, July 27). Study confirms school-to-prison pipeline. *U.S. News & World Report.* Study Confirms School-to-Prison Pipeline (usnews.com)

Davis, L.M., Steele, J.L., Bozick, R., Williams, M.V., Turner, S., Miles, J.N.V., Saunders, J. & Steinberg, P.S. (2014). RAND Correctional Education Survey. In *How effective is correctional education, and where do we go from here? The results of a comprehensive evaluation* (p. 57). RAND Corporation.

30   *Jeffrey Stein*

Fuetsch, H. (2017). The progressive programming facility: A rehabilitative, cost-effective solution to california's prison problem. *The University of the Pacific Law Review*, 48(2) p. 463. https://scholarlycommons.pacific.edu/uoplawreview/vol48/iss2/20/

Institute for Scientific Analysis (2017, January 25). *John Irwin, criminologist.* [Press release]. John Irwin, Criminologist 1929-2010 – Institute For Scientific Analysis

Kenneth Hartman. (n.d.) Retrieved from https://www.prisonradio.org/correspondent/kenneth-hartman/

Korte, G. (2016, June 24). Pell grants for prisoners: Obama to give inmates a second chance at college. *USA Today.* https://www.usatoday.com/story/news/politics/2016/06/24/pell-grants-prisoners-obama-give-inmates-second-chance-college/86312598/

Mace, W.L. (2014, June 5). A peer-to-peer approach for campus mental health: Becoming self-empowered. *Psychology Today Blog.* https://www.psychologytoday.com/us/blog/campus-confidential-coping-college/201406/peer-peer-approach-campus-mental-health

Mukamal, D., Silbert, R., Taylor, R. M., & Lindahl, N. (2015). *Degrees of Freedom: Expanding College Opportunities for Currently and Formerly Incarcerated Californians.* Stanford Law School, p. 41. https://www.law.berkeley.edu/files/DegreesofFreedom2015_FullReport.pdf

Neuroscience Research Institute. (2022). *The benefits of peer support in mental health treatment.* https://www.neuroscienceresearchinstitute.com/peer-support-mental-health-treatment/#:~:text=The%20following%20are%20just%20a%20few%20of%20the,groups%20aren%E2%80%99t%20just%20places%20to%20receive%20help.%20

Sum. A., Khatiwada, I., McLaughlin, J. & Palma, S. (2009). *The consequences of dropping out of high school.* Prison Policy & Center for Labor Market Studies, Northeastern University, Boston, Massachusetts. Microsoft Word - The Consequences of Dropping Out of High School.doc (prisonpolicy.org)

U.S. Department of Education, National Center for Education Statistics. (2020-2021, Winter). Undergraduate graduation rates. [Press release]. Fast Facts: Undergraduate graduation rates (40) (ed.gov)

Weir, K. (2013, November). Feel like a fraud? *gradPSYCH*, 11(4), 24. https://www.apa.org/gradpsych/2013/11/fraud

4 The Freedom & Captivity Curriculum Project

Linda Small

Freedom & Captivity

After being told to be quiet, the young woman continued to laugh. Four heavily armed guards seized her, threw her onto the concrete floor, cuffed her hands behind her back, and dragged her away. This was day two of my incarceration. The brutality, cruelty, and apathy toward a fellow human being shocked me. As daily conflicts raged around me, I searched for alternatives to the norms of acceptance, detachment, or answering violence with violence. I vowed to find a better way to accept accountability, reduce harm, and resolve conflict.

That was 12 years ago. I was unfamiliar with the word abolition and its potential to disarm violent practices in the name of harm reduction. I ached for recognition, a sign that I was more than a number, an inventory to be counted or examined at will. I endured being chained to a wall underneath the courthouse, shackled and paraded in public, and strip-searched by strangers hundreds of times. These searches strip every inch of your clothing, dignity, privacy, and power. Sometimes, the need to be seen as fully human felt truly overwhelming. In 2020, a beacon of hope arrived when Erica King of the University of Southern Maine and Dr. Catherine Besteman of Colby College walked into the Southern Maine Women's Reentry Center. As I listened to their presentation about the project, a delicious quiver ran up my spine. I was in awe of the power, beauty, and vitality of the ideas they shared. Their energy, guidance, and love have sustained me throughout this project and beyond.

I took my first abolitionist college course with Erica and Catherine as I finished my bachelor's degree in the Second Chance Pell program, a federal project that reopened Pell Grants to individuals experiencing incarceration. My years of accumulated questions about the trauma-inducing tactics of the carceral state found a home. I was a budding abolitionist. Dare I claim that out loud as a captive in this punishing cultural environment? How did this internal revolution affect my self-image? I had to find out.

Diving deeper into abolitionist ideas in 2021, I participated with the other women from the Southern Maine Women's Reentry Center in the Freedom & Captivity Initiative and Abolition Night. These public events raised the voices of currently and formerly incarcerated people through podcasts,

DOI: 10.4324/9781003394426-5

32 *Linda Small*

performances, film, art, music, and poetry that explored restorative, transformative, and abolitionist practices for Maine's future. Our makeshift family of sisters, mothers, daughters, and aunties of the reentry center joined the statewide humanities-driven Freedom & Captivity Initiative. Through dance, song, poetry, and narratives, we uplifted the voices of incarcerated women, demystified stereotypes, and allowed our vulnerability to tell the story of our humanity. We laughed, cried, and dared to speak our truth. As I moved toward my release date, those events symbolized my first snips at the razor wire into freedom.

My process of flushing the psychological sewage of the carceral state from my mind began with my involvement in the Freedom & Captivity Curriculum Project. My progress would not have been possible without Dr. Besteman, the support of host Colby College, and the generous support of an ACLS sustaining public engagement grant. As the curator of the Freedom & Captivity Initiative and Curriculum Project, Catherine's fearless dedication to abolitionist practices and pedagogy gathered talent from across Maine. Her projects provided a platform for currently and formerly incarcerated people to express hope, reveal vulnerability, and shift the common narrative about who is impacted by the criminal legal system. The initiative's year of outstanding performances, exhibitions, podcasts, and artwork culminated in a dynamic website of archived brilliance, the foundation of the Freedom & Captivity Curriculum Project.

In 2022, while still incarcerated in Maine, I turned on a computer and searched for the link to our first Freedom & Captivity team meeting. This virtual gathering would include 15 people, both in and out of prison, working for 1 year to develop curricula from the materials generated in the Freedom & Captivity Initiative. When the meeting began, we formed subgroups for specific areas. I requested to be part of the working group developing the course on "Loss, Repair, and Transformation." I had an intimate relationship with loss and hoped the excruciating and ever-present pain I lived with would counter my lack of curriculum design experience.

The Zoom screen opened to a sea of familiar and unfamiliar faces. Catherine greeted me and asked how I was doing. She smiled, and I smiled in return. My ease grew as people introduced themselves, and I discovered that the diverse team was each connected to the work of collective care for formerly and currently incarcerated people. One formerly incarcerated member, Bobby, was part of our first meeting. He was a vibrant, humble, and wise voice in our Freedom & Captivity team. I took a deep breath and relaxed in the glow of belonging. Subjected to years of oppression and isolation, I felt bereft of human contact and intellectual discourse. I yearned for a space to speak my mind about the carceral state without fear of reprisal, judgment, or ridicule. Even in our virtual space, I felt a warm embodiment of safety and community. I had found my people. What followed was a story of mutual devotion, radical love, and transformation for the facilitators and students alike in our pilot program.

The Freedom & Captivity Curriculum Project   33

No one could imagine that, during our pilot class, we would lose our beloved Bobby. Bobby was a giant teddy bear who greeted everyone with soft, warm hugs full of radical love. Our team was the loving family I needed. We processed our grief together and poured our heartbreak into our curriculum. A tribute to him and the power of community. The challenging work of building the curriculum began. How could we guide and share a journey of personal discovery about the meaning of accountability, radical love, restoration, and transformation in the wake of harm? One beauty of creating the Freedom & Captivity curriculum was the awakening of these ideas within me. As we designed, shared, and wrote, learning was a community experience shared with knowledgeable and warmhearted team members.

Our first step was scanning the Freedom & Captivity website for curriculum material. The process induced visceral responses in me. Anger and sadness merged as I viewed Yannick Lowery's contribution, *Burn* (Lowery 2020) a paper collage of police, protesters, and flames. The paper collage spoke to me of our inability to move beyond racial divides. Maine's incarceration rates stood at 255 white people and 1,553 black people per 100,000 people (Prison Policy Initiative, 2018). In his call for active resistance, Joseph Martinez preached in his poem "Forgotten Prophets" (Martinez 2020) about children in solitary confinement, the condemnation of the wrongfully accused, and numbers replacing human beings. The soul-baring, and sometimes hopeful, personal reflections in pencil, coffee grinds, toothpaste, and other media used by imprisoned artists rendered me emotionally exhausted. Yet, incarcerated people inspired me with their raw reflections, extraordinary talent, and capability to reach beyond the bars of what I experienced as an utterly demented and unjust system of violence.

Our curriculum was divided into 13 weeks, each focused on a particular topic. For me, the most taxing work was on chapters that resonated with my experience, including "The Impact of Incarceration on Families" and "Women, Grief, Shame, and Parenting." I had lived and witnessed these stories; even so, they became more concrete, final, and viciously real in the narratives of others.

Living in prison was an illusory state. The physical, emotional, and mental isolation blocked the horrors of life on the outside, and I was left to imagine one of two things: a snapshot the day I was taken away in chains, or, conversely and even more disheartening, a picture of life moving forward seamlessly without me. While exploring the Freedom & Captivity website, I watched videos of people with incarcerated loved ones, heard their words, and felt their pain as they told stories of loss, grief, and loneliness. The website became a living organism that seemed to speak in sighs of despair, screams of defiance, and whispers of hope. It was an immersive experience, which did not allow for holding trauma, emotions, and reality at arm's length. As I read poems by daughters without mothers, narratives of parents disconnected from their children, and horrifying statistics, the reality was grim and crushing. According to the Prison Policy Institute (2018), about 52% of women with minor children report living with their child(ren) at the time of their arrest.

"The deep despair felt by both parent and child amounts to a colossal but largely invisible crisis: the mass punishment of over 1 million children."

The Words of One Lost Child:

Once I hit 7
I moved in with my grandparents
Mom was taken.
Where did she go?
Will the bad guys bring her home again?
Mama, come home
I miss
You.
At the start of age 8
I never understood why
I felt so alone at such a
Young age
I still laughed with my friends
And made sure my Barbie Dolls were okay
But why didn't anyone check in
On me?

("Through the Lens of a Child,"
Katie, 2022)

During this time of research, I sensed that a seismic shift in my thinking was on the horizon. The relationship of education to collective liberation and social justice became the thread that wove through my search of the archived material. Could the Freedom & Captivity curriculum experience raise critical consciousness to promote social change? After completing the research and writing the curricula, we moved into Phase Two of the project: teaching ourselves the curricula in a pilot class. The course asked participants to journal their thoughts and feelings. Participants and facilitators formed a community of mutual support and discovery as we reflected on the coursework. Together, we set community guidelines for participation, including self-care practices during challenging conversations. Class conversations about grief, loss, forgiveness, and potential political issues about public policies and practices could stir uncomfortable or overwhelming feelings. The group honored this possibility by establishing guidelines that allowed people to turn off their cameras, take a break, or the right pass, as sharing was voluntary. Weekly modules contained a vocabulary list with preliminary definitions to help understand unfamiliar terms, or the class could define restorative justice, reconciliation, the carceral state, or others for themselves. The class navigated new territory and needed language to discuss their vision for dealing with harm, accountability, and transformation. The vocabulary lists remained fluid for the group to decide if terms were missing, obsolete, or unclear in their meaning.

The curriculum team and the students of the pilot course met on Zoom one night a week for 2.5 hours. Each week, the curriculum expanded on the previous material and discussion. The facilitators introduced weekly goals and reviewed the group's expectations. At the start of class, each person introduced themselves, shared their pronouns, if desired, and answered a circle question. In the beginning, these opening circle questions encouraged sharing in unintrusive ways, "If you were no longer part of society, what would your community be losing?" As the group moved into mutual trust and discovery, the circle questions expanded accordingly, "How have you taken accountability for a harm you have caused or a law you have broken?"

The classes introduced case studies, artwork, videos, and narratives with small group discussions followed by sharing among the group. When a participant suggested that we let the group talk among themselves, I stepped back as a facilitator while the class experienced the material together and guided their own conversation. They discussed the loss of a loved one who was incarcerated, characterizing it as "death by incarceration." Shaky voices and tears expressed unhealed grief and the lack of closure when incarcerated people don't return home. There were unsolicited moments of silence to honor and reflect on sharing. This stunning display of group cohesion, support, and empathy was beyond what I had anticipated, and I attributed the extraordinary connection to the artists' contributions drawn from the Freedom & Captivity archive. The powerful stories, communicated through art, created an emotional connection. We felt empathy for the despair, sorrow, and remorse expressed through poetry, painting, and narratives. These memorable stories helped us understand one another's experiences and foster a sense of a larger community with men and women we have never met.

The experiences of incarcerated people and their loved ones told through narrative, poetry, and art were the core of our curriculum. Through the Freedom & Captivity stories and research of family policing, racial discrimination, and inequitable distribution of wealth, power, and education, I recognized that the carceral state was not the prison industrial complex but an American way of life. Facts about the carceral state enhanced the power and credibility of voices inside the razor wire. As the world's largest incarcerator, the United States holds 2.2 million people, a 500% increase from a half-century ago, at an annual cost of $100 billion (Prison Policy Initiative, 2018). Maine incarcerates more than the original NATO countries (Prison Policy Initiative, 2018), spending $436.6 million in FY 2022–2023 (Maine Legislature, 2022). Half the people the United States incarcerates are parents of minor children. In 2018, about 113 million Americans had an incarcerated or formerly incarcerated family member. One in four adults in the United States has had a sibling incarcerated, one in five has had a parent incarcerated, and one in eight has had a child incarcerated (Forward US, 2018). It was challenging to decide which chilling facts to include when researching data for the "Women, Grief, Shame, and Parenting" week.

According to a Marshall Project study, mothers and fathers who have a child placed in foster care because they are incarcerated—but who have not been accused of child abuse, neglect, endangerment, or even drug or alcohol use—were more likely to have their parental rights terminated than those who physically or sexually assaulted their kids (Marshall Project 2018). Pine Tree Legal Assistance explained that the Maine Department of Health and Human Services only needed a phone call from family, neighbors, or any community member about *suspected* child neglect to open an investigation, which can lead to a permanent record for a parent (Pine Tree Legal Assistance 2017). I wondered about the power of the Freedom & Captivity curricula to help people unpack oppressive social norms, reflect on privilege and power, and consider the role of capitalism in the choice to spend more on incarceration than education.

The United States disproportionally warehouses the poor, mentally ill, BIPOC, and other perceived non-conforming people. America justifies this social inequality through narratives that categorize these groups as dangerous, problematic, and needing control. Whose interests are served by this inequality and mass incarceration? How have individuals reconciled these facts with meaningful accountability, radical love, and abolitionist ideals of harm reduction? What meaning do justice and equity hold in our individual and collective lives? How might we bridge the polarization and confirmation biases about personal beliefs through dialog? These haunting questions were merely symptoms of larger societal issues. Everyone is affected by the carceral state.

Self-identification with the values and norms established by power and control hold people hostage and criticism of cultural beliefs becomes an attack on the self. I came face-to-face with my inability to separate who I was from my beliefs and values. There lay the rub. If I was unwilling to hold my personal truths up to the light of abolitionist practices, there would be no transformational learning or action. My evolution has been a continuous state of being. Early on, I had no clear vision but stumbled around in incarcerated darkness. I knew there was something terribly wrong but lacked the vocabulary or potential solutions. After 10 years of carceral oppression, Erica and Catherine introduced me to abolition and opened my eyes to a new perspective.

As we continued to build the Freedom & Captivity curriculum, education became a catalyst for abolitionist change. In facilitating the pilot course, we cultivated a brave space for people to envision a different way of resolving harm, brainstorming within the community, thinking out loud, and embracing different lived experiences. Many evenings, I arrived

> Emma
> so reconciliation can come before forgiveness.....huh....never considered that.
>
> Jackie
> That makes a lot of sense.
>
> Lily
> maybe reconciliation isn't the full healing of forgiveness.
>
> Taylor
> DEEP

at class exhausted from my day but the flow of rich ideas energized me. Our class on Zoom included a vibrant chat that ran parallel to the conversations unfolding over the course of the class period.

The Freedom & Captivity curriculum created a choice. It did not sell the ideals of an abolitionist society but instead provided facts, narratives, and information about the carceral state. Its authors and students were free to adopt, disregard, or reflect weekly on the material presented. A cultural shift was possible but it would happen one person, one heart, one mind at a time.

I was living in captivity and dreaming of freedom when the project began. I tried not to be swayed by the narrow scope of isolation. Often, I wondered if I would be an abolitionist without my personal experience within the carceral state. Changing hearts and minds required more than abolitionist ideals. Until we addressed the deep-seated and embodied ways of knowing ourselves and one another, we could not replace the carceral state with restorative practices. It was futile to change the prison industrial complex without addressing our

Clara
And I think lack of reconciliation, or irreconciliation, can be intentional and necessary for further growth.

Lucas
Also true ^^

Emma
Yes. And there has to be agency and choice in whether to reconcile and rebuild the relationship in a new way.

Lucas
Invariably, neither forgiveness nor reconciliation can be forced without causing further harm ^^

Taylor
Reconciliation on the other hand can/does get forced to disastrous ends... 😔

Lucas
Not only fall through, but actually risk trapping people in the original harm/victim cycle.

Emma
Right—reconcile is maybe like acceptance but not forgiveness
 like a truce?

Lily
Yes. An agreement to stop the hating and violence.
 Some people never learn that skill.

Lucas
I suppose reconciliation can take many forms, and while it can be related to forgiveness, it may or may not need to be connected or dependent one on the other.

view of ourselves and the "other." It became clear that incarceration was not a prerequisite for abolitionist thought.

In the middle of curriculum writing, I was released after 12 years of incarceration. In this joyous upheaval of emotion, wonder, and possibilities, the Freedom & Captivity curriculum project grounded me. The team was my family and I relied on them for belonging, purposeful work, and solace. The work became more than a project for us. We became radical love in action. I had the privilege of feeling and sharing their warmth in a new way. Unbounded by walls, razor wire, or rules that managed my access to people, places, and knowledge, I was able to finally hug my adopted family. This was not allowed while incarcerated, and it was transformational to leaving behind my identity as a number and restoring my humanity. Until writing this reflection, I had not considered the significance of being one of only two people working on the project who was currently incarcerated. Miraculously, it did not matter, not only to me but to the rest of the team. It wasn't until deep

Jackie
Agreed, Lucas.

Lucas
Always learning ^^

Clara
Yes, and I also think you can have forgiveness without reconciliation, right?

Lucas
Definitely, Clara!

Clara
Repair is a beautiful thing. Really.

Lucas
Yes, repair should be meaningful and harm should be accurately reflected and represented. And accountability should not be one-sided.

Clara
Isn't that the hardest thing? Sharing accountability?

Ophelia
Thank you so much for that It's really good to hear and I'm happy to know that accountability is mutual. There are many little things that go into harm.

Lily
I'm thinking of the underlying accountability of all harm.

Taylor
When we harm others, we harm ourselves... full circle. ◑
Fascist regimes indoctrinated the people to police each other for special benefits from authoritative power so that

into the work that I knew my inclusion was an act of radical love. Their loving kindness transcended the darkness of self-doubt, and I believed I was capable of what they saw in me. The safety I felt fostered healing for years of trauma, isolation, and uncertainty. More than words, the facilitators and participants breathed life into their definition of radical love. They honored the divine spark in everyone with loving care, accepted the imperfection of self and others, and were gentle in disagreement. They were radical love in action.

As we envisioned a new way of being in the world, one participant shared, "I love where we wound up, coming full circle with the idea that if people were to collectively hold a set of universally accepted principles, we would eventually eradicate the harms and maladies, like hunger, poverty, and violence, that plague our current culture." If people who were strangers just a few weeks prior could create such beauty from the community, that awakened me to the possibility of a kinder world.

I am an abolitionist but acknowledge that we cannot dismantle or

```
they could divide and conquer
the people.... just like car-
ceral cultures... *sad face*
```

In vulnerable moments of growth and sharing, our group held one another in tenderness.

Julia
```
Adriane that was so moving,
thanks so much for sharing such
a painful and powerful story.
```

Kate
```
Radical love takes strange forms.
```

Jack
```
Thank you for sharing that im-
possible situation with vulner-
ability. I hope you feel you're
here now surrounded by people
who care. Holding you and your
heart in the light.
```

Clara
```
I'm feeling this so deeply to-
night, everyone. Thank you
```

Kate.
```
This is a special class tonight.
```

Clara
```
We are getting at some of the
messiness of repair. Thank you.
```

There was lightness and some fun along our learning journey. The following was an exchange in catching a typo in the curriculum.

Lucas
```
draws = drawers (is that mans-
plaining? Or just over editing?)
```

Lily
```
thanks for the over explaining
Lucas.
```

abandon our current carceral system without providing evidence-based, viable, and scalable alternatives. Helping to build the Freedom & Captivity curriculum was my most noteworthy abolitionist achievement to date. We created space for ideas to breathe, for reflection of one's personal liberation under the guise of freedom, and for the possibilities of a different vision. A vision that embraced equity, fairness, accountability, radical love, and harm reduction. The Freedom & Captivity curriculum did not provide answers, it asked questions to enlighten the underlying causes of systemic discrimination, financial inequity, and powerlessness. The answers lie in the hearts and minds of its learners whose actions move us deeper into the status quo or lovingly toward change. I hoped that the Freedom & Captivity curriculum "will become an agency of progress if its short-term goal of self-improvement can be made compatible with a long-time, experimental but resolute policy of changing the social order" (Lindeman, 1926, p. 104).

Lucas
You're welcome, Lily!

Jack
Wear clean draws.

After an emotional conversation about loss, the group released some stress through humor.

Clara
I cry a lot too, Julia.

Taylor
Me three! Cry Queens.

Clara
Cry Queens!

Taylor
Lacrimal stimulation produces pain killers in the brain that assist with coping processes.

Lucas
Taylor, you're killing me!

Lily
Boo Hoo babies.

Emma
omg I sobbed and would have done anything to not in front of you all.

Lily
We love that about you, Emma. Cry away.

Taylor
I got shoulders for ya

Emma
Ugly crier.

Ophelia
Fighters in this group!

References

Forward US. (2018). Every second: Families are losing time. https://fwd.us.

Katie. (2022). *Through the Lens of a Child*. Freedom and Captivity Curriculum Project.

Lindeman, E. C. (1926). *The meaning of adult education*. New Republic, Inc.

Lowery, Y. (2020). *Burn*. Freedom & Captivity. https://www.freedomandcaptivity.org/burn/

Maine Legislature. (2022). CJPS biennial budget pages. Maine.gov. https://legislature.maine.gov/doc/5941

Martinez, J. (2020). *Forgotten Prophets*. Freedom & Captivity. https://www.freedomandcaptivity.org/forgotten-prophets/

Pine Tree Legal Assistance. (2017) Maine child protection: What happens when DHHS investigates a household? Pine Tree Legal Assistance. Maine Child Protection: What happens when DHHS investigates a household? | Pine Tree Legal Assistance. https://ptla.org

Prison Policy Initiative. (2018). Maine Profile. Prison Policy Initiative. https://www.prisonpolicy.org/profiles/ME.html

The Marshall Project. (2018). How incarcerated parents are losing their children forever. The Marshal Project. https://www.themarshallproject.org/2018/12/03/how-incarcerated-parents-are-losing-their-children-forever

5 Humanizing the Numbers
A Photographic Collaboration

Jamal Biggs and Isaac Wingfield

Humanize the Numbers is a collaborative photography project that brings together a class of undergraduate students from the University of Michigan and a group of 16 men housed in a Michigan Department of Corrections (MDOC) facility. Through the Prison Creative Arts Project (PCAP), the University of Michigan has a long history of arts programming in Michigan prisons. For more than 30 years, PCAP has facilitated art workshops in area prisons, including visual, literary, and performing arts. This workshop was the first of its kind for PCAP, bringing cameras into prison so that across 12 weekly workshops, each participant could build a portfolio of images that reflect their experience (Image 5.1).

Like the project, which you'll see is rooted in collaboration, this chapter was written jointly and collaboratively, uniting our voices, and bringing together our two perspectives: Jamal's as an accomplished artist serving a Life Without Parole sentence and Isaac's as a university-based faculty member.

This project was first proposed in 2014 as part of a visit by artist Mark Strandquist from Washington, DC to the University of Michigan. This coincided with an exhibition at the university of *Windows from Prison*, a series of photographs Strandquist made in collaboration with people from Washington, DC, who were incarcerated across the Federal prison system.

Under most circumstances, a camera in prison is considered contraband and would be a major offense. The state of Michigan is conservative when it comes to granting any exceptions to this policy, so this was a significant request. Because of PCAP's lengthy relationship with the MDOC, we brought the idea directly to the MDOC Director's office, and after a brief conversation with staff in the Director's office, we submitted a formal proposal for the workshop, which they approved. With the Director's endorsement, eventually we received approval from the warden (Images 5.2 and 5.3).

In the fall of 2015, the idea of bringing the cameras inside became a reality when a small group of five students and one faculty member were escorted across the courtyard of Thumb Correctional Facility with one digital camera. That first workshop cohort had only six participants from inside the prison.

DOI: 10.4324/9781003394426-6

Humanizing the Numbers 43

Image 5.1 Paint over photograph. By Jamal Biggs, 2016.

This small class size allowed us to experiment and find the best ways to photograph collaboratively. There were a number of constraints, from squeezing into a little conference room to including participants from juvenile units in the facility who couldn't show their faces and bringing one camera inside on only two occasions.

By the second cohort, in fall of 2016, together we formed a clearer vision of what is possible and what we wanted to accomplish together. Now, we were able to bring multiple cameras in every week, so there was more hands-on time with the cameras. We discussed the constraints we were working under in the prison system, often using this as a starting point for

Image 5.2 The Creator. I came to prison with blood on my hands; I will leave with paint on them. By Johnnie Trice, 2015.

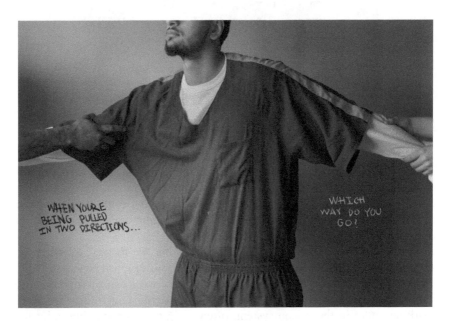

Image 5.3 Choices. By M, 2015.

conceptualizing images. We considered who images were made for and who needs to see them: MDOC leaders, prison advocacy organizations, friends and family members, and the public. Having these things as a starting place helps guide our creativity.

These photography workshops are unique from prison-sponsored programs, which are often run by prison staff, i.e., current or former officers, counselors, or other individuals who have been trained to view and interact with prisoners in a specific way. As a result, many of them, knowingly or unknowingly, have an "us-versus-them" or "supervisor-versus-subordinate" mentality, not allowing prison staff to see a prisoner as an equal. This is not the case with university faculty and students, who do not have the same training and can form their own opinions about the workshop participants. Those in prison easily pick up on these differences.

Building mutual trust begins on the first day of the workshop when participants meet each other. In our workshop together, Isaac asked me how I'd like to be addressed. I said by my first name, "Jamal," and he identified himself by his first name, "Isaac." This small gesture distinguished him from prison staff, who are always prohibited from using first names out of fear of overfamiliarity. Unlike programs run by prison staff, university faculty and students never use the threat of issuing misconduct reports to gain compliance and do not speak to prisoners as if they're superior to them—something prison staff often do. As a result, some prisoners do not feel comfortable confiding in prison staff out of fear that it may be used against them but may be more comfortable opening up in the workshop's environment of respect and trust between all parties.

Trust is further built by the humility and genuine interest everyone shows toward each other, relating to one another as equals. The university students don't judge the men in prison due to their circumstances or lack of knowledge, instead valuing and respecting them and their opinions. We often have broader conversations, sharing aspects of our history and personal stories, continuing to build trust. Facilitating these candid discussions with empathy, respect, and humility leads to a culture of collaboration and openness. This results in greater meaningful breakthroughs in learning for everyone, as well as social and emotional growth.

Experiencing the dignity of the workshops helps build confidence and self-esteem, which many men in prison lack. In a socially restrictive environment, it challenges men to overcome their fears or social anxiety, which are exacerbated by the realities of incarceration. Creating a welcoming space that helps men reconnect with the outside world becomes a breath of fresh air that can sustain a person, giving them a sense of relevance and purpose in a time when they are otherwise isolated from society.

Although it is part of a university course, the workshop doesn't have a syllabus, tests, grades, or a strict schedule. Instead, participants move around the room, working on their own projects and helping others on theirs. This all makes the workshop feel casual and free-flowing, so learning is easy and fun.

Since the course does not require previous experience for students who enroll, it helps put everyone on equal footing, learning the skills together. As everyone learns together, some people find that they are more naturally inclined to work with cameras, while others become more interested in developing the ideas being communicated through their images. Everyone works together, helping and advising anyone who is struggling. People come alongside one another and assist each other as a photographer and/or a model in each of the projects.

Even though many of the men—especially those serving lengthy sentences—have never touched a digital camera prior to the workshop, they are excited about the hands-on learning experience. Despite the abundance of concern by prison authorities associated with us using cameras in prison, a lot of care goes into making everyone feel it isn't a big deal and encouraging everyone to freely explore and experiment with the equipment. This puts at ease any initial trepidation about handling the cameras.

The class shares not only how to use the cameras but also how to consider what messages participants want to convey with images, as well as how to get those messages out. Each participant carefully thinks about what they want to say and makes images that they feel speak for them. This allows participants to learn not only the technical aspects of photography but the creative side as well.

One of the driving elements of the project is to flip the structure of the space. When university-affiliated people come into prison, they are inherently the ones with power and authority. In this collaboration, the university still holds more power. However, from the beginning the voices of those in prison are central to the process, relying on their perspective to provide direction for the work. Allowing their vision to take center stage, the project pushes for their ownership and authorship in every way possible. Practically, this means recognizing each participant's ownership of their image rights and only sharing images they want to be seen. We also seek out participants' recommendations for where the resulting images should be displayed (Images 5.4 and 5.5).

Sometimes, we hang backdrops to hide certain aspects of the space. We also use props that are already present in the space or that the men from prison bring with them to the workshop. For example, we utilized the desk, books, and blackboard of one of the classrooms, along with men posing as students being tutored, to capture the story of being a tutor in the prison's GED program. Some men bring photographs of memorable past events and incorporate them into different shots. There are even instances where participants creatively incorporate their paintings with some of their photos, invoking a sense of fantasy.

During 12 weekly meetings, we have many conversations about our process, about the constraints we are working under, and about life lived under these constraints. Sixteen men from the prison facility, one faculty member, and no more than eight students from the University of Michigan are together

Humanizing the Numbers 47

Image 5.4 My children to this day do not really understand why I cannot come home. Each and every time they visit, when it's time to leave they cry, which breaks me down on the inside. My children and family no longer trust the police or the justice system, they have experienced firsthand the injustice that has been done to me. I constantly remind them that all police are not corrupted, but it's hard for them to trust police when I'm still fighting to get out of prison for a crime I am actually and factually innocent of. By LaVone, 2016.

in one room. We meet in classrooms, the visiting room, or in a multi-purpose meeting/storage room, depending on the prison's schedule. Regardless of the room's intended purpose, we make it a space to explore life through photographs. As the workshop progresses, we are able to explore the complexity of those stories and the personal impact of the criminal legal system.

At first it was almost impossible for any of us to imagine such a program existing inside a prison, considering the concerns Michigan prison staff have about cameras in prison. Attempts to expand the project to other facilities have been unsuccessful because many MDOC staff perceive cameras as a significant custody and security issue. This tension brings awareness to the workshop's fragility and heightens the sense that the workshop might be ended at any time by the MDOC administration.

Even years into the project, it can still be difficult trying to align two very large and slow-moving institutions: the university schedules classes months in advance, and the MDOC can take more than a month to approve a workshop. Our continual success in bringing cameras inside these prisons would

Image 5.5 Being aware of how college and learning helped change my thinking, I now try to help spark that change in others by working as a tutor, helping other prisoners obtain their GED. The greatest reward is in helping individuals get their GED who didn't believe they could, for whatever reason. Working with them for weeks and months and seeing that surprised look on their face and joy in their heart when they finally get the news, "You've passed!" is priceless. By Jamal Biggs, 2016.

not be possible without PCAP's historic institutional relationship with the MDOC.

Across 7 years of workshops, there have been workshops at two facilities, under three wardens, with four different Special Activities Directors—our direct contact at the facility. These transitions can be bumpy, and at times the support from the MDOC Director's office helped smooth over any difficulty. These shifting relationships result in fluctuating expectations from one workshop to another. At times we end up renegotiating longstanding practices in the workshop, sometimes as small as how we address each other: can we use first names, or do we have to use last names like the prison staff? Seeing the creative expression of men in the workshop and the positive outcomes is helpful in maintaining support from staff inside the facility (Image 5.6).

There are also benefits of operating independently from the system, as we have the freedom to determine more parameters of the program. Prison-sponsored educational and vocational programs in the state of Michigan often exclude large groups of people from being able to participate—specifically lifers or people with significant time left in their sentence. This is not the case

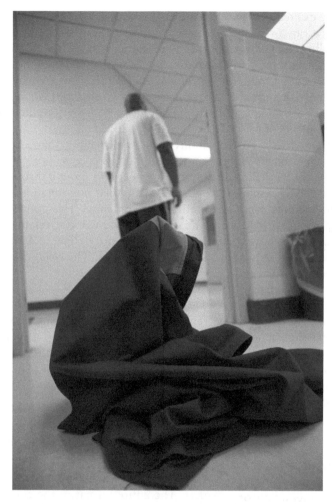

Image 5.6 As I continue to make progress in life, I am determined to leave my bad choice behind me. I am now prepared to become a pillar in the community. I have truly outgrown confinement. By Corey, 2017.

for *Humanize the Numbers*, which allows people an equal opportunity to participate, regardless of their sentence or conviction. Because this is such a rare opportunity for men with years left on their sentences, the number of requests to participate greatly surpasses the capacity for each cohort, which is limited to 16. Although the number of men participating in the project is small, the impact is deeper and more profound for those lucky few.

Having a Life sentence means being excluded from participating in most of the classes and programs offered by the MDOC due to the requirement that someone has to be within a few years from their release date to qualify.

Lifers were excited that was not the case with this workshop. It was a huge honor to be one of the few who was granted the privilege to attend this class and allowed the rare opportunity to share my story beyond these prison walls. Even as a Lifer, I still have dreams, as well as a driving desire to better myself. It's great that *Humanize the Numbers* recognizes this. As another workshop participant said, "That once a week [workshop] would carry and balance out 3 or 4 months [of prison life], lifting your spirits, allowing you to see society outside of prison" (D. Turner-EL, 2022).

Given that we held six workshops at the same facility, that relational history helps each cohort settle in more easily. It has become fairly typical that men starting the workshop already know something about it through a friend who was in the workshop or from someone in their housing unit who would show their pictures every week after the workshop. This continuity helps build rapport and provides a foundation for good working relationships.

The workshops have a consistent focus on storytelling, cultivating conversation and dialogue about shared experiences. The open dialogue and broad-ranging discussions are transformative and influence the image-making process, breaking down barriers in both prisoner-to-volunteer and prisoner-to-prisoner relationships and helping us connect on a deeper level than we would have otherwise. Even if they know the faces of most of the guys in the workshop, many men haven't had much interaction or conversation with the other participants prior to the workshop. Hearing a number of their personal stories and working together to capture each other's story through photography, we learned a lot about one another and built friendships. Now, whenever workshop participants see each other on the prison yard we now greet one another rather

The *Humanize the Numbers* workshop remains one of the most unusual and significant creative experiences I've had in my life. Not only were the physical setting and the people I interacted with deeply unconventional for a college course, but the learning style was not something I'd really experienced in any profound way before. We, the students, were teaching another group of students photography skills, but it was about so much more than that. The entire format of the course was "outside the box." Photography was a medium through which we were able to get to know and learn from a group of people who we probably would have never interacted with otherwise. We were learning via teaching, and learning in real time about the effect creative outlets and opportunities have on people in radically different circumstances than privileged college kids.

This experience—calling it a "course" doesn't really encompass everything—had a significant impact on my understanding of both learning and teaching.

than just passing by, recognizing the unique and special bond we shared from the class.

At the end of the semester, the undergraduate students in the course complete a written reflection on the experience. This exercise allows them to process exactly what they are learning, often realizing for the first time the stereotypes and assumptions they held about those touched by the criminal legal system. Students' comments demonstrate that they are profoundly impacted by the experience and awakened to the realities of the system from a different perspective. This provides a new and unexpected lens on society. One student addressed this in her end-of-term reflection on the collaborative workshop:

I'd previously assumed that learning was something one primarily experienced in a school, for academic purposes. The *Humanize the Numbers* workshop really expanded my perspective. No other course I took during my time at the University of Michigan led me to such intense personal reflection on my limitations, biases, and beliefs. I also learned that working closely with a smaller group of people, especially consistently and over longer periods of time, is a powerful tool for social change and action. It was an unusual learning experience in that there wasn't a "correct" or predictable way we were supposed to run the workshop; we had guidelines and rules, of course, but our experience was dependent on the people we worked with in prison and their goals for the photography work they did.

Humanize the Numbers was one of the most memorable experiences of my 4 years at the University of Michigan, academic or otherwise.

– Sarah Posner

I was mentally prepared for the emotional culture shock between my life experiences and life inside the prison, and the thoughtful and intense discussions in class. I was not prepared, however, for the time outside of the class, workshop, editing and projects that I spend thinking about this experience. It is as though a new part of my brain has been activated, and the neurons there are constantly excited.

(Z. Taswell, 2020)

Learning the individual stories of people in the prison system opens students to an expansive new way of seeing and understanding the world. This becomes a key point of growth for students and can prove transformational. They begin to see behind the walls of the prison system—that it is not a system of faceless masses, but a group of unique individuals, each of whom is profoundly impacted by the criminal legal system. As one student wrote in his reflection, "This is something I cannot unlearn, and my perception of the world is forever altered" (S. Stewart, 2018) (Images 5.7–5.9).

Image 5.7 Anti-mug$hot. By Sankofa 360°, 2019.

Because students learn about the system by coming alongside those most directly impacted, students' understanding is inherently more personal. It gives students a human-scaled view of an expansive system. This individualized scope of learning also spurs students to grapple with their own perspectives and outlook. They see what is often an invisible system, and they begin

Image 5.8 My father, Lensey Earl Mason, was killed on August 16, 1974. I gaze at the scene where his life was tragically taken. At 4 years old, August 16, 1974 was the day I lost it all. By Connell Howard, 2018.

Image 5.9 Tired of the Chaos. By DLG, 2019.

to understand ways in which they have been isolated from it or are complicit in it as they grapple with their own unexpected prejudice.

Humanize the Numbers photography workshops lifts up the voices of the silenced, allowing their voices to travel well beyond the prison walls. Instead of being hidden and suppressed, through their images and words those in prison become important contributors to society's conversation on our crime and punishment problem. Because the images produced are intended to go out into the world, the workshop is inherently outward-oriented. Given that this is a limited opportunity for everyone present to get their message out, knowing that it will come to a close after only a few months gives the workshops an intensity not present in classes on campus. When you are incarcerated, this opportunity represents a rare chance to share your vision and your story with the world.

In the workshops, we have also decided where and with whom we wanted the images and messages to be shared. This broadens understanding, challenges negative stereotypes, and thus provides support to impact changes in public policy and safety in constructive, comprehensive, and beneficial ways.

The title of the project, *Humanize the Numbers*, came from our very first workshop in 2015, where one participant suggested that bringing a camera into prison could serve to literally "humanize the numbers." Our hope is that, even in some small way, it does just that: helps us all see people inside prison as more than just a number. If the project can do that not just for the people most involved, from the university or the prison, but also for judges, prosecutors, legislators, and for the voting public, then it will have been a great success (Images 5.10 and 5.11).

54 *Jamal Biggs and Isaac Wingfield*

Image 5.10 Loss of identity. By June, 2018.

Image 5.11 I am not a number. My name is José Burgos, I was born in Ponce, Puerto Rico. I am a brother, an uncle, a friend, and a mentor. I am not a number. By José Burgos, 2018.

Permissions

D. Turner-EL, personal communication (Unpublished Interview), 2022. Reprinted with permission.

S. Stewart, personal communication (Workshop Reflection), 2018. Reprinted with permission.

Z. Taswell, personal communication (Workshop Reflection), 2020. Reprinted with permission.

Section II
Collaborating in and through the System

6 Scaling Walls
Dismantling Asymmetries Through Empowering Song

André de Quadros, Wayland "X" Coleman, and Krystal Morin

We—Wayland, André, and Krystal—have been engaged in Boston University's *Prison Arts Project* before we named it *Race, Prison, Justice Arts* (RPJA). Over 10 years ago, André went into the Norfolk prison as part of Boston University's Prison Education Program; Wayland was one of the students; and Krystal has co-led the *Prison Arts Project* since we co-founded it with two other colleagues—Judy Braha and Bradford Dumont. The course that Wayland took in prison gave rise to the Empowering Song approach (de Quadros & Amrein, 2022), described by Bryonn Bain (2023) in these terms:

> Empowering Song uses music to reclaim our humanity in inhumane places. It smuggles imagination into dungeons, turns creativity from contraband into commissary. Under the envious eye of armed guards, it unlocks more knowledge on the prison yard than most scholars on Harvard Yard; runs rivers of refuge through deserts of despair; and liberates the spirit of community by any melody necessary... Empowering Song is to music what Pedagogy of the Oppressed is to education, and Theater of the Oppressed is to drama ... they subvert the status quo by democratizing the school, the stage, and the studio.
>
> (p. ix)

In foregrounding our chapter, we position ourselves in relation to the work. Holland et al. (1998) argue that each of us belong in unique constellations of relationships, race, histories, and identities, what they term *figured world*. In the next section, we narrate our figured worlds.

Our Figured Worlds

Wayland—Who Am I?

The only crime that I have committed is being born black and poor in Amerikkka. I was born in the racist south of Birmingham, Alabama, to poor parents living well below the poverty line. I was named Wayland Coleman,

DOI: 10.4324/9781003394426-8

and although my name serves as an identifier for my individual image, it does not suggest who I am in the grand scheme of the nation and society that I was born into. In the national and historical scheme of Amerikkka's white supremacy, my birth into a poor, black body, placed me in the criminal category—the most socially denounced class (not necessarily the "criminal" itself, but, essentially, the poor and black one). Because my birth nation decided post-slavery that black people would be society's deviants, I was strategically and politically targeted for incarceration as soon as my mother was pregnant with me. "One out of every three Black boys born today can expect to be sentenced to prison, compared 1 out 6 Latino boys; one out of 17 white boys" (naacp.org, 2023).

So, who am I? As a youth, I was an 11- or 12-year-old who would steal a sandwich from a convenience store, not because I wanted to upset the socio-economic fabric of upper and middle-class society, or to confirm for white people that brown skin was criminal, but because I was hungry, and I wanted to eat it. However, according to our society's model, I was not some poor, hungry kid; I was a thief—a specific label for a poor person who dares takes a crumb from the over-sated king's table.

In 1997, I was arrested, and in 1998, I was tried and convicted of a murder I did not commit, by an all-white jury. This inmate thing that I would be identified as, placed me in an environment where my birth society supported the idea of my being dehumanized, oppressed, repressed, isolated, abused, harassed, and tormented for the remainder of my life. So, once I was given a number to replace my name, I was much worse than a black teenager superpredator. I was a black inmate.

André—Who Am I?

I encountered race for the first time when my family went to Australia during the White Australia Policy. I never realized what it meant to be brown until then. I was made brown in the way that Farah (2022) recounts in his book, *America Made Me a Black Man: A Memoir*. The experience of being brown has had a powerful sense of self-making for me. When I came to the United States, I was not expecting to be shocked by American cruelty, arriving as I did just before September 11. As an act of resistance, I searched for a way to find meaning and difference, a search that led me to one of the darkest spaces in Boston, the Norfolk prison. I went to the Norfolk prison, fully anticipating that conventional pedagogies would not work in the incarcerated space where folx were more interested in telling stories, expressing themselves, and dreaming through artistic creation. This led to the formation and synthesis of the Empowering Song approach (de Quadros, 2015, 2016, 2017, 2018a, 2018b, 2018c) described here. This approach has found pedagogical application in a variety of settings from prisons and homeless shelters to refugee settings and beyond.

Krystal—Who Am I?

Like many privileged, white Americans, critical examinations of race were woefully absent from my upbringing and education. Growing up in rural New Hampshire, I was especially deluded about myself and the world I lived in, in the way that Baldwin (1972) describes in his writing, *No Name on the Street*. It was not until college, the U.S. presidential election of 2008, and university teachers who brought new perspectives into my life and prompted me on a journey to lift the veil of a white supremacist, ableist, heteropatriarchal lens. The first time I came into close contact with the carceral system was not out of necessity but through meeting and engaging with André. Since then, this work has continuously invited me to better understand my own humanity, and my relationship to anyone deemed "other." My work in settings of incarceration and particularly utilizing the Empowering Song approach has helped me to see the cultures of domination and control that proliferate American systems. This work has led me to meet and learn from some of the most beautiful, brilliant, and insightful souls I have had the honor of knowing. It has brought me into conversations and exchanges that made me feel inspired, alive, and have led me to engaging in activism to dismantle these systems of oppression. This work has helped me to see the arts as a vehicle for liberation and the potential for every space that I have the opportunity to construct, to reflect the kind of just and equitable society we desire to live in.

The University, the Prison, the Arts, and Story

Wayland enrolled in the Boston University Prison Education Program. Through academics, he began to feel that people had seen the human in him, and not the monster. He remembers waking up on the morning of the first class not knowing what to expect, given that it was yet another monotonous day in prison has never been anything to wake up excited about. He writes:

> Another day of overzealous prison guards wanting to stop and frisk me every hundred yards, or to ravage through the stuff in my cell. Another day of my incarcerated peers' hyper-masculine attitudes that often lead to a face getting punched, or worse. I yawned at the thought of having to get out of bed, and for a moment debated going back to sleep, where I would be spared the stress of the day that awaited me. "You gotta get up X," I reasoned with myself, "you got school." I washed my face, brushed my teeth, and made my morning cup of coffee, and prepared to live once again, the repeating day that I'd lived for over a decade.

The classroom was a small space in the education building of the Norfolk prison. Several tables lined the floor space, two chairs parked at each table. Wayland sat at one of the tables directly in front of the teacher's desk—a worn block of wood, seemingly saddened from serving much of its life in prison.

62 *André de Quadros, Wayland "X" Coleman, and Krystal Morin*

The music theory books in front of each person suggested that the course would be about the biographical histories of old, white classical composers. Wayland remembers wondering if the professor would be able to make the subject interesting, considering that most of the class listened to hip-hop music. As he looked around, he saw worried looks on his classmates' faces confirming his thoughts.

He writes further:

> The classroom door suddenly swung open, exposing an enthusiastic man - André de Quadros, who didn't greet me with a handshake. Instead, he extended his arms as if he were a great eagle and welcomed me in for a hug. Awkward, but soothing, I thought. I'd never walked into a classroom and hugged my professor, but the humaneness of the gesture felt good. Shortly after the greetings, he addressed the class. "You guys don't have to worry about the books," he said. "We're not going to be using those. We needed to have some kind of textbook for the class," he explained with a slight laugh. "Are we allowed to move the furniture?" André asked. After a short discussion, the old sad desk was pushed into a corner of the room, the tables were deemed useless, and were marginalized to lining the walls, and the chairs were organized into a circle. The strange class took its first breath and became a space for me to breathe for the next seven semesters. I went to bed that night replaying in my mind and emotions, the activities and bonding that took place in the strange class. I've never danced in any classroom setting or held hands with my classmates. We held hands, I thought. All my classmates were people who lived in my environment, but many of whose names I hadn't known. On that night, however, I could say all their names. I visualized André's gray eyes that had enchanted me, and the kindness and friendliness that they exuded. What did they see? I thought. André hugged me, I added to the thought, which dropped another log into the fire of emotional confusion. I thought about the conversation that he and I had during the class break. André traveled the world and organized choirs. I also discovered in our brief conversation that he was a bit of an activist, which explained the hug a little. I smiled. André sees the human through the oppression, I thought. I closed the curtains of my sleepy eyes. I couldn't wait to open them to a new day where I could once again enter the new space of the strange class.

Race, Prison, Justice Arts

Writing from the Outside

André and Krystal came to this project with an intense desire to create proximity between the inside and the outside, not just as those incarcerated and not, but also between people of color and white people and privileged and unprivileged. RPJA sought to make us proximal to incarcerated and formerly incarcerated individuals through deep listening and respect for their stories, experiences, and the humanity we share. In the process, we anticipated that our participants might feel destabilized and yearn for more layers of understanding. For us, the questions became: In this disrupted and questioning state, how can we learn to activate ourselves? How can the arts become a bridge that enables us to engage our creative souls in conversation with this proximity?

Participants on and off the Boston University campus clearly had a desire to address issues of race, injustice, and mass incarceration after the intensely explosive summer of 2020 following the killing of George Floyd, Breonna Taylor, and many others at the hands of police. As faculty, keenly interested in the arts and social justice who have a decade of experience teaching in incarcerated settings, we wanted to take action as well. We were intent on introducing students to facts linking race and mass incarceration in the US and the power of the arts as a force for change inside and outside of carceral settings.

RPJA was formed as an open dialogue sparking activism through the arts.[1] We resonate with educator and philosopher Paulo Freire's (2000/1970) *Pedagogy of the Oppressed*, in the fourth chapter for which he discusses the role of dialogue as central to empowerment. Our approach also aligns with artist and activist Augusto Boal's Theatre of the Oppressed (1993), in which Boal argues for co-creation as fundamental to empowering through the arts. In the Norfolk prison classroom, a typical session was part of a semester-long trajectory organized around themes, such as "I once was lost but now am found" and "Remember me, but ah! Forget my fate."

We engaged a collective of undergraduate and graduate students, faculty, staff, and community members from varied programs across Boston University who participated in either a short-form co-curricular workshop or a semester-long course to explore race and the American incarceration system as a form of systemic injustice. With them, we focused on the lived stories of Black and Brown incarcerated and formerly incarcerated individuals who have found expansion and personal discovery, as well as a path to activism, through the arts. Throughout each experience, we presented special guests sharing first-hand accounts through a variety of media including visits, written stories, artwork, poetry, phone calls, and interviews. Each artist's story served as the catalyst for the creation of artworks that amplified the untenable situation in our country today. Through these experiences, we intended to:

- Create common ground with participants from across the university;
- Center and respond to stories of Black and Brown incarcerated and formerly incarcerated individuals;
- Engage in creative play and collaboration that cultivates the students' own voices;

- Engage participants in responding artistically to injustice, and to honor and illuminate marginalized voices;
- Initiate dreaming, visioning, and building together; and
- Publicly share the fruits of the work made in response to their introduction to arts as activism.

The culminating process of RPJA continues to be the creation of a public virtual gallery that exhibits the creative work of currently and formerly incarcerated artists as well as that of our participants. In 2021, we launched the gallery to the public through a virtual community conversation event featuring some of our guest artists, community supporters and participant voices, to speak to the power of activism in the arts, and to share their big take-aways were in this process.

The following reflection from Vijay Fisch, a student participant in RPJA during the spring of 2023, demonstrates the impact and learnings from his participation in visits to Suffolk County Jail, where he engaged in sharing, discussion, and creative exercises.

> I thought it was a beautiful and transformative experience. All of my preconceptions of prison before entering were based on my own prejudices, most of which included racist and classist stereotypes that had been built into my understanding since I was a child. From movies to music, the words through which I could explain a prison were "dirty, dangerous, and decrepit." Meeting incarcerated people and talking with them has completely reshaped my understanding of the condition and reality within American prisons.

The Bird and The Fox by **Wayland X. Coleman**

> A bird in a box with hopes and dreams,
> To fly atop its box and sing,
> Begs the sly-eyed fox, oh please,
> Please restore its broken wing.
> The sly fox grins a slippery smile,
> And gestures towards the wind-blown trees,
> And laughs out to the poor ole bird,
> Only time can free the leaves.
> Only time can free the leaves,
> He gestures towards the wind-blown trees,
> HA HA HA HA HA, poor bird,
> Only time can free the leaves.

The synergy and alchemy involved in deep listening and art-making fueled by empathy can often revolutionize a person and transform misunderstanding to full comprehension. Based on interviews with our participants, we realized that transformative methods in our project changed lives, opened hearts, inspired new forms of artistic expression, and encouraged risk in creation, as well as open-mindedness, collaboration, and uplift.

Conclusion and Implications

So, what do we make of this work? How can we begin to understand what we are doing when the process has such far-reaching consequences? The very day we were finalizing this chapter, André received a message from an attorney, "This is … I am here now meeting with Jack Mcintyre, formerly of Norfolk, who is now released on medical parole, due to terminal illness. He loved your classes … He says you brought hope to Norfolk." That seems to be an affirmation of an approach that worked intentionally to create opportunities for story-telling. How, we ask ourselves, did that lead to hope?

Meanwhile, as we write, Wayland has been placed in the extended cruelty of solitary confinement. Wayland is a central figure in RPJA. His activism and infinite reservoir of hope found expression in this article (Coleman, 2020), but there are numerous other examples of narratives that he has produced over the years.

We see our practice of the arts as a space to center human connection, community-building, and to share meaningful experiences in a process that seeks to cultivate hope in one another alongside recognition of extreme brutality. Through the narrative arts, we invite participants to connect deeply to their own identity, dreams, and big ideas. When we center the arts as a means for dialogue, there is no space to remain neutral, anonymous, or even complicit; rather, we can deepen our own relationship to our shared human experience and the world we live in and to be energized for changing the world.

Note

1 See https://burpjp.weebly.com/ for more information.

References

Bain, B. (2023). Empowering song: Music education from the margins (pp. ix–xiii). Routledge.

Baldwin, J. (1972). No name in the street. Dial Press.

Boal, A. (1993). Theater of the oppressed. Theatre Communications Group.

Coleman, W. (2020). Remember me for the love that I have in me. In A. de Quadros & K. Vu (Eds.) My body was left on the street: Music education and displacement (pp. 96–103). Brill.

de Quadros, A. (2015). Rescuing choral music from the realm of the elite: Models for twenty-first century music-making – Two case illustrations. In C. Benedict, P. Schmidt, G. Spruce, & P. Woodford (Eds.) The Oxford handbook of social justice in music education (pp. 501–512). Oxford University Press.

de Quadros, A. (2016). Case illustration: I once was lost but now am found: Music and embodied arts in two American prisons. In S. Clift & P. Camic (Eds.) The Oxford textbook of creative arts, health and wellbeing (pp. 187–192). Oxford University Press.

de Quadros, A. (2017). Music, the arts, and global health: In search of sangam, its theory and paradigms. Journal of Folklore Research, 54(1–2), 15. doi:10.2979/jfolkrese.54.2.02

de Quadros, A. (2018a). Nurturing vulnerability in imprisoned manhood: A spirit journey. In K. Hendricks & J. Boyce Tillman (Eds.) Queering freedom: Music, identity, and spirituality (pp. 187–200). Peter Lang.

de Quadros, A. (2018b). Community music portraits of struggle, identity, and togetherness. In B. Bartleet, & L. Higgins (Eds.), The Oxford handbook of community music (pp. 265–280). Oxford University Press.

de Quadros, A. (2018c). Identity, belonging and struggle: Mobilizing community and transforming individuals through music. Min-Ad: Israel Studies in Musicology, 15(2), 13–22.

de Quadros, A., & Amrein, E. (2022). Empowering song: Music education from the margins. Routledge.

Farah, B. J. (2022). America made me a black man: A memoir. Harper Collins.

Freire, P. (2000/1970). Pedagogy of the oppressed (M. B. Ramos, Trans.). Bloomsbury.

Holland, D., Lachicotte, W. Jr., Skinner, D., & Cain, C. (1998). Identity and agency in cultural worlds. Harvard University Press.

7 "Disappearing Acts" and Education as the Practice of Freedom

Feminist Pedagogy in Carceral Spaces

Laura E. Ciolkowski

My story in this chapter opens with disappearance, turns to despair and then rage, and finally settles into the feminist refuge, described so powerfully by great teachers like Paulo Freire and bell hooks, of education as the "practice of freedom" (Freire, 1970, p. 62). This feminist tale of radical pedagogy begins inside a women's prison, in the company of the 12 students enrolled in my for-credit college course "Introduction to Gender and Sexuality Studies." Well-accustomed to the everyday exercise of carceral control that shapes the prison spaces in which I teach, I was nevertheless thrown off-balance by the administration's sudden change of heart about our course content. In week two of the semester, I was informed that two-thirds of our pre-approved course materials would be removed immediately: this is the inaugural "disappearing act" of my title.[1] Soon after the decision came down, officers confiscated our course packets and were directed to remove handfuls of poetry and prose. The following class session, each student was handed back an emaciated stack of paper held together with a rubber band, jagged edges in the spaces where the pages had been torn out.

People who struggle to survive behind bars and, to a far lesser degree, those of us who spend time teaching in prison, are familiar with the queasy feeling of living in a world turned upside-down, the experience of standing steady one minute and then suddenly losing your footing when the environment you thought you understood has warped and changed into something you no longer recognize or know how to navigate safely. People inside understand that prison is profoundly disorienting by design. It is a twilight zone, in the words of those who have experienced it, in which the il-logic of discipline and the erratic exercise of power wear people out, bearing down on them with the crushing weight of confusion and inconsistency. The animated video project "Welcome to the Zo," based on thousands of letters and essays written by incarcerated people and collected by the American Prison Writing Archive, captures the challenges of surviving in prison and the "deliberately disorienting rules and impossible tasks" (Keller, 2020) that shape the daily experience of incarceration in America. In the Zo, prison jargon for The Twilight Zone, carceral rules and even the definition of "right" and "wrong" are

DOI: 10.4324/9781003394426-9

68 *Laura E. Ciolkowski*

constantly in motion, making day-to-day survival risky and freedom from harm or space for healing rare.

The surprise of the week two raid on our course content—along with the arbitrary nature of the disappearance—the removal, for example, of June Jordan (but not Angela Davis), and bell hooks (but not Audre Lorde)—made little intellectual, or curricular sense but was entirely consistent with the enraging unpredictability and randomness of life inside the Zo. After the remaining pages of the course packets were returned to students in the class, we sat for some time in silence, 12 bodies dressed in green (plus one in "street clothes" and identified by an instructor visitor's badge), sitting on tablet arm school chairs arranged in an imperfect circle. Together, we held feelings of shame, despair, and what Lorde would surely celebrate as the anger that ultimately would drive students to gain even deeper insight into the carceral logics that work to hierarchize, devalue, and dehumanize them. How might students' anger over the prison's refusal to recognize their intellectual autonomy inspire them to analyze and explain the complex systems of power that, as Lorde would say, hold all of us locked in their "teeth" (Lorde, 1997, p. 281)? How could our collective anger over the indignities of censorship and the control over access to knowledge prompt us to make theory about the structures of power that discipline bodies and shape education in carceral spaces? We all understood, as we sat in the classroom, that we were at a significant crossroad with an urgent decision to make about the semester ahead: (1) give up on a tuition-free college course in which the lion's share of the physical content has been disappeared, or (2) embrace the feminist challenge, without books but with our collective histories and lived experience of power and oppression to guide us, of co-creating the themes and direction of our work, clarifying our learning objectives, and intentionally carving out the critical space to sharpen and practice feminist analysis.

Lorde reminds us: "when we turn from anger we turn from insight, saying we will accept only the designs already known, deadly and safely familiar" (Lorde, 1997, p. 283). Our refusal of the "deadly and safely familiar" inspired us to build a robust feminist learning community in prison. The humiliation students experienced led directly to the commitment to imagine a daring new educational path. This is the daring that, bell hooks tells us, can be found at the root of all feminist liberation projects:

> I am grateful for the many women and men who dare to create theory from the location of pain and struggle, who courageously expose wounds to give us their experience to teach and guide, as a means to chart new theoretical journeys. Their work is liberatory. It not only enables us to remember and recover ourselves, it charges and challenges us to renew our commitment to an active, inclusive feminist struggle.
>
> (hooks, 1994, p. 74)

"Disappearing Acts" and Education as the Practice of Freedom 69

The unanimous decision of our group was to rebuild rather than abandon the course, centering our work on weighty questions about power (how is it exercised? What shapes does it take? How can we build and share it with others in the service of feminist social justice?) and the production of knowledge (who gets to be a "knower"? what gets to count as knowledge? who gets to decide?).

The commitment to chart this "new theoretical journey" embodies the kind of liberatory education that most of the students in the class had been denied in their formal educational life inside under-resourced schools located in predominantly under-resourced communities. Adrienne Rich once noted, reflecting on her experience teaching working-class students of color in the educational opportunity program SEEK (Search for Education, Elevation, and Knowledge), that educationally disenfranchised people like the students in my class "have had language and literature used against them, to keep them in their place, to mystify, to bully, to make them feel powerless" (Rich, 1979, p. 63). These students have been rewarded for passivity and silence and punished for making theory from the many threads of their lived experience. The educational histories of the students in the class and, statistically, the educational histories of people in prison, are for the most part riddled with the "unresolved trauma and shame" (Daniels, 2022, p. 18) created by the presumption of their intellectual deficit and by a dismissal of their historical knowledge, creative capacity, and visionary spirit. Leigh Patel makes this point so powerfully in her decolonial exploration of the colonizing, standardizing, and subjugating spaces of educational institutions in the US. Patel describes the ways that our schools and universities frequently erase not only knowledge built out of lived experience but also personhood. She formulates a compelling critique, following practitioners of critical pedagogy like Freire and hooks, of the approach to learning that Freire has disparagingly dubbed "the banking model." Education in the "banking model," according to Freire:

> becomes an act of depositing, in which the students are the depositories and the teacher is the depositor. Instead of communicating, the teacher issues communiques and makes deposits which the students patiently receive, memorize, and repeat. This is the "banking" concept of education, in which the scope of action allowed to the students extends only as far as receiving, filing, and storing the deposits. They do, it is true, have the opportunity to become collectors or cataloguers of the things they store. But in the last analysis, it is the people themselves who are filed away through the lack of creativity, transformation, and knowledge in this (at best) misguided system.
>
> (Freire, 1970, p. 53)

70   *Laura E. Ciolkowski*

Success in the banking model is measured not by the development of critical consciousness or by the practice of freedom, but by "how well people fit the world the oppressors have created, and how little they question it" (Freire, 1970, p. 57). I take Freire's critique of the banking model very seriously, especially as a feminist teacher in prison who thinks a great deal about how this approach to education differentially impacts people and confers upon them rewards or punishments depending upon their location inside multiple and interlocking systems of domination and oppression. The practice of feminist teaching is never about depositing knowledge from above. Rather, it is always about supporting students to ask questions and unlearn the answers we have been given: answers about who we are when we enter the classroom, who we could be when we leave, and about what counts as knowledge within and outside the academic and institutional spaces in which we study, grow, and learn in community with others. Feminist teaching everywhere, but especially in prison, is about supporting students in their efforts to develop and grow the practice, as Bettina Love has put it, of "mattering, surviving, resisting, thriving, healing, imagining, freedom, love, and joy" (2020, p. 2).

The "disappearing act" that launched this chapter and the attempted erasure of the knowledge and dignity of the 12 students in the class is, therefore, the beginning rather than the end of this story. This is because, committed to reimagining our course together but barred by the Department of Corrections from adding new, unvetted materials after the start of the semester, our course became a feminist exercise in education as the practice of freedom. The sudden disappearance of our course texts along with the authority these texts represent, opened a unique opportunity for students to embrace the position of active knowledge producers rather than simply the passive receivers of wisdom coming down to them from above. The feminist critical analysis of power (our central theme) and the act of theorizing systems of difference and inequality were not proscribed by a set of course texts or directed by an instructor. Rather, the feminist practices at the heart of our work in the class were driven by students and grounded in their knowledge and experience of living inside racialized and gendered systems of power and, even more specifically, their experience of surviving within the walls of carceral institutions built to silence, punish, and control them.

We began our "theoretical journey" with an invitation to visualize the racialized patterns, gendered rules, and economic relationships at work in these systems of power. This was an opportunity for each of us to make sense of and build theory about our world. It was also a chance to study the cartographies of power that are typically so normalized and depoliticized that they either escape notice (although their effects are always *felt*) or they exist in forms that are simply illegible to us. This class project began from the provocation that systems of power shape all aspects of our lives, sometimes in ways that we clearly see (who is the CEO and who cleans the corporate offices? Who owns property and who is unhoused? Who sends people to prison and who is behind bars?). But more often, systems of power operate in ways

"Disappearing Acts" and Education as the Practice of Freedom 71

that remain largely invisible to us. How can we expose the outlines of these systems in order to analyze, disrupt, and dismantle them? The students and I began by composing a detailed "visual map" of a familiar place: our high school or elementary school, a place where we worked as an employee, or the neighborhood or street where we or our family lived. In the following session, we displayed our maps on the cinder block walls of the classroom and took some time to complete a "gallery walk" in which each of us could travel around the room, meditate over, and enter into a critical conversation with the maps created by our peers. We each had a stack of notecards on which to record and then attach our thoughts and ideas to each map. Finally, we came back together to talk about what we saw and, collectively, to theorize about the rules or patterns (social, cultural, racial, economic, gender-based, for example) that govern the spaces in which we live and move.

This exercise draws on concepts from our original course syllabus. It is very much in feminist dialogue with the ideas of the Combahee River Collective (2014) on "interlocking" oppressions; Peggy McIntosh (1989) on race, privilege, and positionality; Chandra Mohanty (1984) on "structural domination and suppression"; and Kimberlé Crenshaw (1991) on "intersectionality," for example. But it clearly did not need to begin there. Students mapped the relationships among tangled systems of gender, race, and power and the structures of domination that scholars like Crenshaw and Mohanty dissect in their work. One student's carefully wrought drawing of the place where she grew up included tree-lined sidewalks, public parks, and backyard swimming pools on the white side of town juxtaposed with busy streets choked with idling buses, cop cars on patrol, liquor stores and pawn shops on every corner, and Black men congregating in front of crumbling high-rise housing projects. Aside from the ways that policing is so starkly racialized and gendered in this student's illustration of her neighborhood, this map prompted us to wonder about who gets to show up in certain spaces and why. We asked, how might a feminist accounting of these spatial patterns enable us to see and demystify the economies of power that would otherwise remain hidden? Our analysis opened up an important discussion about what geographer and abolition-feminist Ruth Wilson Gilmore calls "the organized abandonment" (2007, p. 178) of vulnerable communities. Gilmore is interested in the human consequences of abandonment and dispossession by the state, including the impact of massive reductions in social welfare programs and state and municipal funding for healthcare, education, and housing. Her research, which I was able to describe for students in our class discussion, offers powerful supporting evidence, including empirical data, for the theories that students developed to explain the acute social and economic disparities depicted in so many of the maps shared with the group.

Students' insights into organized abandonment, vulnerability, and precarity in their own communities and histories finally led us to an indispensable question at the heart of feminist social justice projects: Why are some people and some communities worthy of nurturing, care, and attention

72   Laura E. Ciolkowski

while others are disposable or subject to surveillance and carceral control? In a traditional classroom, these questions might frame an outstanding research paper or undergraduate thesis, in which a combination of primary and secondary sources could support the insights and incipient theorizing that arise from student's knowledge, experience, and critical insights into the abandonment that Gilmore describes. While the lack of internet access and research support in prison meant that this kind of scholarship would not be possible for us, our collective work nevertheless modeled a key feminist pedagogical practice and accomplished several fundamental goals: it privileged the critical lens and knowledge-seeking projects of students who are directly impacted by the forces they describe, and it set the groundwork for future research that draws on the work of scholars like Gilmore but is framed by the critical questions generated from the richness and complexity of students' lives.[2] In prison (and outside it), education as the practice of freedom is about exercising one's right to know, to learn, to speak, and to practice self-determination and autonomy even in the face of carceral forces that insist that people living in prison, like the students in the class, are not entitled to exercise these fundamental rights. Love asks, "How do you matter to a country that would rather incarcerate you than educate you?" (2019 p. 2). This question, perhaps more than any other, hovered over our work all semester, as a reminder of where we sat as we grappled with the analytical and historical questions at the core of our project and also as a source of inspiration for the creative feminist critical labor in which we were engaged.

The feminist poet-teacher-visionary Alexis Pauline Gumbs beautifully illuminates the meaning of freedom in educational spaces in a story she tells about the young Harriet Tubman. Before Tubman became a nurse, a spy, and an underground railroad conductor, she was an enslaved woman who refused to live as a slave. Tubman refused to accept the ontological condition of enslavement because, Gumbs tells us, "she believed in her freedom more than she believed in the structures that were incompatible with her freedom" (Brown, 2017). Gumbs gives this brand of imaginative flight a name (she calls it "fugitivity"), and she gives the quality of existing in the state of fugitivity a label ("Harriet Tubman-ness"). Tubman embodies the creative labor that is at the heart of our best feminist freedom projects and that is also, in my view, at the center of the most impactful and generative prison classrooms. As Gumbs illustrates, Tubman devotes her life to fighting the brutality of a system that dehumanizes and enslaves people *at the same time as* she directs her energy and the energy of others toward building an abolitionist future in the present. Tubman imagines, she wills into being, and models for others what it *feels like* to live in freedom: "Harriet Tubman-ness...is the practice of refusal of enslavement and it is also the practice of generating a community beyond ownership" (Brown, 2017). It is an intentional divestment from the oppressive institutions that seek to dehumanize, isolate, and keep us

"Disappearing Acts" and Education as the Practice of Freedom   73

in our place, and it is also a courageous gesture to imagine freedom and co-create something new.

By upending the tightly structured 15-week college syllabus that was originally intended to guide our class through the semester, the week two disappearing act also reminded us that living (like Tubman) and learning (like students in the prison classroom) inside institutions is a very tricky business. Regardless of how badly we want our institutions to love us, nurture us, share our highest values, and catch us when we fall, we came to understand that our educational institutions will not (cannot) save us. Instead, as Freire and hooks insist, and as many students illustrated so clearly in maps of their elementary and high schools, our educational institutions are built to sort, hierarchize and also to punish and discard those who do not assimilate or conform, as so many incarcerated students who arrive to the class already a product of the "school to prison pipeline" (Ritchie 2017) know so well.[3] One student's map, for example, depicted predominately white students in the "honors" classes, Black and brown students in the school's basement auto shop, and law enforcement officers ("school resource officers" or "SROs" who, like police, are empowered to arrest students) posted out front.[4] This map and several others just like it gave us a compelling entry point through which we could think and theorize about systems of economic, racial, and gender injustice and the histories of surveillance, policing, and other forms of violence with which these systems are so deeply entangled. In a powerful critical moment in the class, students "connected the dots" for each other between the exercise of power and control in a carceral institution like a prison (or other carceral spaces, like juvenile detention facilities, with which some students in the class were also familiar) and the reproduction of racial, gender and class hierarchies and the culture of punishment in a disciplinary space like a school. This critical work is deeply feminist because it is rooted in an analysis of power that remains attentive to the intersecting axes of race, gender, class, and sex that govern social relationships and disciplinary formations. It also elevates a model of feminist theorizing that centers the insights, questions, and critiques that arise from students' intimate knowledge of surveillance and policing in school and prison.

My story of feminist pedagogy in carceral spaces may appear to be firmly located in the prison classroom, but it really lives in the imaginative spaces and deeply generative "healing places" of theory, like those that hooks discovers when she finds "a place of sanctuary in 'theorizing,' in making sense out of what was happening. I found a place where I could imagine possible futures" (hooks, 1994, p. 61). Our gender and sexuality studies college course without books prompted me to wonder how education as the practice of freedom might support students in their feminist efforts to illuminate, navigate, and push back against the intricate systems of power in which they must survive/thrive? It made me think even more deeply about how this work can help us to strengthen the muscles that carceral life is designed to

74   Laura E. Ciolkowski

atrophy: imagination, and the belief in liberation, futurity, and change. As Freire understood, the work of teaching and learning must be joyful, and it must always be centered on "hope" (Freire, 2014). But not the kind of blind, unreflective hope that is all about beauty, sweetness, and light. As Mariame Kaba has put it, hope in the service of social justice is not a feeling that we hold but a "discipline" (Kaba, 2021, p. 26) that we practice. Education as the practice of freedom activates hope as a difficult but necessary feminist critical practice that helps us to find our way between the dangers and disappointments of the present, and the dreams and life-changing possibilities of the future. Teaching and learning in prison must nurture and feed the radical imagination that enables us to create these dreams and possibilities. The hope that I aspire to practice, inside and outside prison, is grounded in the principles of liberatory education and feminist pedagogy and lifts up the courage, confidence, and collective care that we need to think differently, dismantle systems of domination and oppression, and build something new.

Notes

1 In prison, all course materials must be submitted for review many weeks in advance. Everything that appears on a syllabus and any supplementary materials that enter the prison classroom, such as a video or a deck of slides, must be cleared well before the start of the semester. The vetting process often feels opaque and it is frequently unpredictable. But, in my experience, approvals are rarely subject to revision once the semester has begun.
2 The Indiana Women's Prison History Project (IWPHP) is an excellent example of what this kind of system-impacted and student-driven work could look like (Jones 2023). A decade-long research project powered by incarcerated and formerly incarcerated scholars and assisted by faculty, graduate students and independent researchers on the outside, the IWPHP created an extraordinary history of women's carceral institutions in Indiana, from 1848 to 1920. Directly impacted students used their knowledge and experience of incarceration to read against the grain of existing archival sources and historical accounts and to pose the critical questions that outside scholars and researchers hadn't thought to ask.
3 In *Pushout* (2016), her study of the criminalization of Black girls in school, Monique W. Morris illustrates some of the ways our educational institutions continue to "[sustain] our society's racial and gender hierarchy" (p. 26). Morris argues that the toxic combination of misogyny and racism and the "punitive learning environment" (p. 157) in many schools has devastating consequences for the academic, social, emotional, and physical well-being of Black girls. In a 2016 interview, Morris explained: "Black girls are 16 percent of girls in schools, but 42 percent of girls receiving corporal punishment, 42 percent of girls expelled with or without educational services, 45 percent of girls with at least one out-of-school suspension, 31 percent of girls referred to law enforcement, and 34 percent of girls arrested on campus. Too often, when people read these statistics, they ask, 'What did these girls do?' when often, it's not about what they did, but rather, the culture of discipline and punishment that leaves little room for error when one is black and female" (Anderson).
4 Andrea J. Ritchie documents the history and the consequences of police in schools in "Policing Girls," Chapter 3 of *Invisible No More: Police Violence Against Black Women and Women of Color* (2017).

References

Anderson, Melinda D. (2016). The Black Girl Pushout. *The Atlantic* 16 March. https://www.theatlantic.com/education/archive/2016/03/the-criminalization-of-black-girls-in-schools/473718/

Brown, Adrienne Maree and Autumn Brown (Hosts). (2017, December 19). A Breathing Chorus with Alexis Pauline Gumbs. In How to Survive the End of the World. https://www.endoftheworldshow.org/blog/2017/12/19/a-breathing-chorus-with-alexis-pauline-gumbs

Combahee River Collective. (2014). A Black Feminist Statement. *WSQ: Women's Studies Quarterly*. The Feminist Press 42 (3–4), 271–80.

Crenshaw, Kimberlé. (1991). Mapping the Margins: Intersectionality, Identity Politics, and Violence Against Women of Color. *Stanford Law Review* 43(6), 1241–1299.

Daniels, Em. (2022). *Building a Trauma-Responsive Educational Practice: Lessons from a Corrections Classroom*. New York and London: Routledge.

Freire, Paulo. (1970). *Pedagogy of the Oppressed*. New York and London: Penguin.

—— (2014). *Pedagogy of Hope*. New York and London: Penguin

Gilmore, Ruth Wilson. (2007). *Golden Gulag: Prisons, Surplus, Crisis, and Opposition in Globalizing California*. University of California Press.

hooks, bell. (1994). *Teaching to Transgress: Education as the Practice of Freedom*. New York and London: Routledge.

Jones, Michelle Daniel and Elizabeth Nelson. (2023). *Who Would Believe A Prisoner?: Indiana Women's Carceral Institutions, 1848-1920*. New York: The New Press.

Kaba, Mariame. (2021). *We Do This 'Til We Free Us*. Chicago: Haymarket Books.

Keller, Bill. (2020). The Zo: Where Prison Guards' Favorite Tactic Is Messing With Your Head. https://www.themarshallproject.org/2020/02/27/welcome-to-the-zo?utm_medium=social&utm_campaign=socialflow&utm_source=twitter

Lorde, Audre. (1997). The Uses of Anger. *Women's Studies Quarterly*, 25(1/2), 278–285.

Love, Bettina (2019). *We Want to Do More Than Survive: Abolitionist Teaching and the Pursuit of Educational Freedom*. Boston: Beacon Press.

McIntosh, Peggy. (1989). White Privilege: Unpacking the Invisible Knapsack. *Peace and Freedom Magazine*, July/August, 10–12.

Mohanty, Chandra. (1984). Under Western Eyes: Feminist Scholarship and Colonial Discourses. *Boundary 2*, 12/13, 333–358.

Morris, Monique W. (2016). *Push-Out: The Criminalization of Black Girls in Schools*. New York: The New Press.

Rich, Adrienne. (1979). *On Lies, Secrets, and Silence: Selected Prose, 1966-78*. New York: W. W. Norton & Company.

Ritchie, Andrea J. (2017). *Invisible No More: Police Violence Against Black Women and Women of Color*. Boston: Beacon Press.

8 The Brutal Stories That Connect Us

Joshua Fernandez

The Brutal Stories That Connect Us

I'm not quite sure what to expect on my first day of class at Mule Creek State Prison, a sprawling facility full of people mostly seen as gang dropouts, snitches, disgraced cops, molesters, and Jeremy, the man sitting front and center in my College Writing class with enough swastikas tattooed on his flesh to make Hitler sit up in his grave. When Jeremy blinks, SS bolts appear on his eyelids, like a forbidden stop-motion cartoon. He's sitting about two feet away but I'm not uncomfortable. I'm not intimidated. In fact, there's something warm about the bulky man, who stands about a foot taller than I do. He's so close that I could reach out and touch the tops of his ink-filled hands if I wanted. I'm not sure if he's sitting so close because he eagerly wants to learn how to write compositions or because he notices a prominent tattoo on my neck, three arrows pointing southwest, the universal symbol of antifascism and a direct affront to the violent story etched upon his own body.

Like all my students, I give him the benefit of the doubt.

As I'm shuffling around my bag to find the materials for the day, I catch Jeremy staring, examining me, as a doctor might examine a patient with a mysterious rash. And whenever he's not looking, I inspect his tattoos, each one more racist than the next.

The last time I was this close to a Nazi skinhead, we were both bloody, rolling around the street, trying to choke each other to death.

We continue our game of covertly reading each other's artwork until, finally, Jeremy breaks the silence.

"You look like one of us," he says.

"Oh?" I say, caught a little off guard. "What do you mean?"

"You look like you've seen some shit," Jeremy clarifies.

Everyone in the room laughs at this statement, as if they were all thinking the same thing.

The room feels lighter now, and I laugh, too, mostly because it's true. I have definitely seen some shit.

DOI: 10.4324/9781003394426-10

Some Shit

As long as I fight, I am moved by hope; and if I fight with hope, then I can wait.

—*Freire and Ramos, Pedagogy of the Oppressed, p. 92*

Back in 1990, when I was 15 years old, I went to punk shows every weekend. Bands like Operation Ivy, Blatz, Econochrist, 7Seconds, and Jawbreaker filled every weekend with untuned guitars, off key screaming, and sweaty kids slamming into each other and jumping off the stage in euphoric bliss. It was everything a pubescent boy could want in the small city of Davis, California, a sleepy little college town with more cows per capita than punk rockers. When the Nazi skinheads started to come to the shows, dressed in their white laced black boots and red braces, circling the mosh pit like sharks, attacking anyone in their way, our little crew of mostly brown punks shoved off to the side to avoid a beatdown, pretending like it was OK to watch the show from the back of the room. It stayed like that for a while until the skinheads, or "boneheads" as we used to call them, began to multiply. Every show was a game of survival, whoever gets through the night without a boot to the head, wins. Eventually, an older punk, a brilliant, long-winded man who read anarchist theory in his free time, gathered us all together in a room to share a plan: We would go to shows together, never leave each other's side. We would hide weapons in the bushes outside of the venues. When the time came, we'd attack. It sounded like a horrible plan to me, a lanky weakling, infantilized by the comfort of the suburbs. But I agreed. We all did.

"Power in numbers," he said. "Don't be afraid."

It went on this way for years, the punk shows, the weapons, the violence, the blood, the adrenaline of youthful rage, until one day a gang of skinheads showed up to a concert in Sacramento and a brawl ensued. My older friend, the anarchist who gathered us together when the skinheads first started to come around, took a knife to the stomach. His roommate also got stabbed, and later died in the hospital.

After all this violence, the Nazi skinheads stopped coming around. They moved out of the metropolitan area, further toward the mountains. Punk shows went on, but with an air of sadness, the excitement of confrontation now shrouded by the reality of violence, the fragility of life, and the all-too-real prospect of death.

The First Lesson

We can figure out what schooling sounds like to students from inside their ears. Teachers and administrators and counselors are constantly lecturing them on how important schooling is or what it will give them some time in the distant future. All this promoting of school only reveals its failure to motivate with the materials being studied.

—*Freire and Shor, A Pedagogy for Liberation, p. 5*

78   *Joshua Fernandez*

There are other skinheads in my class, but they sit mostly in the back corner, away from all the other people, forming a white bloc, a neatly segregated clump of Caucasians, huddled near the wall clock. Everyone seems wary of me, but they give me extra attention, probably because I'm covered in tattoos—my arms, my hands, my fingers, my neck, and even my head— plastered in images and symbols that tell my antiauthoritarian life story for anyone who looks hard enough.

I begin by telling the class my narrative, how I cheated my way through Chemistry class in high school and, most of the time, skipped school altogether to sit in the library and read books, all kinds of books, from fantasy to how-to guides on survivalism. It didn't matter. I read and read and let the rest of the world play in the background, like a television set in a busy train station. I couldn't stand the idea of sitting in another classroom with an underpaid teacher wagging his crooked white finger at my face while my eyelids drooped to the sound of their droning lecture. I'd rather risk a suspension from school with my face buried in a book. I told them how I didn't finish high school, how I couldn't sit still, how I raged against authority and authoritarians, got fired from all my jobs. I got into fights on the street and turned to drugs at the same time I started sending my poems to literary journals. I recalled the letters I received from the magazines that said, "Dear Mr. Fernandez, Thank you for submitting your work to our journal, but it is not a good fit at this time." The writing wasn't good. It was full of mistakes. I told them how I would stack up my rejection letters like trophies and keep writing, drunk and high as a distant galaxy, until one day, I got an acceptance. And then another. Soon, I could see my name in these little journals. Soon, my girlfriend at the time would break up with me, but before she left, she would pay for my classes at a community college. One day, she dropped me off with a sweet, "Good luck!" I never saw her again. She left and never came back.

I walked into that community college because I had nothing else going on. A writing professor saw value in my words and took me under her wing to show me a pathway from my crumbled life to a job that would sustain a creative life. I struggled and failed and smoked drugs in heroin dens while trying to study for my exams. I ended up in the Sacramento County Jail for getting into a drunken fistfight with my boss.

I told my students how I lived in San Francisco's Tenderloin neighborhood, right on the corner of Hyde and O'Farrell, a haven for drugs and gangs and prostitution. I'd go to the liquor store across the street and buy two 40 oz. bottles of Steel Reserve malt liquor and then write poems while watching the action of the city, the reckless way of a neighborhood sustained by illegal activity, the hand-to-hand drug deals, the sex in alleyways, the occasional dead body in the street. None of this is foreign to my students. This is the life many of them know. It is not surprising or even interesting. It is common.

"Writing is the only thing I can do," I tell my students. "I dropped out of school too early to understand any math."

The Brutal Stories That Connect Us 79

They think it's a joke, so they laugh.

"I am like one of you," I say. "In every way."

The class lets out a collective grin. To them, I am common.

"Oh, so you're fucked up, too?" a white guy with a shaved head calls from the back.

"Exactly," I say. "But isn't that the beauty of it? Now we can all sit here, together, creating knowledge with our own messed up histories."

Rumble

Education as the exercise of domination stimulates the credulity of students, with the ideological intent (often not perceived by educators) of indoctrinating them to adapt to the world of oppression.

— *Freire and Ramos, Pedagogy of the Oppressed, p. 78*

"Hey," I say, searching for a switch I can turn off so the fluorescent lights aren't so effective at illuminating this disgusting room. "Let's learn to argue."

Our college classroom is gross, exactly the way you might imagine a prison classroom. Nasty yellowing linoleum. Mismatched shelving. Institutional clock that ticks too loud. And motivational posters from the '80s that say things like "Achieve Your Dreams" that somehow make the room even more depressing.

"We argue enough," Jeremy says. "We don't need to argue in here."

"Yeah," says another voice in the back of the room. "That's all we ever do."

"Not that kind of arguing," I say.

"Then what?"

I tell them to imagine the last argument they were in.

It's easy for them.

Then I tell them to imagine the moment the argument reached its peak, when both their faces were red, spit flying out of their mouths, and one of them was about to take a swing.

"You got it?" I ask.

"Yup," says Andre, a 20-something kid who got caught up in a burglary gone bad.

"Now imagine you're at that peak, then you take one step back and say, "You know what? You're right about that."

"Why the fuck would I do that?" says one of the skinheads.

"Because you're arguing."

"That's not arguing."

"That is arguing," I say.

"That's weak," someone calls out from the back of the room.

The air conditioning unit lets out a groan, as if it's reminding me to move the lesson along.

"Is it weak or is it brilliant?" I say. "When you're arguing, then you stand back and tell the person you're arguing with that they're right, what happens?"

80 *Joshua Fernandez*

"You lose!" The class laughs.

"No, goddammit," I say, impressed by their stubbornness. "The other person is thrown off guard. The red in their face might go away. They might catch a breath. Their demeanor might soften. They might back off a little bit when they know that their adversary might not be an adversary at all. They might view you as just a person having a dialog."

"Then what?" Jeremy says.

"Well then you attack," I say.

The class bustles with energy. Some students nod their heads at the Machiavellian nature of writing. It's exciting, the possibility of warfare through language. The sleight of hand. The strategy. It's a game. There's a certain bravado to writing, a technique, a carefully planned aggression. And they're all starting to see it, how it's not strait-laced, how it's not just for bookish nerds, how writing can be used to stylishly build, and also to creatively destroy.

"It's like chess," Jeremy says.

"Exactly," I say. "Or, I guess it's like chess. I don't actually play chess."

Jeremy shakes his head: What kind of common fool doesn't know how to play chess?

Some More Shit

> Only by abolishing the situation of oppression is it possible to restore the love which that situation made impossible. If I do not love the world—if I do not love life—if I do not love people—I cannot enter into dialogue.
>
> *Freire and Ramos, Pedagogy of the Oppressed, p. 90*

I remember walking with my mom and sister in Downtown Sacramento, headed back to my mom's car after she took us shopping at Macy's for school clothes. It was summer. The heat in Sacramento in August is like standing in the middle of an oven, everyone drenched in sweat, scrambling to find the nearest air conditioner.

I was 14. I remember how I felt then, like a time bomb, full of hatred for the world. I hated my mom then. She banished her Mexican culture for a life of assimilation, and I despised her for that. I didn't understand why she'd tuck away all that beauty, the quick accent of the language, the rich spices of the food, the colorful artwork, dripping with love, all for a life of safety and blandness and boredom and whiteness. I was proud of my last name, its unmanageable length, the troublesome "z" at the end that traced my family's origin across the border to a place rich with stories of struggle. I walked alongside my mom with shrugged shoulders until I saw in the distance a group of punks and skinheads and I looked for a quick exit. I knew they would see me, a poser wearing a Dead Kennedys t-shirt, walking with my mom and her giant Macy's bag, full of expensive clothing.

The Brutal Stories That Connect Us 81

But it was too late. As soon as they saw me, one of the skinheads leapt up, jumped behind me, slid his arm under my neck and put me in a chokehold. He laughed as he tightened his grip. My face reddened with equal parts lack of air and embarrassment. As much as I tried to wiggle free, the tighter his hold became. When I could feel a tiny bit of life squeezing out of my body, he loosened his clasp and pushed me toward my mom and sister, who were both standing there, frozen in their confusion, as if they weren't sure whether to help me or laugh at me.

"See ya, mama's boy," he said and he skipped off toward his friends who were all smoking cigarettes, laughing at me under a tree.

"Are you OK?" my mom asked. "Who was that?"

The humiliation and shame rendered me speechless and angry. I wished at that moment a bomb would explode and wipe out the entire planet. I hated my middle-class family, with academic expectations, soccer practice, and life ambitions. Something that day solidified inside of me, a deep loathing calcified in my soul that radiated from the inside out, like something worse than anger, a religious sort of hatred that would soon take control.

Don't Make Me White

> ... only through communication can human life hold meaning. The teacher's thinking is authenticated only by the authenticity of the student's thinking. The teacher cannot think for her students, nor can she impose her thought on them. Authentic thinking, thinking that is concerned about reality, does not take place in ivory tower isolation, but only in communication.
>
> *Freire and Ramos, Pedagogy of the Oppressed, p. 77*

After I had been teaching at the prison for some time, one of my colleagues decided that he would teach in the prison. He's a good teacher, serious, open and honest with his students. He's Caucasian, but he doesn't try to be anything else. He's authentic, which is why I thought he would do well at the prison. When I went to observe his class, I noted that he seemed nervous. I could see it in the way his face never relaxed. He looked defensive, or overly cautious, even if he wasn't. He sat at the front of the class on a tall chair and answered questions from students.

When he left the class, so I could hand out his evaluations, one of the inmates, my former student who I knew as a black revolutionary with long dreadlocks, pulled me aside.

"Hey man," he said, leaning in close, but speaking loudly in my ear. "You're not going to let him turn us into white people, are you?"

I jumped back a little bit. I didn't know how to answer the question.

He said it loud enough so the rest of the class could hear. Some of them nodded their heads, as if they wanted to ask the same question.

82   *Joshua Fernandez*

"That's the whole point of school, to turn you into white people!" I joked. "By the end of this class, all of you are going to look like Winston Churchill!"

The class roared in laughter but behind their smiles was true worry. They didn't want more institutional programming. They wanted education, the way they thought of it in their minds. The kind of education that lifts you from one place to another. The kind they talk about in books.

I heard secondhand that the students gave my colleague a hard time that semester. Lots of complaints. Too much confusion. Bad vibes. I don't exactly know what it was, but I assume it had to do with communication. I know the teacher and I know the way he teaches. He's good. He knows his shit. But over the years, I've learned there's something in a prison that you have to do that you don't necessarily have to do on when you're teaching in schools outside the prison. You've got to transcend the institution. Your teaching must go beyond the lesson. Beyond the walls of the classroom. Beyond their pods. Beyond the gates. It must soar just high enough to lift into the sky, undetected, over the electrified fences, past the guards in their watchtowers, this mutual connection of minds, flying over everything into the surrounding fields, free.

Reaching the Sublime

A few weeks into my first-semester teaching at Mule Creek, Essay 1 is due. Jeremy is sitting in his usual spot looking especially pleased with himself.

"What's that smile for?" I ask.

I hardly notice his tattoos, the kaleidoscope of swastikas, anymore.

"Check this shit out," he says, sliding his paper toward me on his desk. "It probably sucks, but I worked my ass off."

"Did you make an argument?"

"Yup."

"Is there a thesis?"

"Yup."

"Did you back up your argument?"

"I think so."

"I'm sure it doesn't suck," I say.

We are close now, Jeremy and I. He helps me in my class when I forget things (which happens often) by reminding me what we are supposed to be doing. He answers questions when the class becomes dull with boredom. He understands what the class needs, and he tries to provide it as best as he can. When the class roars over my lesson, he helps me get them back on track. When I tell a stupid joke, he pretends to laugh. We trade stories of our past lives. I tell him about all the rage I felt from childhood and how I knew I would explode and how they must have felt helpless as they looked on at this little self-destructing boy and how, ultimately, I ended up in jail for beating a

The Brutal Stories That Connect Us 83

Nazi in his face. He understands what happens when all the hostile elements combine in a soul to make it explode into a mushroom cloud of trauma.

When I catch a glimpse of one of his tattoos and say, "By the way, how many fucking swastikas do you have?" he pulls up his shirt to reveal a gigantic swastika on his stomach with a tattoo of a pistol tucked into his waistband, only because he thinks it will shock me. And he's right. I am shocked. I am at once revolted and delighted that a sworn enemy has worked his way into my life. A man who at one time would have choked me in the street has bared his soul, a soul that is permanently attached to mine in this tragic comedy of life, through this sacred act of teaching, teacher and students.

When I get home that night, I'm tired. I've been working all day at the college and then at the prison. Teaching exhausts me. I don't know how anyone does it for more than 10 years. The constant use of my limbs. My voice. My trauma. My joy. My soul. I lay on the couch and shuffle through the essays and get to Jeremy's. It's one of the few essays that's typewritten. Most students don't have access to a typewriter and so hand in their papers in their own scribbled handwriting. Jeremy knows someone who can type out his stuff for him. I'm not sure how that works and I don't ask.

Jeremy's essay is called, "The Hole." I start reading about the first time Jeremy joined a gang, the Nazi Lowriders, how it offered a sense of belonging and brotherhood in his life of loneliness and rage. I read that he killed his first person because of that gang and how the gang led him to prison, where he killed again, and ended up in administrative segregation, commonly referred to as the hole. Jeremy writes that he spent years in solitary confinement, where he had time to think about his life, his family, the love he lost and the mistakes he made. He argued that even though he didn't want to admit it, the time by himself gave him a new perspective on his character, his strengths and flaws. Sure, he could have gained perspective in many, less oppressive, ways, but this was where his life led him and now he's here, tatted up from head to toe with regretful symbols of his past, but the only student in the class who wanders from table-to-table, making sure the other students—Black, Mexican, Native—understand the lessons of the day.

I find myself, similarly with a past of rejection, failure, violence, and mistakes, in a new position: Teacher, the arbiter of grades, the holder of the key. As I read Jeremy's work, full of grammatical errors, typos, run-on sentences, comma splices, formatting issues, and foul language, I notice that I'm crying, not because I'm sad, but because I'm reading a perfect essay, a dialog between a delinquent teacher and damaged student, and these words that come together to form something like a cloud, one of the thick, scary ones, that moves slowly against the sky, above us all, threatening a nasty storm that rains upon the earth, feeding it, crops sprouting where there was only dirt. I read to the end of Jeremy's essay, where he reflects upon a wasted life

84 *Joshua Fernandez*

of rage, hatred, and violence—so similar to mine that it's shocking. He uses the word "regret" when talking about some of his most sinister tattoos, but he also wonders if a feeling like regret can be transformed through writing into something useful, something that resembles hope.

> Dialogue cannot exist ... in the absence of a profound love for the world and for people.
> *Freire and Ramos, Pedagogy of the Oppressed, p. 89*

References

Freire, & Ramos, M. B. (1993). Pedagogy of the oppressed (Ramos, Trans.; New rev. 20th-Anniversary ed.). Continuum.
Freire, & Shor (1987). A pedagogy for liberation: dialogues for transforming education. Bergin & Garvey Publishers.

9 Matters of Life and Death
Art, Education, and Activism on Death Row

Robin Paris, Tom Williams, and Barbara Yontz

"Learning to draw means learning to see. With blind contour drawing, the concern is not on how the drawing looks, but how much attention is paid to the subject. Tonight, our subject is each other, and you should try to draw without looking at your paper." These directions are familiar to drawing students during their first week of class. The exercise requires students to pair up, facing each other, and focus complete attention on one another as they draw the person in front of them. The resulting drawings are often ungainly and lopsided. There is always awkwardness and laughter, and that night with men on death row in Tennessee, it was no different.

This was early in the summer of 2013. It was our first night of a long-running prison art program. We were crammed into a small, locker-lined room surveilled by cameras, carefully watched by correctional officers. There were 16 of us crowded around a painted plywood table that was simultaneously too large for the room and too small for the group. As three outsiders, we had just traversed our first gauntlet of security checkpoints to get there. To enter Unit 2 at the Riverbend Maximum Security Institution, you pass through a metal detector before submitting to a pat-down. Then, you're escorted outside and through two large gates topped with concertina wire before passing through several buildings and a half dozen loud metal doors. The act of navigating this stronghold (or living within it) and tracing the features of a person in front of you presents a litany of striking contrasts: surveillance vs. observation, discipline vs. intimacy, and suspicion vs. trust. Some of these are variations of the contradiction between punishment and rehabilitation that defines the justice system. During that visit, this contradiction was as vivid as the contrast between the person before you and the line drawing on your page.

The lawyer and activist Bryan Stevenson has written about the "power of proximity" in reference to his work in prisons and on death row. "Proximity," he wrote, "to the condemned and incarcerated made the question of each person's humanity more urgent and meaningful, including my own" (Stevenson, 2015, p. 12). For us, this drawing exercise was the first of many moments when we confronted the complex humanity of the men on death row along with our own. In the years that followed, this initial encounter

DOI: 10.4324/9781003394426-11

turned into an ongoing class in the prison, a series of exhibitions and public programs, as well as several other prison initiatives and college-level courses, all committed to recreating the proximity we experienced on that first night.

Prisons are designed to be invisible. Even though this country incarcerates almost two million people, many Americans will never see a prison, especially if their race, class, and life circumstances preclude them from having to see one. Before 2013, the prison industrial complex and the judicial system were abstractions for us. We were educators, however, and were all interested in bringing contemporary political and social debates into the classroom. Our connection with these men began with an exhibition of their art organized by Lisa Guenther, a philosophy professor at Vanderbilt University in Nashville. The show led to contacts, conversations, and an invitation to fill in for her classes during that summer. It was the first time any of us had taught in a prison setting or had direct, sustained experience with those living there. We could not have anticipated that this project would expand, or how it would challenge and grow our activist spirits as well as that of the others involved.

According to its website, Riverbend Maximum Security Institution in Nashville, Tennessee houses 748 people, with 489 considered high risk, including most of the state's male death row population (numbered at 45 at the time of this writing). Riverbend is a relatively new prison; many of its buildings look more like the DMV than the bowels of an unassailable fortress. The prison is divided between maximum security and medium security, and the men are held in distinct buildings referred to as units. Unit 2, the death row unit, features a separate building connected to the first by a fenced walkway for the library, meetings, activities, and classes.

The "overall mission of the institution," the website tells us, "is to house and manage high-risk male offenders, including those sentenced to death, to ensure the safety of the public, departmental employees and inmates, while providing rehabilitative programs." The role of rehabilitation in the American Justice System is a matter of intense debate. According to prison officials, educational programming typically aspires to prepare incarcerated people for life on the outside (though prisons typically operate more like warehouses). When it comes to death row, however, this aspiration is somehow beside the point. When men are sentenced to death, the state effectively declares them beyond rehabilitation. They are relegated to a liminal space that precedes their execution, even as this time may stretch to decades of waiting. If rehabilitation as preparation for life on the outside was off the table, our work could connect men with the outside world. As we made these connections, we began to experience our project as activist as much as rehabilitative.

Activism can be defined in many ways and can be as simple and broad as doing something in pursuit of social change. When teaching, we might make the decision to include discussions of power, inequity, and money, and these discussions may call into question the rhetoric of impartiality or objectivity. In the world of prisons, those discussions often addressed unfair sentencing, racism, poverty, and inequity. In part, our intention was to make our college students aware of these issues and the ways that the language of crime and punishment often sustains inequality and violence. We did this indirectly through books, articles, and other projects, and directly through conversation and collaboration with those who were incarcerated. Regardless of its subject matter, the artwork made inside the prison could be considered activist because of where and how it was created. Some of it was obviously political, but much of it was not. A tenderly rendered bird in pastel on a napkin, a miniature table and chair made from toilet paper rolls, or Impressionist-inspired paintings on the back of cereal boxes showed the ability of these artists to find and express creativity even in such dehumanizing circumstances.

The three of us were associated through Watkins College of Art in Nashville, Tennessee. Robin Paris and Tom Williams were teaching there at the time, while Barbara Yontz left in 2006 to take a position at St. Thomas Aquinas College in New York, returning each summer and winter break. Initially, administrators at Watkins were wary of the project but soon saw its value for students even though we were never supported financially. Though we were not going into the prison officially associated with any college, the fact that we were all teaching in higher education gave a kind of legitimacy to our class, for the men, the staff, and the prison administration. In addition, being associated with the colleges provided consistent connections with new students and ideas the men could engage with.

Our aspirations for the class were mostly guided by the men inside. While they wanted to learn more art skills, history, and theories, they also wanted to create art that addressed their stories and circumstances, and they wanted this work to be seen by the public. Engaging with people on the outside was important to them. To that end, we invited a group of art students from Watkins who were interested in the justice system to participate. Our initial mission was simple: Three arts educators and a group of about 15 art students would collaborate with a group of 13 prisoners on death row to create artworks for 3 months in the summer of 2013. (These men expressed to us that they preferred the honesty of the word prisoners to incarcerated people or other terms.) The three of us met twice a week, once with the men inside the prison and once with the students. Eventually, some of the college students joined our weekly prison visit. The project was designed to educate the college students about mass incarceration and the death penalty and to create situations in which students could directly or indirectly connect with the men inside.

There are complex circumstances as to why so many men spend so many years on death row, and why so many of these years are defined by intense isolation. By the time they are eligible to take classes, they've typically spent many years in prison, with at least 3 years of solitary confinement, and are not the same people as they were when they arrived. We found them to be insightful, tender, and empathetic toward us and our students. They were equally supportive of each other. Insiders are often wary of friendships with their peers; relationships can be risky or dangerous. But the men in our group had solid, almost familial, relations with each other. These bonds helped to maintain a shared sense of humanity in the face of such difficult circumstances.

88   *Robin Paris, Tom Williams, and Barbara Yontz*

Inspired by their relationships, we all decided that collaboration would be at the core of our experiment and designed projects that allowed for connections between men in prison, the three of us, and our college students.

That summer, we designed two collaborative exercises: "Surrogate Projects" and "Add-On (or Collaborative) Drawings." For the surrogate projects, the men composed a list of activities they would do if they were on the outside. Men shared: "Photograph the night sky for me," "buy a homeless man a hamburger and tell him everything is going to be OK," and "take photographs of beautiful libraries" among other requests. We then distributed the list among our group, each receiving a request to enact and document. Once completed, we shared our photos with the men so that they could see what had become of their intentions. The man who asked for a photograph depicting the night sky wrote directly on the photo: "It's been twenty years since I've seen the stars in the open sky."

With the Add-On or Collaborative Drawings, we attempted to create a dialogue between prisoners and outsiders. Each began when one person started a drawing, painting, or photograph, and that fragment would be sent in or out of the unit. Another person would add to it before sending it back, sometimes accompanied by written thoughts. This process continued until both felt the piece was finished. The collaborative drawings yielded diverse forms of communication, sometimes with the partners imagining the others' intent and responding accordingly. Sometimes, the collaborator would add an image that altered the original meaning. For example, when a student sent in a photograph of part of an abandoned house with weeds growing and boarded-up window, one of the men added white lines as a rays of light coming through the broken windowpane showering down on a group of colorful flowers he added among the weeds.

Classes and Exhibitions

Art lessons provided inside the prison were designed based on our skill sets, all presented at the college level. Each week a lesson plan was created, and because no electronics were allowed inside, printed hand-outs of images with artist examples and instruction were included. That first summer lessons on observational drawing (including perspective) were introduced. Eventually, we also taught acrylic and watercolor painting, charcoal drawing, cartooning, printmaking, storyboards, and Asian brush painting (among others). The group was composed of varying skill and experience levels including vastly different thoughts about the purpose of art.

On the night we did acrylic painting, we offered some basic instructions on color mixing with a simple exercise before moving to images of their choice. The students with more experience helped those with less, and we all participated by talking and laughing together. One student, the unit librarian, said he didn't like to paint, he liked to write. But after a few minutes, he began painting a horse. The drawing pleased him so much that, after that class, he made

Matters of Life and Death 89

over 50 paintings on his own. Most were copies of paintings from art history in acrylic paint on cereal boxes. Another night, a local printmaker accompanied us with all the materials needed for printmaking. He gave instructions, and the men made self-portraits using small stamps he brought. These images then became part of a larger project in the Nashville community (Image 9.1).

Exercises like this one were great because they didn't necessitate preexisting skills. Beginning with a level playing field allowed everyone to learn the

Image 9.1 Tyrone Chalmers, self-portrait, from the series Our Town, organized by Bryce McCloud, 2014, print. Funded by the Nashville Metro Arts Commission.

process together. The men decided early in the summer that they wanted the class to continue, so they wrote a proposal to the warden to make our program permanent. After returning to our respective academic institutions, we soon learned that the proposal was approved. After that, the class continued once a week with Tom and Robin in Nashville and Barbara working remotely. We were divided between two institutions in two different states during the academic year coming back together during the summers.

Upon returning to New York in the fall of 2013, Barbara introduced the project to her students at St. Thomas Aquinas, and they began collaborating with drawings almost immediately. She then designed a class for the College called *Art in Prison* that built on the work begun that first summer. The final project in that class challenged students to design their own "ideal" prison art projects based on research and personal concerns. Between 2014 and 2018, she taught this class three times with students from various disciplines sharing ideas with each other as well as the men. She began each semester by asking the students to send their questions to the men inside. The men answered them openly and honestly, and the students responded in kind, revealing their own histories, fears, and anxieties. These were among the most touching moments in the course, as the men provided encouragement with generosity, tenderness, and concern. These classes provide a sense of community for students in the class and prisoners.

Meanwhile, Tom and Robin in Nashville continued to meet with the prisoners for a few hours each week, bringing in lessons on contemporary art, art history, art skills, and creative writing. We also hoped to extend the educational mission of the program to a larger public as the men felt they had much to share that might stop the cycle of poverty to prison and help others avoid the situation they were facing. Between 2013 and 2015, our group organized 11 exhibitions (in campus galleries and elsewhere). Some of them had central themes such as gift-giving, relationships, and mortality, and the men made work to address it. We had students who curated exhibitions as well, based on their observations and experiences. Conceptualizing and working together on exhibitions gave the men a shared purpose and hope that their experiences would be meaningful to others.

Our first exhibition featured add-on drawings and surrogate projects. We also included a survey with two simple questions: "What's the worst thing that's ever happened to you?" and "What's the worst thing you've ever done?" This aspect of the exhibition was inspired in part by one of the students who'd been a victim of a violent crime. When visiting the prison, she told the men about this experience and her ambivalence about participating in the project. To our surprise, they understood. "We've all been in that situation," one of them remarked. This experience complicated our assumptions about who's a victim and who's a victimizer.

In 2015, we organized an important juried exhibition at Apexart in New York City. For this show, titled *Life after Death and Elsewhere*, the men designed their own memorials to call attention to the living death that they endure and, frequently, the hope that they feel despite their convictions. Students from Watkins collaborated with the men on several of these works and helped with the installation. This exhibition featured panel discussions and performances and received reviews and online coverage. This project and the related press served to widen the dialogue about the death penalty and mass incarceration in the community. These conversations were often fraught and complex. Many of the men in our class were convicted of serious crimes. We often found ourselves weighing the grievous harm they were accused of inflicting on others against the people they have become after years in prison. This balancing act wasn't always easy, but Robin re-discovered a famous passage in Aleksandr Solzhenitsyn's *The Gulag Archipelago* that offered some moral guidance. "If only there were evil people somewhere insidiously committing evil deeds," he wrote, "and it were necessary only to separate them from the rest of us and destroy them. But the line dividing good and evil cuts through the heart of every human being." He adds, "During the life of any heart this line keeps changing place… One and the same human being is, at various ages, under various circumstances, a totally different human being. At times he is close to being a devil, at times to sainthood. But his name doesn't change, and to that name we ascribe the whole lot, good and evil" (Solzhenitsyn, 2002, p. 75). As we pursued this project, we used Solzhenitsyn's belief in the human capacity for change to see the men and ourselves in light of his example (Image 9.2).

Image 9.2 Life after death and elsewhere, Apexart, New York, NY, September 10–October 24, 2015. Courtesy of Apexart NYC © 2015.

Expansion and Conclusion

At the time we began this project, Watkins College of Art was a small but vibrant independent art college. It has since become part of Belmont University in Nashville. St. Thomas Aquinas College is a small liberal arts college just north of New York City. Neither institution had funding sources to support this prison program. Some administrators supported the effort, but they did not help with finances, course release, or administrative support. We were on our own. And while this reality created challenges with time and money, it also allowed the project to grow more organically and in line with prisoner interests. Even though our academic institutions did not have formal relations with our prison education program, the program affected the institutions and vice versa.

When COVID shut down all programs in the prison in March 2020, we continued the spirit of the project in the community and university classrooms. During the pandemic, Robin taught an Honors Class "Art in the Age of Mass Incarceration" for two semesters at Belmont University. In both classes, she brought in speakers, filmmakers, and artists who addressed the circumstances of justice and mass incarceration in America. Formerly incarcerated artists were included to discuss their art practice during imprisonment and after release. Towards the end of 2023, Belmont University will also host an exhibition of works by Ndume Olatushani. He spent 28 years in a Tennessee prison, including 20 on death row, before being exonerated. His show will include the voices of men currently on death row, with Robin and Tom building courses around it.

Barbara is currently teaching in college programs in two prisons in Nashville and one in New York. In fact, her knowledge of prisons and prison education through this experience at Riverbend aided in the design and acceptance of a College Education program in 2018. Together with several colleagues, she developed a college prison program at St. Thomas Aquinas in New York, which now offers BS degrees in Social Science at Sullivan Correctional Institution in Fallsberg, New York.

Our projects together profoundly influenced each of us and all those who worked on them, including those who attended the exhibits and lectures. What began with a modest drawing exercise ultimately provided a forum for the prisoners to raise awareness of issues surrounding incarceration and the death penalty and created a sense of purpose that gave them hope. We observed that throughout the process, the men gained confidence in their abilities to make, exhibit, and understand art. They told us that creating the work and interacting with faculty and students gave them a shared purpose, while our sustained connections with each other are a reminder of our shared humanity regardless of circumstances. Most of the men have lived on death row for the greatest part of their adult lives and have much to share regarding their experiences as young men, when different circumstances could have created significantly different outcomes. As Gary Cone, who lived on death row for almost 30 years remarked, "No one wants to be remembered for the worst thing they ever did."

References

Solzhenitsyn, A. (2002). *The Gulag Archipelago, 1918-1956: An Experiment in Literary Investigation* (T. P. Whitney and H. Willetts, Trans.). HarperCollins.

Stevenson, B. (2015). *Just Mercy: A Story of Justice and Redemption*. Random House.

10 An Achingly Realized Sunset

The Importance of Prison Creative Writing

Jason Kahler

It starts—as most good stories do—in the library.

During my incarceration at Federal Correctional Institution-Elkton, I worked in the Education Department, helping fellow prisoners earn their General Educational Diploma (a high school equivalency). The library, a generously sized room, was well-stocked with books by prisoner donations, and sometimes GED workers would staff the check-out desk.

One day in December, Jim, a fellow prisoner, was in the library looking through the book catalog when he turned to me and asked, "I heard you teach English?"

I recognized Jim. We stayed in the same housing unit, and he's big, nearly a head taller than me. At the time, he had long salt-and-pepper-mostly-salt hair beyond his shoulders. He looked like a tough biker dude. If prison social politics are a lot like middle school social politics (and they are), then he and I would not sit at the same cafeteria table (and we didn't).

Still, I told him I was and asked what I could do to help him.

Jim explained that he liked to be reminded of Christmas around the holidays. It was a tradition he kept during his incarceration and he asked if I had any recommendations for stories. He quickly listed books he knew. I scrambled through the book catalog and landed on David Sedaris's *Holidays on Ice* and *Barrel Fever*. I told Jim that Sedaris's work was funny but poignant and might fit the bill. But, I told him conspiratorially, Sedaris is gay and some of his pieces deal with his love and family life. I didn't want Jim to be caught unaware.

He leaned over and said quietly, "I don't care about any of that like some of these knuckleheads do. By the way," he extended a giant bear-paw of a hand, "my name is Jim."

It's difficult to describe a prison buddy as a friend, but that's what Jim became to me. He never failed to surprise me with his insight, his faith, his heart, and his sincere wish to reenter the world and do better. It was less surprising, then, the day he arrived at my bunk with a small stack of poetry chapbooks he'd received in the mail. He had contacted a prisoner book exchange and the chapbooks had been a part of his haul. Though he shared that he didn't always understand poetry, he'd read them and thought I might like them and wanted to pass them on.

DOI: 10.4324/9781003394426-12

Within the pile were some selections of prisoner-produced writing published by the ID13 Project out of Kent State University. The ID13 Project—named for the 13th Amendment, which outlaws slavery except as punishment for a crime—is dedicated to providing a voice to incarcerated writers. According to the books, the project held workshops within prisons and then packaged the edited work they produced in small collections. In addition to my work in the GED program, I was teaching Poetry Writing in the Adult Continuing Education (ACE) program, a volunteer enrichment program that all federal prisons conduct in some capacity. I thought my students would appreciate hearing from someone else, so I wrote a letter asking the ID13 people to consider conducting a workshop at Elkton.

I got a response the next week.

Because organizing a workshop would take some time, why not just take the work my student writers had done already, let KSU students give some feedback, and make a chapbook after some revisions?

My journal entry for that day reflects my excitement:

September 3, 2019: 7:26 PM

Fighting a cold.

But the real news is that someone from Kent State's ID13 Prison Literacy Program responded to my letter I sent a little while back. They will look into expanding their program into Elkton and are interested in publishing a chapbook of Elkton writers' work. *So* exciting! It hasn't happened yet, but that's a neat opportunity. I am happy—beyond happy—for the guys.

The kids have their first day of school today. They also had a can drive today, so I'll call in a little bit.

Our collection, *Through Fences* (2020), became available just after I returned home.

The story of our little book and the challenges of creating it are illustrative of both the powers and the problems of prison arts programs. They exist at the intersection of reality and good intentions. What we learned in the process of making *Through Fences* can prepare organizers and course developers for what they'll find on the other side of the bars and how they can best use their limited resources. In this chapter, I share some of our classroom practices and assignments and place them within the context of the environment my students and I experienced at the time.

While justice-impacted and formerly incarcerated people share some of the same stories, everyone's experience in the system is unique. What we did and how we got by was very particular to our time and place and the institution's staffing at the time. I wouldn't presume to claim that I know what it's

96 *Jason Kahler*

like for someone else at a different place, with a different charge or sentence or family history. Maybe my students, who were in the same rooms as me, would describe something different.

A BRIEF NOTE ON WORD CHOICE

In advocacy circles, there's a push to use terms like "justice-impacted" and "formerly incarcerated person" to refer to people in or formerly in jails or prisons. I appreciate the intention of using language that puts the person first.

Incarceration is a dehumanizing experience to begin with, and the use of the "Inmate" label is a deliberate attempt by some guards to remind us of who is going home at the end of the day, and who is not.

For brevity, I use the word "Prisoner" unless directly quoting from an outside source.

Adult Continuing Education

The Poetry Writing classes I taught were part of our ACE program. Most institutions are required to conduct ACE courses as described in the Bureau of Prison's Program (BoP) Statement issued in 2002.

The Statement outlines the BoP's intention:

> PURPOSE AND SCOPE §544.80. In consideration of inmate education, occupation, and leisure-time needs, the Bureau of Prisons affords inmates the opportunity to improve their knowledge and skills through academic, occupation and leisure time activities. All institutions, except satellite camps, detention centers and metropolitan correctional centers, shall operate a full range of activities as outlined in this rule.
> <US Department of Justice, Federal Bureau of Prisons, 2002, >*p. 1*

The first listed objective of the BoP's Education Program addresses what they hope prisoners will gain from participation:

a Inmates will be advised of and afforded appropriate opportunities to improve their knowledge and skills through academic, occupation, and leisure-time programs. (p. 2)

Ensuring that ACE courses are made available to prisoners in their care is one of the warden's responsibilities. ACE classes can cover a wide variety of topics, like financial planning, basic skills, and consumer education. Prisoners who complete ACE classes get a certificate and a note placed into their records.

The Program Statement discusses ACE classes:

b Adult Continuing Education. Adult continuing education classes are organized differently in different institutions. Additionally, non-education staff members sometimes share responsibilities for developing and supervising

An Achingly Realized Sunset 97

these activities. Therefore, no national standards are established for class size. However, when full time staff or fully funded contractors provide instruction, ordinarily at least 15 students should be considered necessary to justify program continuation. (p. 12)

During my time at Elkton, ACE classes resembled the looser description, and no ACE classes were taught by anyone other than prisoner volunteers, who shuffled into the Education Department at the beginning of every course session to lay claim on topics, rooms, and times. We'd be reminded by the staff member in charge of the ACE program that business courses were always popular and that we should make plans to limit the number of copies we'd need for class.

Teaching and taking ACE courses filled up time and gave some of us a sense of purpose. For some, ACE courses became a source of income—business course teachers often worked on other prisoners' business plans as part of the prison's underground economy. Access to basic office supplies is advantageous.

For outside volunteers looking to implement arts classes inside of jails or prisons, the ACE Program is a helpful structure that may already exist within the institution. While this doesn't guarantee that Education supervisors will be amenable to outside groups, ACE provides a language and a pathway to begin the process of introducing arts education to the program.

Implementing programs and classes can be a frustrating process. During my time at Elkton, some staff members provided opportunities for prisoners to learn, become better people, and serve their time productively and with dignity. These staff members were dedicated to serving the underserved. They did their best within a broken system. These are the people you'll need to find if you're hoping to start new programs in a prison. They are champions. But you may need to wade through multiple levels of apathy and bureaucracy to find them.

When it came time to teach the class, I wanted to quickly move my students into writing a new way. If they considered themselves poets already, I wanted them to try something new. And if they didn't think of themselves as writers, this first assignment would allow them to write *as* someone else, sort of a way of tricking themselves into being writers.

* * *

Assignment One

Write a poem as someone else. Adopt their voice, their cadence, and their vocabulary. Try to understand what that other person would consider worthy of a poem. What forms would they choose? What topics would interest them? Do not judge that person; you're not writing a critique of who they are through your poem. Instead, try to authentically write *as* that person, tackling a subject they would consider and writing in a way they would write.

* * *

Our Poetry Writing Class

For our class, I wrote assignments based on the models I provided. I was fortunate that I could make copies of the poems I requested from home. Our library also had some helpful anthologies I was able to mine. Outside groups will, of course, have an easier time assembling sample poems.

We had some rules:

- Never write about a staff member
- No pornography
- Use language in a way that attracts the right attention
- Keep feedback focused on the words on the page
- Remember: staff could read your work at any time

We stressed taking risks. You'll see the assignments often ask the writers to try something new. My writers were like many writers—a little insecure about their work but also protective. We were asking each other to be vulnerable, which is scary enough, but within a prison it's especially challenging. FCI-Elkton isn't a dangerous prison, but it's still a prison, and many of the people living there had been in places that *were* scary.

My writers carried baggage that made honesty difficult. Simply being in the room for class could be considered a betrayal of codes in certain circles. Going to class, playing the game of prison on the administration's terms, being anything but resistant to the rules and wants of the people in charge— to some prisoners, this was a sign that you couldn't be trusted, that you'd switched to the other side, that you thought you were something more than just another convict. It was a self-defeating philosophy that discouraged making productive use of your time away.

* * *

Assignment Two

Write your own "rant." Direct your rant in any way you'd like but focus on stringing together long lines and phrases like we saw in "Howl." Think about how this poem would work if you performed it out loud.

* * *

As a capstone project, writers collected all their poems into a small chapbook of their own, complete with dedication and collection title. We discussed naming their books after a theme they found in their collections or choosing the title of their favorite poem to represent all of them. My favorite approach is to select a meaningful line to use as a title for the collection.

I believe the important aspect of this final day of class is that writers can leave feeling like something is "done." Days stretch endlessly in prison—that's usually a good thing because "excitement" that breaks the monotony usually signifies a lockdown in response to some sort of incident or security concern and is rarely the result of anything positive. That makes any cause for celebration a welcome addition to the routine.

Most of my students sent their collections home. Finally, there was something different to discuss in letters, a new aspect of life away. For some, it was a step toward reconciliation.

* * *

Assignment Three

Using the poem "This Morning" by Charles Simic as a model, write a poem that speaks to someone or something else. Try to make a connection to that audience in a unique way, like how Simic is reminded of a story that he relates to the ant.

* * *

The Problem of Technology

Access to technology is a major hurdle if prison writers hope to get their work noticed. While there are some literary journals and magazines that specifically make allowances for incarcerated writers and continue to accept hardcopy submissions, many journals are moving toward exclusively electronic submission systems. It's also becoming more common for journals to request payment with submissions. A three-dollar fee to cover the cost of the submission system subscription hits differently when you earn a quarter a day and need to buy new shoes.

Additionally, it's difficult for prison writers to even find venues to consider their work. As emerging writers, my students were unfamiliar with literary journals, and without the ability to discover them online, they were shut out of that world. When a publisher sends a copy of one of their journals to a prisoner, the impact they have is beyond measure.

Institutions can have wildly different policies when it comes to technology. At Elkton, we had no Internet access beyond the CORE Links email system, and that charged a hefty per-minute fee. For professional-looking writing, prisoners relied on half a dozen typewriters and needed to provide their own ribbons (available for purchase at the commissary). The Education Department had a handful of computers for GED students to use to practice their online tests, but in my time there, those were always checked out.

100 *Jason Kahler*

For our first book, *Through Fences*, we were fortunate to have outsiders type our work for publication. (Before committing to this assistance, teachers should understand that prisoners have a lot of time on their hands and get pencils and paper for free. Include submission line limits so your volunteers aren't faced with mountains of typing.)

Unfortunately, the only guaranteed way to avoid issues with technology is to assume incarcerated writers have none. Even when resources are available, access to these resources is tenuous and can be revoked for any number of reasons.

* * *

Assignment Four

Build a metaphor across the entirety of your poem like we saw in Tupac Shakur's "The Rose That Grew from Concrete." Try to be subtle—don't go giving everything away! On the other hand, don't make your poem so impenetrable that we can't figure it out.

* * *

Feedback and an Audience

My students greatly appreciated the opportunity to have someone read our work and give substantive feedback. Incarceration is an isolating experience. Some of my students hadn't heard from friends or family from the outside in quite some time.

Care must be given to balance the support you'll want to give the writers with the professionalism of a teacher or an editor. Some of the writers may still be on their journey toward understanding how to appropriately interact and communicate with others. Your readers may need some protection, and the writers may need some reminding. Incarcerated writers who have been abandoned by family and other loved ones may misinterpret the support and encouragement given by readers and editors, leading them to presume relationships between themselves and readers that don't exist. Incarcerated people may push for correspondence to become more personal than appropriate. Unfortunately, too, some people in prison do not understand personal and private boundaries or may revel in pushing beyond them. Our experience was overwhelmingly positive, but I kept an eye on the correspondence going back and forth, and I would recommend reminding outside readers that personal information should only be shared in a limited capacity, and only after consultation with the manager of the program.

I was fortunate that I had the means to pay for outgoing mail and the opportunity to return comments from the KSU students to my writers, and that afforded me the chance to peek at the back and forth. We also directed everyone to keep comments focused on the work, and the editors did not provide personal information beyond their first names.

* * *

> **Assignment Five**
>
> Write about place.
>   You can write about prison if you'd like, but don't feel obligated.
>   Make the poem focus on the material things that represent that place. Let the reader feel how they should feel without telling them how they should feel. Be specific.

* * *

The Power of Prison Arts Programs

The reality of prison arts programs is that their results are hard to measure. In his essay, "Limits of Prison Education," James Austin (2017) articulates the challenges of advocating for prison education of any sort. The difficulty, he writes, is that evidence of prison education's ability to prevent recidivism and reincarceration is impossible to quantify because so few prisoners have access (usually due to their relatively brief stints behind bars) and because prisoners who do complete programs are self-selecting and therefore presumably more likely to remain free regardless of their prison experiences.

People who set policies and budgets want proof that the money they spend has a measurable impact. Because those sorts of results can't be properly researched, Austin argues, prison education should be used to reduce populations by counting toward earlier release.

While I agree they can and should be reduced, the federal system has shown no interest in reducing the overall prison population in any meaningful or sustained way. For instance, while the population fell significantly during the COVID-19 pandemic and lockdowns, these reductions were a result of closed courthouses unable to feed the prisons new people and, sadly, prisoner deaths. In the years after the pandemic, populations began to rebound (Sawyer, 2022). That means that increased attention to supervised release and the enaction of legislation like the First Step and Second Chance Acts are not being implemented as intended.

That's depressing, but it shouldn't be cause for abandoning prison arts programs. Rather, it should solidify and intensify the work advocates and volunteers do for incarcerated writers. Help rarely comes from inside the system, and when it does, it's been ripped free by the tremendous efforts of those who care about the people living and making art behind bars. The work they do matters, even if it doesn't matter in the way some people would prefer.

The classroom can be a great equalizer. Inside, people who've previously lived a gang lifestyle, pleaded guilty to fraud, visited bad places online,

102 *Jason Kahler*

pointed guns at people, can learn that they each have something valuable to say and there are those willing to listen. I'm not saying poetry can keep someone out of jail, but it can be part of the process we go through to become the people we were really meant to be.

It's hard to describe the excitement the writers expressed when they learned their work could get published "for real." It was another thing, too, especially considering the tough lives some of them had experienced and the horrors they had seen, to watch them shake with nervousness over the prospect that someone might read their work and get a glimpse inside their heads.

That includes my friend Jim, who I teased was entirely at "fault" for the whole book-thing, anyway, but was so inspired by our efforts that he submitted poems of his own. One of them, a meditation on who he was before and who he is now, appears in *Through Fences*.

The proper response to inhumanity is humanity, not the inhumanity prisoners experience in our justice system. The impact of the arts is increased in the places you least expect to find it.

Why are the arts important?

The answer is the same, within prison walls and without.

The arts teach and promote empathy with those who would be artists and with those who would be the arts' audience. It's a reminder that you and I are alive, and no matter where we've been, we're here now sharing together, even if just on a page or, like the writers of FCI-Elkton, through fences.

Final Thoughts

Every so often, I return to my final journal entry written inside Elkton:

February 18, 2020: 7:12 PM

I am packed.

Saying official goodbyes a little at a time. Went to Education to say goodbye to my students in the afternoon. My boss in the evening.

My dinner: a big pizza burrito made with stolen cheese, cooked in a mop bucket, washed down with a foxy Andrew made for me.

Tomorrow—what will it look like? Different than this. A little the same.

I got here 29 months ago tomorrow. I've been extraordinarily lucky.

I was never really scared. Never alone. I laughed more than anyone would think.

I followed my rules: Get home as soon as I can, Work my program, Help others. I think I did my best.

Goodbye, Elkton.

In sharing our story, I'm hoping to inspire groups who would bring their expertise to incarcerated people. The impact you'll have is challenging to measure, but your efforts are appreciated, even if the people who are grateful struggle to articulate their thanks.

But be realistic in your expectations, too. My experience indicates prisoners are responsible for their own transformation and the programs that facilitate it. When you decide to help—and please do decide to help—understand the inertia of the system you're approaching. Be patient and be bold. And don't forget the greatest challenges have the greatest rewards.

From the outdoor recreation area at Elkton, you can watch nightfall behind the hills that stretch to the horizon on the other side of the fence. You can watch the moon climb above the barbed wire. It seems close enough to touch. In winter, ice freezes on wire and glistens like a star. The night stars are drowned-out but the yard lights, so you can go years without seeing them. But one night while I was there, the facility lost power. In the sudden darkness, the stars became visible from the housing unit windows, a reminder of what you might find—anywhere—if you look hard enough. The sunset out of view behind the buildings, but as Kyle's poem reminds me, we never forgot it was there, and we could remember it.

> But these poems, these bits of collective humanity, don't dissolve when we close the book. Like the light in Kyle Marrufo's achingly realized sunset, they stay to transform us. We carry them with us, just as when the sun sets the "light has not died/Only scattered .... "
>
> *Trasker (2020, p. II)*

References

Austin, J. (2017). Limits of prison education. *Criminology & Public Policy, 16*(2), 563–569. https://doi.org/10.1111/1745-9133.12301

Sawyer, W. (2022, January 11). *New data: The changes in prisons, jails, probation, and parole in the first year of the pandemic.* Prison Policy Initiative. Retrieved February 17, 2023, from https://www.prisonpolicy.org/blog/2022/01/11/bjs_update/

Trasker, K. (2020). *Through Fences: A Poetry Collection by Writers in FCI-Elkton.* The ID13 Project.

US Department of Justice: Federal Bureau of Prisons. (2002) *Program statement 5300.21: Education, training and leisure time program standards.* Retrieved February 17, 2023, from https://www.bop.gov/policy/progstat/5300_021.pdf

11 Transcommunal Peace, Cooperation, and Respect for Diversity

A University/Prison Multi-Partnership Approach

John Brown Childs, Flora Lu, and Sarah Woodside Bury

Introduction

Directly outside an auditorium on campus, a truck pulled an unusual attachment: a trailer, larger than the vehicle itself, dubbed an "interactive prison cell." Visitors could step into the trailer to view the bunkbed with a mannequin in the top bunk and a basic metal toilet and sink, all behind bars. Informative text on the wall next to the cell described the consequences of incarceration, prison policy, the prison industrial complex, alternatives to incarceration, the economics of incarceration, as well other pertinent information, including statistics. A replica of a visiting room was also on view. Participants were able to sit in the confines of the cell and listen to audio recordings of the day-to-day sounds of prison life.

Inside, the auditorium filled with students, staff, faculty, and community members to listen to a panel of three extraordinary speakers: Santa Cruz Barrios Unidos (SCBU) Director Daniel "Nane" Alejandrez, himself an alumnus of University of California, Santa Cruz (UCSC), where the panel took place, Donnie Veal, the Outreach Coordinator for Underground Scholars, a UCSC program supporting a prison-to-school pipeline for formerly incarcerated and system-impacted students. The third panelist was UCSC Distinguished Professor of Sociology, Craig Haney, who has studied the longitudinal impacts of imprisonment and solitary confinement. The panel was part of a student-organized conference, Practical Activism, in February 2023 (Images 11.1 and 11.2).

The panelists spoke from their unique and complementary perspectives. Craig referenced his involvement in the famous Stanford Prison Experiment by his then-graduate advisor, Psychology Professor Phil Zimbardo in 1971, which was planned as a 2-week simulation of a prison environment to study power dynamics and deindividuation. The experiment was stopped after only 5 days as participants chosen to be "guards" enacted increasingly brutal psychological abuse of participants who were "prisoners." He used that as a larger window to reference his copious studies documenting the profoundly harmful and inhumane repercussions of a carceral system that perpetuates

DOI: 10.4324/9781003394426-13

Transcommunal Peace, Cooperation, and Respect for Diversity 105

Image 11.1 US incarceration and imagining abolition panel at the Practical Activism Conference at UC Santa Cruz in 2023. Credit: Flora Lu.

Image 11.2 Santa Cruz Barrios Unidos' interactive prison cell at the 2023 UC Santa Cruz Practical Activism Conference. Credit: Flora Lu.

106 *John Brown Childs, Flora Lu, and Sarah Woodside Bury*

structural violence, including the practice of years-long solitary confinement that has been demonstrated to be torturous for even a few days (Haney, 2003). Donnie highlighted the importance of higher education in reintegrating formerly incarcerated and system-impacted people, speaking about his own experience overcoming multiple challenges to build a sense of belonging at UCSC.

But it was Nane and the members of SCBU—who have undertaken decades of grassroots, community work around violence prevention, restorative justice, and culturally-salient healing—that best represented the real-world impact that the Practical Activism Conference seeks to spark. Nane spoke poignantly about the intergenerational harm of incarceration within his own family, the growth that was catalyzed by his years as an undergraduate at UCSC, and his daily efforts to rehabilitate and reintegrate those who are currently and formerly incarcerated. In the face of the dehumanization perpetuated by systems of mass incarceration, SCBU seeks to provide a curative space, what Nane refers to as "medicine," as part of its abolitionist efforts.

At the conclusion, Nane expressed excitement about the combined UCSC/Soledad CTF class offered for the second time that spring, through John R. Lewis College, that brings diverse partners together. In this chapter, we describe the significance of this course called "Transcommunal Peacemaking and Cooperation," and the efforts that brought it to fruition. We first discuss the foundational efforts by Nane and John Brown Childs as part of the SCBU prison project at Soledad CTF and then the involvement of John R. Lewis College in the creation of a combined course for UCSC undergraduates and incarcerated men in which they learn with and from each other. Inspired by and grounded in the philosophy and praxis of transcommunality, as developed by Childs, the course is an innovative example of a collaboration between a state facility, a community-based organization, and an institution for higher education in an effort to promote nonviolence, social justice, and solidarity across difference.

Transcommunality and the Barrios Unidos Prison Project

Transcommunality: From the Politics of Conversion to the Ethics of Respect defines transcommunality as "a way to maintain particularistic, rooted affiliations and to create broad constellations of inclusive cooperation that draw from multitudes of distinctly rooted perspectives, emphasizing an ethic of respect in which mutual recognition and acceptance of diverse, and even divergent, perspectives occur among partners. This ethics of respect can lead to transformation of interacting participants as they learn more about one another and thus alter their outlooks" (Childs, 2003, p. 22). The ideas in Childs' book are inspired and shaped by the Haudenosaunee (Iroquois) "Great League of Peace," a pre-Columbian innovation that established protocols for ending violence through guidelines of respectful interaction.

Transcommunal Peace, Cooperation, and Respect for Diversity 107

Childs also drew inspiration from the Civil Rights movement, which he supported as volunteer at the University of Massachusetts, Amherst, helping to organize a contingent headed to the March on Washington for Jobs and Freedom in 1963. In 1965, as a member of the group, Friends of SNCC (the Student Nonviolent Coordinating Committee), Childs went to Montgomery, Alabama to aid in their voting rights campaign. As a man of mixed heritage—enrolled member of the Massachuset Tribe at Ponkapoag on my maternal lineage, and African American from Marion, Alabama on my paternal side—Childs' transcommunal peacemaking work is a form of following in the pathways of my ancestors.

Today, these guidelines are fundamental to the success of the class that constructively challenges the overall prison institutional environment, often characterized by intense group antagonisms and conflict. The guidelines offer a practical resource for how those incarcerated men in CTF who want to do so, can work together constructively. In turn, such positive interaction provides a foundation for effective, collaborative social justice action among diverse groups both inside the prison and in the wider world. As participants in the class communicate with, and are released back to their communities, these lessons of cooperation across group lines help to create stronger bonds among diverse groups. For social justice to advance, there must be peace within and among communities that are today wracked by deadly violence. No one is better placed to create that kind of community peace than the incarcerated men who can bring transcommunal guidelines into practical reality. It is for this reason that the men who complete the class in CTF are known as the "Peace Warriors," who pledge to support non-violence and positive community development. For the UCSC students involved, the class broadens their range of human understanding through the direct work that they do with their incarcerated counterparts, while also opening doors for future networking opportunities for reinforcing strong cooperative communities. As one UCSC female student remarked:

> During our group interactions, I appreciated everyone's contribution to the discussion and the different lenses that were offered. Additionally, something else resonated with me....I realized that we were in a space where women were respected and listened to, [and] we were equally contributing to dialogue with men from all walks of life.

In the trasnscommunality course, the brothers (or relatives as they are referred to, never "inmates" or "prisoners") have the opportunity to develop their critical thinking and knowledge about political, cultural and social movements while working with in a group of people with diverse backgrounds. This is in stark contrast to daily life in an institution characterized by "internal unseen walls of group against group in prison," as Craig Farrell, a formerly incarcerated Vietnam Veteran, puts it. The classes include honest, thoughtful, and caring discussion and mutual learning among participants

108   *John Brown Childs, Flora Lu, and Sarah Woodside Bury*

and facilitators. In those spaces, in those moments, men have shared that it feels like they are not in prison. Within the classes, there is more useful, honest, self-reflective, and analytical discussion, dealing with issues including inequality, racism, and sexism, than is commonly found in society.

In the same way, another UCSC student says:

Seeing how passionate and driven these men are to change the community within prison was truly inspirational. Getting to have discussions with the men up close really bulldozed stereotypes....It was a great feeling to let them know that they are seen.....as students and leaders.

In 2014, prior to UCSC student involvement, a diverse group of men at Soledad CTF who participated in the Transcommunal Peace and Cooperation Classes, as well as in Kingian nonviolence certification workshops run by Kazu Haga of the East Point Peace Academy in Oakland, founded the Cemanahuac ("One World") Cultural Group. The men of CCG produced a video in 2019 speaking about the impact of transcommunality from which we, with permission, will quote. As Ramon Mora, now Chair of the Cemanahuac Executive Committee and a long-time transcommunal activist and scholar in CTF, puts it:

The Cemanahuac Cultural Group is grounded in two philosophies, Transcommunality and Kingian Nonviolence. The goals of Cemanahuac are to promote peace, mutual respect, multiculturalism, and social justice...Our long-term goal is to institute constructive interconnections among people of all walks of life, drawing on Dr. King's Beloved Community approach to nonviolence, and the transcommunal method, with its emphasis on the Indigenous Iroquois Longhouse model of peace and cooperation that respects both diversity and our common humanness.

The CCG group established a circle of "Peace Warriors," people who have studied transcommunality and have committed themselves to its practice. As Jonathan Butler says, "Peace Warriors believe that humanity possesses the ability to achieve a positive future. Peace Warriors stand with those who do not know how to stand for themselves." Biljie Varghese adds that,

being a Peace Warrior means that I get to be part of a continuing a historical legacy of those who believe that all human beings are equally human, and should be treated as such, and who believe that the antidote to the insanity of hate is grounded in peace, love, and non-violence. I love doing this activity because I know it works. I love seeing diverse people come together on the basis of their shared humanity; learning about each other and forming friendships.

Being a Peace Warrior is not just the absence of violence, but the enactment of positive peace. This is seen in the example of Chris Diep, who shared, "In 2013, I arrived in CTF State Prison where I encountered the man who murdered my best friend. I harbored hatred and anger toward the man...Kingian nonviolence taught me that 'Positive Peace' is to have reconciliation. Today I am able to call the man who took my best friend's life, my friend."

Reflecting on his earlier days, another leader in the CCG, Enriquez Rivera shared, "Before, all I knew was to resolve things through violence. If I can save somebody from going through what I did, with all the pain and violence I caused, by now using Martin Luther King's nonviolence, then that is going to be my life's goal." For Peace Warriors Ramon, Jonathan, Biljie, Enriquez, and others, maintaining a vow of nonviolence within the prison is an extraordinary act that requires deep courage.

The transcommunal work by CCG has been largely welcomed by wardens in the California prison system, especially at CTF. The recidivism rate for the men who are involved in this effort and released on parole is zero (Nane Alejandrez). After the Transcommunal Peace and Cooperation classes began Soledad, a select set of CTF residents (including those quoted above) were so committed to these teachings that they took the initiative of starting their own Transcommunal Peace and Cooperation classes around 2016 with Nane Alejandrez, and John Brown Childs as partners. These classes are characterized by rigorous homework assignments and well-developed themes for group discussions based on the readings. Class participants model useful ways to interact, through both agreement and constructive disagreement. Several hundred men have now gone through these classes. Childs says that their enthusiasm for learning and strong work ethic puts them on par with the best students he has taught at Yale, Harvard, the University of Utrecht, and the University of California. The effective organizing of these classes by the incarcerated men defies negative stereotypes and the impacts of prison life, while offering practical pathways for personal and societal growth. In this model, the people who are incarcerated are not the recipients of curricula or training; they are co-producers of knowledge, equal co-instructors, and educational colleagues. The class organizers at Soledad CTF, who have become teachers, are pushing the concept of transcommunality in new, exciting directions—including the idea of the combined class with UCSC.

Working toward Social Justice and Community at UCSC

The University of California, Santa Cruz (UCSC) is one of the 10 campuses that make up the University of California system and is located on Monterey Bay, where the ocean meets the redwoods. UCSC was established in 1965 and is a public university that combines the intimacy of a small liberal arts college with the depth and rigor of a major research university. Committed

110 *John Brown Childs, Flora Lu, and Sarah Woodside Bury*

to providing its 17,500 undergraduates with a transformative and personalized educational experience, it is organized into ten colleges that each comprise a unique living and learning community within the larger university. These residential colleges have different themes, and they offer students the opportunity to participate in both academic and non-academic activities and events that are meant to enhance their intellectual and social life and that of the campus.

Founded in 2002, College Ten is the youngest and one of the most diverse of the colleges at UCSC. Of our 1500 undergraduate students, more than 60% grew up speaking another language either in addition to or instead of English, and more than 30% are "First-Gen," the first members of their family to attend college. Despite being the newest college, College Ten already has some of the oldest and most robust programs designed to realize its theme of "Social Justice and Community." This theme lies at the heart of its programs, which engage the community in and beyond the campus, empowering our students to become justice-and-equity-minded change agents. Right before its 20th anniversary, College Ten was named after the late civil rights icon and congressman representing Georgia, John R. Lewis, becoming the first UCSC college named after a person of color.

When College Ten became John R. Lewis College, we clarified five core principles that frame how our theme of Social Justice and Community articulate with the life and legacy of John R. Lewis: (1) standing up against injustice, racism and discrimination through nonviolence; (2) centering student leadership and voices; (3) recognizing the humanity and interconnectedness of all peoples; (4) being of service to others; and (5) persevering in the face of adversity and suffering.

The Transcommunal Peacemaking and Cooperation course—which closely articulates with JRLC principles 1, 3, and 5—was 2 years in the making, requiring many visits with the warden and leaders of CCG, as well as emails and meetings with various administrators and staff at UCSC. Course proposals were drafted and submitted to the university to establish two sections of the course: one for UCSC undergraduates and other for the attendees at Soledad CTF. However, when the class was first offered, we were not able to find the funding support for a tuition waiver to enable the CTF section for CTF to be unit-bearing. The CCG men felt that it was more important rather continue without credits because they felt it was much more valuable to both UCSC students and CTF students for the shared knowledge, wisdom, and experience of this course.

It was in community with these remarkable men that CLTE 125a: Transcommunal Peacemaking was offered as a UCSC course in Winter 2019, sponsored academically by College Ten, with co-sponsorship from the Barrios Unidos Santa Cruz prison project and the CTF Cemanahuac initiative. For much of the quarter, UCSC and CTF students held combined class sessions in which they learned together at CTF. For these joint sessions, UCSC faculty and students would leave campus in the early afternoon to drive the

Transcommunal Peace, Cooperation, and Respect for Diversity 111

Image 11.3 UCSC students of the first transcommunal peacemaking class in 2019, in front of Soledad Correctional Training Facility. Credit: Flora Lu.

65 miles to CTF, often not returning to campus until after 9:00 p.m. In the class, mixed UCSC/CTF small working groups were designated, and the bulk of the time together was spent discussing the readings, sharing perspectives, and reporting back to the entire group (Image 11.3).

In this space of transcommunal learning, the atmosphere was one of deep mutual respect and recognition of our shared humanity and interconnection. As one UCSC student reflected:

> I was surprised by how comfortable I felt in the group's discussion of the text. There was an overwhelming feeling of hope inside the chapel that reaffirmed my desire to work towards a better society through transcommunality. I want to work with young people after graduation, and bring this message to them.

It was not just the UCSC students who were uncertain about how they were going to be received. A man who has been incarcerated for two decades— "over 80 percent of my life"—marveled at the ease with which the UCSC students interacted with their CTF classmates, saying he had expected them to be nervous, uncomfortable, and judgmental, based in part on media stereotypes of prisons and inmates. "There was no judgment. They were comfortable and saw us as students, as humans," he wrote. "[The opportunity] has restored my hope. Thank you" (McNulty, 2019) (Image 11.4).

Image 11.4 Meeting of the joint UCSC/CTF transcommunality class in 2019. Credit: Nane Alejandrez.

This restoration of hope was impactful to all involved in the class. Another UCSC student remarked:

> One of the moments that I found particularly poignant was when one of the men reminisced on his youthful experience of when he was first introduced to violence, He recollected his parents teaching him that if ever found himself in a physical dispute that he must fight back.... He spoke of his moral dilemma of engaging in violent aggressions.... [that had] consequences at school in terms of detention or other academic probations....He pointed at the class *Transcommunal Peace Studies Reader* – 'This, no one taught me this.' He explained that...in his youth...no one was explaining peaceful tactics or how to engage in communication geared toward understanding each other.

The second iteration of the class is underway, after a long hiatus due to the COVID-19 pandemic. For the first time, and in all following classes, the CTF students will also receive UC credit through UCSC Extension.

Conclusion

There is a dire need in these times for engaging with others across difference, for reaffirming our shared humanity, fostering redemption, and healing, and finding ways to move beyond strife and violence. The men of Soledad CTF have experienced poverty, educational inequity, systemic racism, and abuse, yet some of them, at risk to themselves, are Peace Warriors working toward transcommunal and nonviolent interaction for all. The course, Transcommunal Peacemaking and Cooperation, gives UCSC undergraduates the opportunity to learn with and from incarcerated men at Soledad CTF in Soledad, CA and offers the students in the prison the opportunity to participate in a credit-bearing class from the local University. The course centers on peacemaking, solidarity, unity that respects diversity. All the students, be they at UCSC or in CTF, contribute to constructing transcommunal ways of being that exemplify the egalitarian, compassionate "Beloved Community" of which U.S. activist and political leader Martin Luther King Jr. spoke.

References

Childs, John Brown. (2003). *Transcommunality: From the Politics of Conversion to the Ethics of Respect.*

Haney, C. (2003). Mental Health Issues in Long-Term Solitary and "Supermax" Confinement. *Crime & Delinquency*, 49(1), 124–156. https://doi.org/10.1177/0011128702239239

McNulty, Jennifer. (2019). *College Ten Class Connects Students with Soledad Prison Inmates: Building Peace through Dialogue and Personal Transformation.* UC Santa Cruz Newscenter, March 28, 2019. https://news.ucsc.edu/2019/03/childs-soledad.html?utm_source=04-09-2019&utm_medium=email&utm_campaign=tuesday-newsday

Section III

Voices of Teaching Artists and Scholars

12 Writing About Art

Duston Spear

It is time for visitors to be allowed inside the prison walls, for volunteers who teach yoga, music, and art, as well as adjunct professors, to carve a siloed college campus inside six bare classrooms that serve as GED sites for high school during the day. Many faculty members are paid by institutions to teach classes in the prisons. In this way, I have been teaching at Bedford Hills Correctional Facility for 20 years as an adjunct faculty member in Marymount Manhattan's College program.

Clad in my downtown artist's wardrobe of all black, I am a dark silhouette against the backdrop of hunter green, New York state's uniform for incarcerated people. I lived for three decades in Soho, a neighborhood of factory lofts that artists converted to homes and studios. In 2002, I moved north of the city to give my younger daughter a gentler environment to recover from a year in treatment for cancer. Still unable to walk without crutches, we'd spend most afternoons driving around this rolling horse country that felt foreign to both of us. One afternoon, I drove by two women's facilities across the street from each other like anachronistic centaurs. Their matching yellow signs read "Taconic and Bedford Hills Women's Facilities." I had fresh feelings about being trapped in a society I didn't want to be a member of; seeing this as an opportunity, I decided to apply to teach in the College Program.

I've taught women here as young as 16 and as old as 70, all seeking a special connection with art. Looking to art to help redefine themselves-this could be as simple as making a pencil drawing from their child's school portrait. Deborah was in my first studio class two decades ago; she was beyond excited to magically render her small son's likeness with charcoal and an eraser. I still run into Deborah in the College Learning Center room, and our greeting is always, "Value drawing!"

When our college went remote in March of 2020 at the start of the Covid-19 pandemic, the director of the program set up an elaborate system for delivering papers and schoolwork to the women. Assignments were sent through the prison mail, gathered, sorted, and then delivered to professors to be read, responded to, graded, and returned. Unable to teach studio art in this format, for the first assignment, I sent in brief histories of two artists with reproductions of their artworks and requested that students write

DOI: 10.4324/9781003394426-15

118   *Duston Spear*

essays with an enticing introduction, a body that compared the two artists' work, and a conclusion based on their personal reaction to the artworks. My response to each paper was a long letter, specific to every student, commenting on their essay and encouraging them to think about art and artists in new ways. There was a sea-change in this epistolary approach to teaching art. My students, liberal arts majors, were thinking about art more deeply, and they were engaged in challenging discussions with me. They were braver in their opinions than in any comments they'd made in class when they were surrounded by peers.

I was also enrolled in a remote program myself, completing an MFA in Writing from the Vermont College of Fine Arts. I wanted to design an art course for my Bedford Hills class that incorporated the benefits of the remote format, specifically the value of having one's teacher as an advisor, and art as the focus, of discussion. This class, "Writing About Art," is an essay-driven approach to becoming a visual thinker.

**

We are meeting in person again. It's early evening when my students pour in from the main hallway of the education building to the first classroom on their left. They've followed the asphalt footpaths conjoining all the prison campus buildings to arrive for the College Program at 6:30 p.m. Their uniforms, in assorted shades of green from repeated machine-washing, form a spectrum, a dozen variations of the original color. Mingled smells of peppermint candy and hand-rolled tobacco fuse with the frigid air. College classes are held at night, for most students after their jobs, for some after caring for a baby, and for everyone, after dinner.

At the first meeting of the new writing course, each student chooses a pen name. I believe in using a moniker specific to this class because it helps establish them as art writers, individuals, and not just "ladies" as they are often referred to by the Correction Officers. Despite having taught in other colleges, I learned how to be a teacher in this College Program. Outside prison, my students in studio art classes started using subtle earbuds, graduating to noise-canceling headphones, to "get in the zone while painting." They preferred to look at Rembrandt's self-portraits on their iPhone screens, finding it easier than studying the full-color 8 × 10 glossy print handout. In the Bedford Hills class, there are no electronic distractions allowed. Classes last two and a half hours, without a break to go to the cafeteria or text friends. My lesson plan is always longer than the classroom time allocated, and humor is inserted where possible. The grade is a great incentive. The grade matters. Our students are very motivated.

"Chessy" has asked me to review her topic essay, due at the end of the semester. She's reading my notes, sitting at the corner of the big gray teacher's desk, while the other students enter the classroom and scoop up their folders fanned on the surface, labeled with their pen names. Inside they find returned essay papers, relevant articles, and an image by an artist for the group prompt that begins each class meeting. Clear plastic backpacks, the insides stuffed with school papers, are used to stake the table and chair each student will stick to, like college students everywhere, for the semester. For her essay Chessy went back into the artists we studied and felt herself "tethered" to the sculptor Camille Claudel in Belle Epoque Paris, and further back to the late Italian Renaissance in the fierce paintings of Artemisia Gentileschi. She has found her voice through this genre of creative writing—a perceptive new writer able to read images as clearly as text. She begins with a strong opening thought, "My respect for Gentileschi and Claudel acts as a tether to them, holding me, I feel connected to them. Our desire to create, to give life to the lifeless, links us together as sisters through the decades."

In another essay, "Klover" describes *Clotho,* Claudel's sculpture of an elderly woman with a great swath of hair, as "a cloak and protection that serves as a crown." *Clotho* standing only 90 cm tall was sculpted from life, a model in Auguste Rodin's studio well into her 80s. A mass of heavy hair cascades down around her lined face, past her shoulders creating a shawl with the currents of a river.

The students have been following the same three-part formula for their essays that we established in our remote class, beginning with an engaging introduction meant to entice the reader into reading further. Chessy choses to establish her admiration for her subjects without revealing that she's in a carceral environment, while Klover puts the reader inside the grounds of the facility, relating her sense of dread while walking to class through a sea of green before being "washed over by the palettes of the artworks we will study in class." For her final essay "Rabbit," she will compare *Columbus Day Painting* (2020) by contemporary artist Titus Kaphar to the often-unattributed historical paintings found in lobbies of government buildings. Kaphar's painting wraps the conquering Spaniards in raw fabric, leaving the tiny images of two Indigenous peoples untouched. Rabbit's voice is determined right out of the gate: "Although many people find historical paintings to be works of truth, others find the same paintings to be works of lies. Artists like Titus Kaphar refuse to let what happened to Indigenous peoples, to African Americans, to enslaved women, go unseen."

Each class starts with a prompt for a short writing exercise to focus the students, and to wipe the experiences of the day away and allow them to be fully present in the class. After studying a handful of solitary people trapped inside staged urban landscapes by Edward Hopper, I give the prompt: "Write yourself into the story of the Hopper painting I handed you." With 15 minutes to write their responses are urgent and imaginative. "Star" thinks the nude woman sitting with her back to the viewer in the painting, *New York Interior*, is sewing her wedding dress, "but she's old and not really getting married." For another class, I've added images of paintings by Abstract Expressionist Joan Mitchell to their folders for the prompt. Mitchell was an active member of the New York School of Painters in the 1950s and 60s, and

120   *Duston Spear*

her canvases, bursting with vivid colors and a cacophony of brush strokes, were heavily shaped by poetry. In class I pass out copies of a John Ashbury poem that influenced her artwork and the students do an impromptu round-robin reading. We were halfway into the semester at that point, and I thought the students were up to the challenge of combining the sister arts, painting, and poetry. The room is silent for the allotted time to write before "Tarzan" catches my eye, indicating she's ready to share. She's written her response to her vibrant copy of a painting in a few short lines, a prose poem, finishing with "I am trying to understand the ball of emotions circling inside my head and then I look at a piece of Joan Mitchell's art and suddenly I see all of my emotions inside a frame." The students show their approval with finger snapping, moved by their colleague's raw admission to surrendering to this small reproduction of a painting which, I tell them, is actually the size of the blackboard.

Another week, I start the class with a prompt that is not based on a re-production of a work of art. Instead, I set up a still life on top of a desk in the center of the room. A round cardboard globe sits cocked on its axle, poised on top of the teal-colored wool scarf that I wore into the facility. Two detective novels, found on a shelf, and a lined notebook are stacked near the globe. "What do we know about the person this still life represents?" I ask the room. Clues are flung out rapid-fire: "A writer of detective novels." "Someone who travels." "Or wants to." "A woman, look at that scarf... wait, Professor, that's your scarf."

I challenge them: "Your prompt tonight is this: Describe a still life you would compile for a painting about someone else, someone you know." This is a big leap from looking at a finished painting, recalling images up from memory and composing in the mind's eye. "Slim" is the first to share her piece. She explains that her still life would be a table with a lamp that resembles a Heineken bottle, a calendar crossed off to show the days until a birthday, a pack of Newport 100s in a baby-blue ashtray filled with half-smoked butts. She has imagined a still life for her aunt, and with her description, she seamlessly fuses her new knowledge of still life into describing the corporeal absence of someone. "Shelly" articulates through her writing the elaborate care her father gave to a still life he created in their home, a wall display of samurai fans and swords. She describes the pride of place this display held in their living room, both evoking and interpreting his creation of that household still life in a different lexicon.

After the prompt, I give a casual but prepared lecture on Frida Kahlo. Her self-portraits always bring out animated commentary. Before our discussion, I used the old Dada trick for writing poetry. I put cut-out lines of random text in a bowl and have each student take four phrases, then I divide them into two groups and have them "throw a poem," scotch taping it to white paper before sharing it with the class. Our discussion of Dada leads to the random dreams portrayed in Surrealism and *What the Water Gave Me*, Kahlo's 1938 painting of her feet at the end of a bathtub, often referred to

Writing About Art 121

as her visual biography. Tableaux from her dramatic life float like dreamy islands inside the water. I keep them in the two groups to work on outlining their next essays. One group will write a short paper that emphasizes "Kahlo painting from the site of pain," and the other group will focus on "Kahlo painting from the site of obsession." They refer to the notes they made during my presentation, along with source materials appropriate to each subject for them to share. They can study together, suggest ideas to one another, or work alone. Once we have established a comradery, about a month into the semester, I have each student pass her rough draft to her neighbor to read during the workshop part of class. Sounds simple enough, but in this carceral environment where the students live, work, eat and socialize together, sharing their writing can be a challenge. "Only encouraging comments please, help the writer with her ideas," I remind them. Adding that they should write their notes in the margins and attribute each comment with their pen name.

Learning about, discussing, and writing about art helps students think critically. "Albany," writing her Topic Essay on socially engaged art, states, "Sometimes it's okay to be behind the scenes to make a difference. Picasso was behind the scenes when he painted *Guernica*. The three women who started Black Lives Matter were also behind the scenes. It's okay to use your words or your art to educate people about what's going on around them."

Discovering how an artist's backstory, true or manufactured, affects our interpretation of each work, Prana writes, "When both Kahlo and Claudel created art, it was dissected, scholars and critics used their art to analyze each woman's personal life. This is just an opinion from the perspective of someone who has an understanding of having so much taken that it stands to reason why Camille Claudel (institutionalized for the last 30 years of her life) would want to hold on to or destroy what little she was left with."

Tarzan decides to dig deeper into Mitchell's abstractions for her final paper, she connects to Joan Mitchell's art through self-discovery and understanding what they can help her accomplish in life, she has found the painter's language inside a visual cacophony of gestures; "I understand what I can delete from my life, what I can build, and how I can express myself through learning from Mitchell's art," Tarzan says. Legacy's conclusion is elegant in its simplicity, "Art is just one big form of expression that comes in various shades."

There is a wide range of ages and life experiences in a prison classroom— many students are mothers; some are incarcerated for violent crimes; often, they are perpetrators as well as victims. Discussing Artemisia Gentileschi's rape trial and the cult of personality that has been used to justify her aggressive approach to Biblical scenes on canvas, I focus on how Gentileschi uses her woman's body to paint her subjects. While studying her version of *Judith Beheading Holofernes* one student points to Holofernes's bent legs on the bed, slightly open; she notes this is a "vulnerable, women's pose." Excellent observation. My job is to help them find the message to be found in the work of art even as the artist's backstory creeps in. Frida Kahlo's stream of surgeries and her history of miscarriages can spark hard memories for a few students. One student uses her experiences of multiple operations to weave through a critique of Kahlo's work. "Yeah, backache without medication is challenging," I say to "Ariel," who has used her first draft about the Mexican painter to focus on her own surgeries, "but how does Kahlo's image in *The Broken Column*, of a Roman column holding up her head, her torso slit in half, straddled by a therapeutic corset, how does the artist paint pain? Do these nails piercing her skin invoke a valid interpretation to the nerve pain you describe having? Go into the painting and find specific places where your experiences at the site of pain overlap and tell the reader why, always *why*."

I simply keep pulling it back to the art, to write in a genre not as rigid as academic writing, not as confessional as memoir, writing that can be steered through the portal of Fine Arts and away from the single incident or series of abuses that has put them all in green uniforms, seated them in three straight rows of high school desks, limiting everything except their imaginations, their newfound ability to associate and dissect with some empirical history. To become visual thinkers.

13 Beyond This Door
Photographic Vision and Carceral Experience

Evan Hume

As I was preparing to teach my first photography course as part of a college in prison program, I revisited foundational and influential photographs and texts to consider how I could relate them to photography as an artform in prison. In his introduction to *William Eggleston's Guide*, John Szarkowski writes that, "Whatever else a photograph may be about, it is inevitably about photography, the container and the vehicle of all its meanings" (1976, p. 6). It could be said that photography created in prison is inevitably about prison. Photography is a medium that traditionally depends on light and surface to render an . When photographing in prison, all surfaces are part of the carceral space. Although a photograph can be taken in such a way that the location is not obvious, the context in which it was made should not be dismissed. Context helps us perceive "the whole picture," enriching our visual experience and allowing us to access the personal, social, and cultural significance of a photograph.

During the summer of 2022, I taught an introductory digital photography course to students enrolled in the Moreau College Initiative (MCI) at Westville Correctional Facility in Westville, Indiana. MCI is a collaboration between Holy Cross College and the University of Notre Dame in partnership with the Indiana Department of Correction that gives incarcerated students at Westville the opportunity to earn an Associate of Arts Degree from Holy Cross College. After completing the associate degree, students may work toward a Bachelor of Arts degree at Westville, or at Holy Cross College after release.

The MCI program offers a rare opportunity to creatively use cameras in a prison classroom setting. Whenever I shared with someone that I was teaching photography at Westville, I was met with surprise: "Students are allowed to use cameras in prison?" I soon learned that there are limitations and restrictions on how the cameras can be accessed and used in prisons, such as only using the cameras in the school area of the facility and not photographing identifiable architecture. From the start, these created teaching challenges for logistics as well as photographic content.

Before the beginning of each class, I would ask the officer to unlock the storage room containing several digital single-lens reflex cameras and other

DOI: 10.4324/9781003394426-16

124   *Evan Hume*

art supplies. The storage room is only accessible with the assistance of the correctional officer on duty in the school section of the prison. Once opened, I retrieved the camera kits for the students before they came from the dorms. At the end of each class, I carefully accounted for all the kits and returned them to the storage room before the students left. Outside of class time, the students had limited opportunity to use the cameras for class work during brief weekly study hall hours, but some students were unable to use this time because it overlapped with other classes. In a typical college photography class, class time is devoted to instruction and students take photos outside of class. In this case, I had to build in significant class time for photographing during class. We were also limited to working with files taken straight from the camera's memory card without possibilities for digital editing. There is no internet at the school and no editing software could be put on the computers. However, I was able to make inkjet prints for the students in Notre Dame's digital print studio and bring them to class so that they could see their work with more accurate color and detail than the monitor in our classroom could provide.

On the first day, I asked students what came to mind when they thought of photography. "Paparazzi" said one. "National Geographic," said another. A few mentioned nature photography and expressed interest in photographing the garden next to the school building that their garden club was tending. The associations that the students offered all spoke to an understanding of photography as a kind of document. The notion of photography as a visual record, an observation, and a reflection of experience, would become a common theme throughout the course and in the work the students made.

I introduced the history of photography starting with proto-photographic practices, such as the use of the camera obscura by painters. From there, I discussed the innovations leading to the announcement of photography's invention in 1839[1] and some of the aesthetic and technical developments that took place over the course of its first century. One of the first photographs we analyzed together was Alfred Stieglitz's *The Steerage* from 1907, a classic example of the documentary mode merging with modern art. The photograph shows passengers on a ship travelling from New York City to Europe, with some people on an upper deck in the top half of the composition and others in a lower deck in the bottom half. I asked the students what the photographer seemed to be showing us in the photograph. A student immediately chimed in, "I see different classes. The people on the top look like they're wearing nicer clothes than the people on the bottom." The other students agreed. He went on to say, "It makes me think of how we find differences between each other in here. Maybe somebody got more food at chow, maybe somebody has something we don't, but we're all in the same situation. We're in the same boat." The student perceived that although there may have been socio-economic disparities present among the passengers, there was a shared experience. Many of the passengers were immigrants who had come to the United States to find work and were now returning to Europe, either because

Beyond This Door   125

they were turned away or had temporary work visas (Whelan, 2000). Differences among the passengers in *The Steerage* was this student's "punctum," to use a term from Roland Barthes (1981, p. 27) to indicate the element in a photograph that serves as a point of personal, emotional connection to the viewer. The student related the content to his own experience.

Though the scope of photographic capabilities has expanded with the rise of digital processes, within the limitation of prison, we work with photography's basic principles—harnessing light and composing form within a rectangular frame. However, this is not to say it is a simple or easy process. Szarkowski writes:

> Photography is a system of visual editing. At bottom, it is a matter of surrounding with a frame a portion of the one's cone of vision, while standing in the right place at the right time. Like chess, or writing, it is a matter of choosing from among given possibilities, but in the case of photography the number of possibilities is not finite, but infinite.
>
> (1976, p. 6)

While this may mostly ring true outside the prison, where the photographer can roam freely and point a camera toward any subject, photography in prison only offers finite possibilities. A photographer's work is often a response to their environment, but in prison, spatial restriction is taken to the extreme and subject matter is limited. The only spaces the students can use cameras in are the classrooms and occasionally the garden outside the school building. We also needed to avoid any identifiable architecture. With this in mind, the first project I assigned was a still life. To begin, I shared photographs by artists who have worked within constraints to make creative s.

The still life has been a photographic genre from the very beginning. The oldest surviving photograph by Louis Daguerre taken in 1837, 2 years before his announcement of photography's invention, shows an arrangement of sculptural plaster casts sitting by a window in Daguerre's studio. The low light sensitivity of his photographic plate demanded that he photograph a still subject; an exposure time of about 20 minutes was needed to form a fully detailed . Even a person trying to sit completely still in front of the camera for that amount of time would have resulted in motion blur and thus a loss of sharp detail. Additionally, Daguerre's early photograph was not simply a random assortment of objects arranged to test his process. As art historian Geoffrey Batchen (2004) notes in his analysis of Daguerre's still life, the choice of subject is deliberate, establishing a direct connection between photography and fine art. The plaster casts in the picture directly reference the visual language of Neoclassicism, a dominant art movement of Daguerre's time. In the center of the composition are the plaster heads of two putti, winged children often representing romantic love (think Cupid) and associated with Phaethon, the Greek god of light (Batchen, 2004). Daguerre, an academically

126   *Evan Hume*

trained painter, transported a subject of the traditional arts into photography to suggest his invention was an artform in its own right (Batchen, 2004).

Edward Weston's *Pepper* from 1930 is an instance of, in the photographer's words, "making the commonplace unusual" (1975, p. 40). In this photograph, Weston uses a single object as his subject, a twisted pepper. By photographing it up-close against a dark, non-descript background, the picture is bereft of environmental context and the sense of scale is ambiguous. Some students met the photo with bewilderment when viewed without knowing the title. The picture can just as easily be seen purely in terms of curving lines and organic form as it can be recognized as a close-up shot of a uniquely shaped vegetable. Weston, to my mind, is not photographing the pepper to make it a symbol or metaphorical representation of a feeling, but rather the photograph shows how the decisions of the photographer, and the properties of the camera can translate an everyday item into an abstraction where form and content are inseparable, yet still be recognizable.

A more contemporary and playful approach to the still life genre while working within a set of parameters can be found in *Quiet Afternoon* by collaborators Peter Fischli and David Weiss. In this series of photographs, the artists create temporary sculptures from objects found around their studio. Common items such as bottles, utensils, and produce are often stacked on top of one another with a delicate sense of balance, photographed on flat surfaces against blank backgrounds. The seemingly intuitive, improvisational combinations resist fixed interpretations and offer a process for creating a variety of outcomes from limited options.

The MCI students are allowed to bring books and other items such as school supplies and snacks that they can fit in their net bags to class, so for the next meeting, I asked them to bring objects they were interested in arranging and photographing. They were able to use any of the classrooms and study spaces to set up and photograph their objects. The only available light came from overhead fluorescents and natural light through the windows. Cloudy days are not uncommon in northwest Indiana, and the first day shooting the assignment was one of them. The lack of bright light made photographing more challenging for the students. Their exposures required longer shutter speeds and so with no tripods to use, they had to find ways of stabilizing their cameras on desks and stacks of books to reduce motion blur that can occur from the camera moving at the time of exposure. The still life photographs the students made revealed that, even within a restrictive situation, photography still offered a range of possibilities in how their chosen subjects could be documented and ascribed meaning.

Steven Foernzler brought items he had purchased from commissary, essentially a prison's "store." In his photograph, the objects sit on a wooden classroom desk with a blackboard in the background, all evenly lit by the fluorescents in the ceiling directly above (Image 13.1). In the center of the composition is a bright green 20-ounce bottle of Mountain Dew. Balanced on top of the soda bottle is an orange spoon with green and white mints on

Beyond This Door 127

Image 13.1 Photograph by Steven Foernzler.

either end. A tube of cookies in orange packaging forms a strong diagonal, leaning against the left side of the soda bottle. To the right of the bottle a rectangular pack of instant ramen noodles labeled "CHILI FLAVOR" sits on top of a small blue and yellow container of Kraft cheese spread. His playful arrangement takes inspiration from the work by Fischli and Weiss that I shared in class, but these seemingly unremarkable goods that could easily be found at any convenience store on the outside take on a different significance in prison. In prison, they are precious commodities that can only be obtained from commissary every few weeks using an account with money provided by family or acquired by working a job while incarcerated. The classroom setting of the photograph frames the assemblage as a learning experiment. Partially visible on the blackboard behind the items are Steven's initials written in yellow and pink chalk, the artist signing his work.

Adam Clendenning used clothes for his still life, a standard-issue shirt and pair of pants (Image 13.2). In one of the classrooms, he draped a light blue button-up with a white shirt underneath and a green beanie on top over the back of a chair. The legs of the dark blue pants hang from the chair's seat to meet a pair of black shoes on the floor. The silhouette formed by the clothes sits next to a table in the school's library. Cases of books with different neon-colored labels on the spines repeat throughout the background. When the photograph was presented for our group critique session, many of the students immediately perceived what the photographer later stated to be one of his intentions in arranging this picture—the phenomenon of someone being in prison one day and released the next, leaving their uniform behind as if they had just vanished into

128 *Evan Hume*

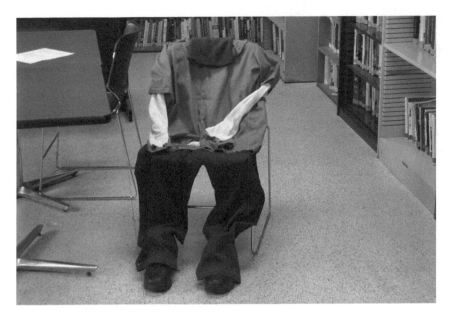

Image 13.2 Photograph by Adam Clendenning.

thin air. It was something almost all the students had experienced with dorm mates leaving over the years. While it must be a strange experience to have a friend you see every day suddenly be gone, there is a sense of hope and optimism in the photograph. It envisions the moment when a student's time has been served, and he is released to start a new stage of life. For the students, the classroom setting in the photograph added to the sense of optimism. Although there may be challenges when it comes time for them to leave, they will have earned a college degree that can provide opportunities for a better life.

Nathaniel Dodson's still life that was made based on visual elements resulted in unexpected interpretations (Image 13.3). A red apple wrapped in a small US flag print cloth with a small rock on each side sit on top of a copy of Aldous Huxley's *The Doors of Perception* on a wooden desk. Behind the desk is a closed white door with a padlock on it. The scene is illuminated only by natural light coming into the room from the right side, the window concealed by a metal bookcase containing a stack of prealgebra textbooks. When Nathaniel presented this photograph for critique, he spoke about his choice of objects being guided by color, shape, and texture. His classmates saw more than those elements. One student saw the apple as representing knowledge, something long associated with the fruit. For another student, the presence of the flag introduced political implications. Others connected the title of *The Doors of Perception* visible on the book spine to the door with the padlock in the background. The photographer admitted he had not consciously considered any of these associations but was pleasantly surprised

Image 13.3 Photograph by Nathaniel Dodson.

by his picture eliciting such responses. It was an important moment for demonstrating the connotations that can arise for viewers based on their experiences and beliefs, regardless of the artist's intentions.

To encourage more conceptual thinking, I asked the students to make a series of photographs based on a cohesive theme of their choosing. For this project, we were able to expand possibilities for subject matter and scenery. I was given permission to take the students out to the garden. Some were members of the garden club and were eager to document the work they had done. On the few days we were able to go to the garden, we had to wait until after the regular facility-wide headcount was done, leaving us with just about a half hour to photograph each time, but the students made the most of it.

Conor Jackson took a very personal approach to how he photographed the garden (Image 13.4). His grandmother, who had passed away the previous year, was a nature photographer and he took inspiration from her photographs as well as a letter she had written him. In the letter, she describes the wildlife and natural beauty that surrounded her. Finding instances of beauty in prison seems like an impossible task, but the garden offered a respite from the brick, concrete, and highly regulated procedures of daily life. He photographed his subjects up-close, focusing on the textures and vibrant colors of the flowers and vegetables in the garden. He also photographed a mourning dove with her babies resting in a shaded area of the garden and a bumble bee on a speedwell. The close-up compositions and use of shallow depth of field removed any traces of carceral space, creating that sense of being surrounded

Image 13.4 Photograph by Conor Jackson.

by wildlife and nature that his grandmother had written to him about. One photograph, however, stands out from the rest of his series. It is a tightly cropped, frontal shot of the garden's chain link fence with creeping foxtail intertwined and coming up from the bottom of the frame. When sharing this image with the class, Conor explained that he saw the foxtail weed as representing him and his fellow incarcerated students, dismissed and disregarded by society. The fence was a restrictive barrier, but growth continued around it anyway. This echoed a sentiment I had heard the students express before, that despite difficult conditions and experiences, they were learning and growing.

Joshua Fisher found inspiration for his project in spaces where instruction and learning take place. The students in general are proud to be enrolled in MCI. It is a selective program, with about 30 percent of applicants admitted annually. The students take their education seriously and take nothing for granted. However, there remains a strong sense of isolation in the educational experience, which is what this student wanted to portray with his photographs. The students have a connection with each other through shared experience, but their collective separation from the rest of the world is felt acutely. The pandemic had amplified the feeling of isolation. Classes had to be put on hold for over a year and contact with visitors became more restricted. Joshua's photographs all show the classrooms and study spaces with empty seats, lit only by soft, indirect sunlight coming through the windows. One picture gives the impression of a first-person view of sitting at a desk in a room lined with bookcases (Image 13.5). On the desk is an open book with an indecipherable passage highlighted in pink. A green baseball cap sits

Beyond This Door 131

Image 13.5 Photograph by Joshua Fisher.

just behind the book on the left and to right is a large pink cup of water with "ACE" written in black marker on the handle. An empty blue chair is on the other side of the desk, and just beyond is a wall with a window looking out into a blank hallway, the grid of the exterior window behind the camera reflected in it. With this staged tableau, the photographer visualizes isolation within the context of an education program in prison.

During our final week of class, we read and discussed Nicole R. Fleetwood's "Marking Time," an essay about the practice of portrait photography in prison. Fleetwood has since developed a multi-media exhibition project titled *Marking Time: Art in the Age of Mass Incarceration*, bringing together the work of incarcerated and nonincarcerated artists addressing prison life and culture. She begins the essay writing about her personal connection to prison photography from visiting her cousin Allen, who had been serving a life sentence since 1994 when he was 18 years old (Fleetwood, 2018). On the day we discussed the reading, a student brought some of the photographs he had from family visits during the 13 years of his incarceration. His classmates remarked how they could see the differences in his appearance over time, from the facility where he was first placed to the present at Westville. The student and his family members posed smiling with arms around one another in all the photographs. These pictures from family visits preserve an infrequent opportunity for connection with loved ones but are also reminders of lost time and all the difficulties that come from separation. One student shared that although he was always happy to have his mother and son visit, he felt like he had to put on a mask to hide the pain of separation. He did not want to show or share his struggles so that they would not worry about him.

132 Evan Hume

Fleetwood outlines how portrait photography in prison differs from what is typically associated with incarceration, and I believe the same can be applied to the photography made by the MCI students, providing "an important counterpoint to a long history of visually indexing criminal profiles, such as mugshots and prison ID cards" (2018, p. 79). With various types of painted backgrounds, there is also an aspirational aspect to vernacular prison portrait photography. Fleetwood explains:

> Carceral backdrops project exterior life – a space outside prison walls – and they fall within landscape-painting traditions. While some backdrops reference iconic landmarks, like New York City's skyline, the majority do not project a sense of place or specificity of location. Instead, they represent a sense of nonconfinement, a lack of bars, boundaries, borders – an ungoverned, yet manicured, space.
>
> (2018, p. 79)

An aspirational quality is also present in the creative photography of the MCI students. In his book *Beauty in Photography*, Robert Adams writes that, "The job of the photographer, in my view, is not to catalogue indisputable fact but to try to be coherent about intuition and hope" (1981, p. 24). Despite their personal and shared struggles, the MCI students have a sense of hope, knowing that in a few years' time they will be released having earned a college degree. In a picture made for his final project, Jarrell King photographed the main hallway of the school that all the classrooms are connected to, lined with empty chairs (Image 13.6). The scene is captured from a tilted

Image 13.6 Photograph by Jarrell King.

angle with one-point perspective and lines leading to a door at the end of the hallway. He used a slow shutter speed to create motion blur and introduce a sense of forward movement. On the print, he wrote:

The destiny of the
Future is beyond this door
Tunnel vision with precision to succeed and soar
Time to proceed and explore with hope
Across the naked floor, those chairs
Want to slow the speed of the need for
Me to be free for sure!

(2022)

Note

1 Photography's invention cannot be pinpointed to one year although the earliest surviving image taken by a camera was made by Nicéphore Niépce circa 1826. The invention of photography was announced in 1839 by Louis Daguerre, but it has existed for several years in various forms unbeknownst to the public.

References

Adams, R. (1981). *Beauty in Photography*. New York: Aperture.

Barthes, R. (1981). *Camera Lucida*. New York: Hill and Wang.

Batchen, G. (2004). Review: Light and Dark: The Daguerreotype and Art History. *The Art Bulletin* 86(4), 764–776.

Eggleston, W. & Szarkowski, J. (1976). *William Eggleston's Guide*. New York: Museum of Modern Art.

Fleetwood, N.R. (2018). Marking Time. *Aperture* (230), 76–81.

Weston, E. (1975). *Edward Weston: The Flame of Recognition*. (Newhall, N., Ed.). New York: Aperture.

Whelan, R. (2000). *Stieglitz on Photography: His Selected Essays and Notes*. New York: Aperture.

14 Why French?
Fear and Freedom in Stepping Outside Our Languages

Cecelia Ramsey

The First Day

I had been driving north for 45 minutes in bumper-to-bumper Nashville traffic when it was finally time to exit onto a side road and start making my way up the long, secluded drive leading to the parking lot of the high-security women's prison—a distinctly less populated path. Leaving everything in the car but my key and my driver's license (per instructions), I walked toward the entrance, which was flanked by the kind of barbed wire fences I had only seen in movies. The closer I got, the more imposing they felt. Stepping inside, I began the long, slow wait to be processed by security, followed by a long, slow wait to be allowed to move to the next space. Eventually, I joined a group of 30 or so volunteers gathered in the cafeteria for the mandatory volunteer training session. The chaplain, a tall and powerful woman with an unhurried demeanor, introduced us to the rules of conduct, from the seemingly arbitrary, like shoes must have straps and clothing must be loose-fitting, to the very serious protocols set forth by PREA, the Prison Rape Elimination Act. The chaplain punctuated each phrase with an affirming, unanswered "amen." "Y'all can have no outside contact, no sending emails for inmates, amen? Do not share any personal information with the inmates, amen? There can be no hugging or physical touch, amen?" With the "amens" ringing, somewhere between the barbed wire fence and the litany of regulations, it began to set in that this teaching experience would be unlike anything I had attempted.

The chaplain's words continued to echo in my mind on my drive home, so much so that when I sat on the couch that evening, I pulled out my laptop, started a GoogleDoc, and wrote: "Weirdly inefficient. Its own set of rules. Feels like I've entered another world." Throughout two semesters of teaching elementary French at the Tennessee Prison for Women (now known as the Debra K. Johnson Rehabilitation Center), I acclimated to this other world and to the unique opportunities and challenges it presented for my students inside and for me. The prison classroom is, as they say in French, *très particulier.* It is distinctive, idiosyncratic, particular. And it is precisely those particularities, those constraints, that pushed me as

DOI: 10.4324/9781003394426-17

an educator to become both more creative and more intentional with my choices in ways that apply to any setting.

Preparing to Teach Inside

When I first volunteered to offer the course inside—eager to help, excited to learn—I sat down with the program director to discuss best practices. Take caution not to ask personal questions, she advised. But if you think about the early days of learning a language, it often revolves around personal topics: where are you from, what's your favorite food, talk about your hobbies, describe your family. She warned me to be especially careful with family topics, given that families are often involved in the nature of the students' sentences or their past trauma. While it's difficult to obtain accurate statistics when it comes to disclosing traumatic experiences, surveys suggest that half of the women in correctional populations report having suffered prior abuse, and of that number, over half by spouses or boyfriends, and another third by parents or guardians (Harlow, 1999, p. 1). The challenge became to what extent could I, as a language instructor, be mindful of my students' potential past trauma when designing class activities?

In "French Behind Bars," Ann Masters Salomone describes the blunder of asking personal questions in her language class: it quickly became evident that these methods were "inappropriate." She recounts a cringe-worthy grammar drill that asked students to list what they have and don't have as "especially awkward" given the setting (Salomone, 1994, p. 79). On the other end of the spectrum, some instructors have gone too far in trying to make the content "relatable" for inside students. In a Spanish prison program that has existed for over a decade, the faculty observed that when an instructor tried to impose a topic tailored to the prison setting (discussions about the yard, the chow line, prison programs), the students showed a lack of interest and even objected, pointing out, "prison was where they were, but not who they were" (Drew et al., 2015, p. 38). There is a clear gap with a need for interesting, engaging content that students can connect to, but that does not probe into personal or past experiences.

Fortunately, my colleague Kelly Kidder was already identifying this need in her own language classrooms.[1] She was frustrated by the expensive textbooks and their dependence on pop stars and personal inquiries. "One text I worked with asked students to describe the Simpson family tree and discuss attributes of Jennifer Lopez and Tiger Woods," she explains. "Whether you are talking about students learning inside a prison or students who come from other cultural backgrounds, the assumption that students will know the same famous people—or want to talk about them—is flawed" (Kidder & Ramsey, 2021). As a result, she created her own textbook based around the story of the famous French play *Cyrano de Bergerac* (1897), adapted into a modern love triangle, including comprehension questions and guided grammar activities that help students learn French as they read the story together.

136   *Cecelia Ramsey*

Getting to know the characters provides a shared point of reference for the students and also fuels classroom activities for describing characters' hobbies and families in a context that builds on students' investment in the characters without requiring the students to talk about themselves. As Kidder suggests, "The beauty of teaching through literature is that it allows for personal connections, but it doesn't force them" (Kidder & Ramsey, 2021).

Kidder's text served as the primary workbook for the class, filling nearly 50 minutes of our 2-hour-long weekly class, between pre-reading, reading, and post-reading group work.[2] In addition to the grammar topics of the story chapters, class time varied between activities developing oral comprehension, speaking skills, analysis of images and songs, and critical thinking tied to discussions and discoveries of culture. While many of these activities would normally involve technology (YouTube clips, playlists, audio files, etc.), I had to adjust to delivering content solely on paper and in person. My clear plastic bag—the only kind allowed to be carried into the prison—was filled with flashcards, whiteboard markers, handouts for the students, and pictures to be used as props or taped around the classroom for reference.

Beginning French

When I entered the prison for the first day of class, the barren, cement walls could not dull the buzzing energy and nerves in the excitement of a new semester. I filed through security with the undergraduate students from Lipscomb University who had opted to take a course alongside the students in the university's LIFE program.[3] Once our group had been processed through security, we shuffled our way from checkpoint to checkpoint, waiting for the large metal doors to be opened by an officer, then through the grassy yard, following the concrete path to the designated classroom building where another officer checked us in. Soon, the inside students began to arrive. Some had to pass through multiple security checkpoints to arrive, given that the students are housed in different units, work different jobs during the day, and are forced to go through varying security protocols prior to entering class. Standing outside my classroom door, with officers in sight at the end of the hall, my exuberant greetings of "Bonjour!" were met with reticence and avoidance.

Our first task of the semester: introducing ourselves. I began the class in French with simple, repetitive structures, asking students to tell me their names. My four "outside" students, mid-level French students from campus who volunteered to join the class, were able to help by modeling and practicing the exchange.[4] Second task: the students were given a list of francophone names and were invited to choose a new name for the year, introducing themselves again but with their chosen French names.[5] Next, I held up pictures displaying different emotions and introduced the vocabulary to establish our weekly ritual of asking, "*Ça va?*" (How are you?) at the start and end of class. As I worked my way around the circle of desks, eliciting a response from each student, the outside students all replied that they were *"content"* or *"heureux"* (happy). This is the classroom equivalent of an exchange you know well: How are you? Good. You? Good. Though neither locutor is necessarily feeling good. The inside students, however, reported a blend of emotions—from happy to tired—but all of them included this one word: *"nerveuse"* (nervous). In response, I asked the class (in French) to take a collective deep breath. I explained that I would continue in French, but that they could ask questions in English at any time.

Addressing Fears and Expectations

The ten students who took my class did not necessarily want to take French; once admitted to the LIFE program, they needed to pass a language class to meet the requirement for the Associate of Arts degree. French was the only language offered that year, and since the students were only able to take one class, one night a week, they would have to take French for two consecutive semesters. Though some were naturally passionate about the language—they came into class eagerly each week with new words and expressions they had learned while looking through their French dictionaries for fun—others explicitly told me on day one that they were not looking forward to it. "I heard it was gonna be really hard," one student admitted. Another said she would've preferred Spanish: "My first thought? Ugh. French." These statements are indicative of two shared sentiments: they feared they would not succeed, and they didn't understand why they should learn French.

As an educator looking to offer language courses in a prison classroom, this potential lack of motivation must be considered. Will they be studying abroad in Paris next year? No. Will they get to pop over to a local French restaurant or check out French films at the indie theater? No. Have they encountered a need for French in their lives up to this point? If they have lived in Middle Tennessee, again, the answer is likely no. Then why should they invest in learning this language?

That question has prompted linguists and language teachers to provide countless attempts at an answer, from lists of reasons of benefits to curriculum redesigns.[6] My own approach involved being transparent with students; our syllabus outlined language-specific objectives, but also the guiding principles that would apply beyond the language itself:

Talk-based: Students will be encouraged to ask questions and make mistakes.
Practical: Students will hear about real-life stories and events.
Compassionate: Students will think critically about the complexity (and compromises) of operating in a foreign language.
Discovery-driven: Students will be invited to play, explore, and get curious while learning about the francophone world.

Students naturally leaned into the discovery aspects, wanting to know more about both the language and the culture: Why is soccer called *foot*? Why do

138   *Cecelia Ramsey*

nouns have genders? What does the national motto (*liberté, égalité, frater-nité*) mean to the French and what do those values mean in the United States? But when it came time for a test, we hit our first roadblock. The students took the test at the end of class, and I brought the graded copies back the following week. When the students arrived that night, they were in a panic, hounding me about their grades. All of them told me variations of: "I did awful" or "I know I failed." In reality, their grades were all passing, with a few As, many Bs, and a couple Cs. But the majority of the students were not satisfied with anything less than perfection. Eager to seize the opportunity for an education, the LIFE program students, in my experience, demonstrated an extremely high commitment to learning, studying daily and diligently, asking challenging questions, and incorporating their own passions and interests into their work.[7]

In response to the students' reactions toward test day, I learned not to use the words "test" or "exam," instead referring to assessments as "show what you know" days. In addition, I began providing homework answers and explanations each week along with assignments. Without the ability to ask questions to the professor, to their classmates, or on the internet, students would feel "stuck" throughout the 7 days of uncertainty waiting for the next class, and that "stuck" feeling was not helping them improve, it only lessened their motivation. To help, the LIFE program invested in purchasing each of them a high-quality bilingual dictionary as a resource for looking up words in French or English. Providing ample supports enabled students to focus their time and energy on higher-level questions, but it did not fully soothe the sense of palpable anxiety and rampant self-criticism.

Few of my inside students seemed to have positive associations with in-stitutionalized learning. They reported feeling unsatisfied with their past education, and for various reasons did not remain within the system; this is consistent with the fact that 42% of women in state prisons have not earned a high school diploma or GED (Harlow, 2003, p. 1). My students charac-terized their experiences with institutional learning as defeating and de-moralizing.[8] Overcoming these negative associations took intentional—and consistent—work. Before the second semester began, I added a new clause to my syllabus meant to remind students that the French classroom is not what they dread. I boiled it down to a surprising mantra: mistakes are good, not bad. You cannot learn a language without hitting all the bumps along the way; indeed, those are a sign of progress moving toward greater command of the structures. But for the students, mistakes were mainly associated with failure and punishment, with a sense of loss of control—things we avoid at all costs.

To emphasize our new Rule #1 (mistakes are good), I began to celebrate grammatical errors to reframe them as signs of progress. For example, Nico-lette hated to get things wrong so much that she always wrote translations in English beneath every line of her homework in French "just to make sure" I knew what she meant to say. One day in class, Nicolette tried to use *faire* (the

French verb for "to do, to make") in a sentence, saying, "*Vous faisez* [...]."
While the -ez ending is often used with the pronoun *vous,* it just so happens
that *faire* is an irregular verb. To correct an error out loud, instructors in
language classrooms will often use recasting (restating the student's phrase
but with the correct form) to affirm and correct at the same time. Instead of
recasting this right away, which might feel as if I were pointing out her error, I clapped my hands and went to the whiteboard: "*Vous faisez,*" I wrote,
and told the class this was an excellent, brilliant idea, but incorrect. I asked
them why, then let them discuss with the person next to them. In the ensuing
discussion, the students explained to me the regular verb endings as well as
the irregular forms for *faire.* Because the students were the ones providing
the answers, they not only revisited the grammar point, boosting their skills,
but were empowered to realize how much they know. To further cement the
lesson, I followed up with questions that required students to use the verb.
As I wrote responses on the board, I made a mistake on purpose, letting them
correct me and explain it back. This type of exercise takes time and flexibility
(you never know when you'll get a good error), but it empowers the student
to learn self-corrections as constructive rather than punitive. They also became communal learning opportunities, as opposed to individual mistakes.

Learning to Laugh, or Laughing to Learn

Another defining characteristic of this class was the students' sense of humor.
From the very first day, as we were debriefing the syllabus in English, Latitia
raised her hand and said, "*Je suis fâchée*" (I'm angry). "*Fâchée?*" I repeated,
making an angry face to clarify the meaning. "*Oui,*" she said back, "*fâchée*
because you *parle anglais* right now!" (She wanted us to speak French, not
English.) She delivered this line with a broad, confident grin, and the class
whooped with laughter. They may have entered the classroom with a sense
of dread, but it ended by making a joke—in French!—and asking for more
of a challenge.

On numerous occasions, and with surprisingly little vocabulary to work
with, humor originated among the students. While recapping emotion terms
on week two, I ran through imaginary scenarios and asked them to pre-
dict what characters might feel... "*Jean a un grand examen demain*" (John
has a big test tomorrow), I prompted the class, how does he feel? Nervous,
stressed, tired, they all said, as I expected, until Virginie said, "*choqué! un
examen?!*" (I'm shocked! There's a test?!) Her classmates all laughed, joining
in on the joke, throwing in their own comments.

Humor helped transform the tense atmosphere into one that felt fun and
relaxed, creating a noticeable difference in the students' body language. They
regularly arrived worn out, at times coming straight from their various jobs,
such as operating call centers or doing manual work like cleaning, without
time to shower or eat dinner. On four separate occasions, a student cried in
the minutes before class started while processing a traumatic event (sickness,

140   *Cecelia Ramsey*

a death of a relative, an incident in the prison, etc.) that had taken place that day or week. But at various points throughout the class, body language could be seen demonstrating the opposite of the tears and upset: upright, open, making eye contact with me and with classmates, returning smiles. These social behaviors are significant because antisocial behaviors are considered one of the "big four" risk factors in recidivism (Andrews et al., 2006, p. 116). Since our classroom doors must remain open, a journalism professor who was teaching down the hall would often say to me after class, "What was it this week?" and "Can we join the party?" Near the end of the semester, in a feedback session, Zoë, the oldest student in the group, touched on this aspect of the class by saying, "it cheers you up" and "it's too short."[9]

We met on Wednesday evening from 6 to 8, which always flew by quickly, thanks to engaged learners and intentional breaks to allow for mental rest and incorporate physical activity. If the students had been sitting, concentrating on grammar for 50 minutes, I might institute a quick game in French to review some older, more familiar material. For example, I would ask the students to stand in a circle and go around counting sequentially, starting at zero. At every interval of five, they would have to say something in French, like, "*pamplemousse!*" (grapefruit), and if a student forgot a number, they would say, "*banane*" (banana), then the class would help them find the right answer and proceed. While there is little content objective achieved through the enthusiastic chanting of numbers and fruits, there was inevitably laughter. Quick breaks for movement helped rejuvenate the classroom energy, allowing us to dive back into the text or topic at hand.

Though humor is regularly part of my teaching practice, it seemed to characterize my inside class far more than any other. One possible explanation is the students' willingness to bond with one another. While students on campus can save their jokes and laughter for their friends, students inside seemed to crave and cherish the opportunity to carve out a learning space where their creativity and personality could be freely expressed. Sociologist Meghan Kallman discovered similar trends in her prison courses, noting that unlike the individualistic approach to learning in many American classrooms, "learning in prison is often more a communal practice than an individual one"(2020, p. 329). My own students regularly used French phrases and their French names outside of class, so they claimed, as if it gave them something uniquely shared among themselves. As the class progressed, together they gained a sense of pride and ownership with using the language (Constance liked to say that she would even dream in French).

The students' communal approach matched beautifully with the communal pedagogical approach, where students regularly worked in partners and small groups. I thus moved away from the old teacher-centered approach, though in fact, the classroom looked a lot like an old-school traditional class: no slideshows, no videos, no discussion posts on Canvas. My only tools were paper, whiteboards, and the few approved props I was (sometimes) allowed to bring with me. As it turned out, my most basic, most reliable tool of all

Why French? 141

was myself. So, it was them, and it was me, learning from one another as we developed the skills to communicate in French.

This scaffolded approach, which involves providing the steps to help students move higher and further than they could on their own, resulted in the students feeling like French was "way easier" than they'd originally feared. To illustrate: one night, as groups were writing descriptive sentences, Catherine's group called me over to ask about negation (which we had not explicitly learned). They could say, "she is blonde," but they wanted to say, "she is *not* blonde." As I prompted the group to reflect on what they already knew, Catherine was able to produce, on her own, the correct sentence: "*Elle n'est pas blonde.*" Shocked, the others asked how she knew how to say that. She replied, "I don't know... Because '*Cyrano n'est pas beau*'?" ("Cyrano is not handsome"; this is one of the defining struggles of the story's protagonist, and a sentence used repeatedly). Catherine had so imbibed this line from the story, a description using the negative form, that it came to her when she wanted it, even though we had not yet explained what it meant. Similar to an "aha!" realization, these wins felt "easier than expected" and allowed success to come from the students themselves.

Conclusion

It can be tempting, as language educators, to think that we need our "stuff" (and yes, props and realia can embed the content and make it more meaningful), but at the core, humans acquire language through interacting with each other. Inside the prison, interactivity is all we had. And we treasured it. The communal aspect became fertile ground not just for discoveries about French (*"elle n'est pas blonde"* and *"vous faites"* and so on) but, more importantly, for discoveries about themselves. Inside students may never travel to a francophone country, but they concluded that they were "good" at learning, "good" at school, and "good" at French, rewriting the negative narratives they came in with and looking one another in the eye with a smile as they did so. As they walked out the door at the end of each class, they gave air *bisous* to me, reminding me that the sense of escape and self-discovery afforded by language learning—when done in a context-appropriate manner—may in fact be what every prison education program needs.

Author Note

I taught the class described in this chapter at my former institution, Lipscomb University, Department of English & Modern Languages, as part of the LIFE Program. My thanks to the hardworking program directors, who made the course run as smoothly as possible; to the program founder, Richard C. Goode, an exemplar of Christian service and mentor to many; and to my incredible students, who impacted my life, my faith, and my teaching in ways that escape these brief pages.

Notes

1 While the prison setting may heighten awareness of prior abuse, the same considerations apply to all language classrooms. Instructors can allow room for students to input their personal experiences or opinions without making that the central objective of an activity.
2 To learn more about expanding the notion of "text" and building students' literacy, see Menke and Paesani (2023).
3 The Lipscomb Initiative for Education (LIFE) offers faith-based education at two Tennessee prisons where qualified students can earn credits toward an Associate of Arts, Bachelor of Professional Studies or Master of Arts in Christian Ministry degree. Upon release, students can apply for the Richard C. Goode LIFE scholarship to continue pursuing their undergraduate or graduate degree at Lipscomb. Undergraduates from campus can take certain courses in the prison classroom.
4 Due to the lab component of on-campus language courses, the students cannot take the prison course to meet the same requirements, but I wanted to maintain the dynamic of a blended classroom. When our schoolyear got cut short by the pandemic, the students on campus wrote letters to the students inside, using French, as we maintained our course through correspondence.
5 The students' names in this article have been replaced with French pseudonyms.
6 Regarding course design and the status of language departments in the early twenty-first century, see Geisler et al. (2007).
7 When I learned that we had several singers and artists in the class, I included French songs and designed activities that incorporated drawing or analyzing francophone art. Building on students' interests requires flexibility, but can gain motivation.
8 Some students openly shared their personal experiences with the class, or with me individually in the space before and after class. Though unprompted, they would talk about dropping out of high school, or how they had to learn another language while in the military, or the stigmas they encountered.
9 In addition to limited class time, students taking nightly medication typically had to leave class early when the officers called for them (known as the "med line"). Disruptions and absences—often outside the students' control—are a regular part of prison education.

Works Cited

Andrews, D. A., Bonta, J., & Wormith, J. S. (2006). The recent past and near future of risk and/or need assessment. *Crime & Delinquency*, *52*, 7–27.

Drew, J. D., Duval, J., & Cyr, J. R. (2015). Community colleges and Spanish language instruction: Peer Pedagogy in prison. *New Directions for Community Colleges*, *2015*, 31–40. https://doi.org/10.1002/cc.20141

Geisler, M., Kramsch, C., McGinnis, S., Patrikis, P., Pratt, M. L., Ryding, K., & Saussy, H. (2007). Foreign languages and higher education: New structures for a changed world. MLA ad hoc committee on foreign languages. *Profession*, 234–245. https://www.mla.org/Resources/Guidelines-and-Data/Reports-and-Professional-Guidelines/Teaching-Enrollments-and-Programs/Foreign-Languages-and-Higher-Education-New-Structures-for-a-Changed-World.

Harlow, C. W. (1999). *Prior abuse reported by inmates and probationers*. US Department of Justice, Office of Justice Programs, Bureau of Justice Statistics.

Harlow, C. W. (2003). Education and correctional populations. *Bureau of Justice Statistics Special Report*.

Kallman, M. E. (2020). "Living more through knowing more": College education in prison classrooms. *Adult Education Quarterly (American Association for Adult and Continuing Education)*, 70(4), 321–339.

Kidder, K. L., & Ramsey, C. (2021, November 5–7). *Creating Curriculum and Community in a Women's Prison through Meaningful Language Instruction*. The 62nd Annual Convention of the Midwest Modern Language Association. Milwaukee, WI, United States.

Menke, M., & Paesani, K. (2023). *Literacies in language education: a guide for teachers and teacher educators*. Washington: Georgetown University Press.

Salomone, A. M. (1994). French Behind bars: A qualitative and quantitative examination of college French teaching in prison. *Modern Language Journal*, 78(1), 76–84.

15 Pushing Back/Pushing Forward

Embracing the Margins to Build Non-Punitive Learning Environments in Canadian Correctional Facilities

Nicole Patrie

Teachers in prison have to balance the needs of their students with the demands of the education and carceral systems. In this chapter, I draw on my experiences as a teacher and administrator in carceral environments in Canada. I will share how I attempted to create a non-punitive space in a physical space built for retaliation and how at times that meant confronting the typical practices in both higher education and in corrections.

For over a decade, I worked in an education program inside correctional facilities in Canada. The program was funded by the provincial government and operated by a local community college. Education program staff were employees of the college but worked fulltime inside the facilities. I worked in provincial facilities with students who were either serving sentences of less than 2 years or were pre-trial/pre-sentence.[1]

People in remand (pre-trial) custody told me that not having a release date increased their stress and made planning difficult, and accessing education seemed to add some stability otherwise unpredictable lives. Anecdotally, approximately half of the students in the program were pre-trial or pre-sentence. They could be waiting months to go to trial, arguing for bail reductions, or dealing with court dates and sentencing while attending classes. A small number of students waited years in prison for their trials. Often, these long-remand students would be transferred between provincial institutions in order to relieve population pressures, adding even more uncertainty.

My position as a professional in education who worked exclusively inside prisons, but not *for* prison, put me in a strange situation. When I attended college meetings and events, I often felt like our group of prison educators were outsiders. Our work environment was vastly different from typical campuses, and although we saw our students as similar, others saw only their prisoner status. On the other hand, although I worked in the prisons daily and was well-known among staff, I remained an outsider in that space. I neither wore a uniform nor reported directly through the prison hierarchy. Only sort of belonging to both carceral and education institutions enabled

DOI: 10.4324/9781003394426-18

me to push back on both institutions when our ability to offer educational programming was restricted.

What Is the Purpose of Education?

I started my teaching career in public high school. Having been trained in secondary education, and having gone through the public school system myself, it was a highly predictable experience. In contrast, teaching adults, and adults in prison, was jarring. However, when I reflect on the two experiences, I notice one similarity: a seemingly relentless focus on what comes next, growing up, or law-abiding adulthood.

The purpose of education, in both the public school and schools in prison, seemed to be training students to be socially appropriate, law-abiding adults. Most importantly, to become adults with jobs. Teaching in a rural high school, I observed this through the challenge "Why do I need to learn this?" Many students already knew they would be working on their family farm or ranch, or in local resource extraction. They saw no need for algebra or finance spreadsheets. To be honest, I did not see a need for it either. It seemed as though many students were in a rush to grow up. Government policies reinforced the importance of becoming "adults with jobs" through education reports and directives focusing on early entrepreneurship and developing skills for the 21st-century workforce.

In the prisons, I saw the same preoccupation with the creation of socially appropriate, law-abiding adults with jobs. The implication behind a name like the "Correctional System" is that people need correcting. Similarly, a focus on employment and rehabilitation manifested in "dust them off and patch them up" education practices. For example, the program I taught in was directed to teach shorter GED, life management, and employment-preparation courses. The emphasis was on quick resolution of individual shortcomings for eventual employment.[2] Individual shortcomings were tied to the concept of criminological needs (risk factors of criminal behavior) (Andrews & Bonta, 2010). As an administrator, I was asked to identify which criminological needs were addressed in each course.[3]

I think this view of education along with a focus on criminogenic needs, is short-sighted. The purpose of education is more than molding people into ideal workers. Furthermore, the students I met in prison did not need "dusting off" or "patching up." They were up against serious structural barriers, and the solution (if there was one) was more complex than a diploma or course completion certificate. All people carry within themselves a variety of complex life experiences, past learnings, goals, and a personal understanding of how their worlds work. These all need to be taken into account when designing learning experiences, if we want them to be meaningful.

146   *Nicole Patrie*

Like most people who have taught in high schools, I can relay stories of struggling to complete mandated curriculum, preparing for standardized tests, managing teen behaviors brought on by turbulent new emotions, and meeting with parents who want the best for their children. A packed curriculum prevented me from being a designer of learning experiences. I was instead more of a traffic conductor organizing the most effective way to get students through the material. I was often conflicted because a focus on efficiently delivering curriculum took precedence over students' needs.

When I started teaching adults in prison, I immediately realized many strategies I used to teach in public school would not directly translate. Happily, many of the struggles evaporated (parents of my adult students did not often call the prison). Unfortunately, new struggles rose in their place (addiction, poverty, racism). Ironically, in prison I was freer to teach how I wanted, in more meaningful ways. In ways that honored my students' experiences and who they were.

Adjusting to Adult Education, and Adult Education in Prison

I entered education in prison with an open mind and few expectations. Thinking back, I am not sure I had any preconceived notions about who my students were or what prison was like. In talking to and mentoring others new prison educators, many express surprise that their students are not stereotypical "prisoners" as portrayed in popular media (television dramas such as Orange is the New Black were popular when I was working in prisons). Even without this stereotypical expectation, I was surprised at the differences between my high school students and my prison students.

My students in prison seemed to truly want to be in class. They wanted (and asked for) so much more than the standard workbook-based curriculum. They were avid readers—we set up an area of my classroom as the school library. They were reflective, connecting learnings to their lives. They did homework—they asked for homework. They were artists. They wrote stories, business plans, and poetry. My training as a high school teacher gave me teaching strategies, most of which were directed at convincing students to participate in class and managing disruptive behavior on escalating scales. In my prison classroom, the strategies did not fit. Students needed no convincing, and behavior problems were rare. If course topics were relevant, and they were active participants, they were up for it. For them, education was more than employability and growing up.

In short, they were adult learners. Andragogy helps us to think about how adult learners are different from children and teens. The framework outlines a set of assumptions about learning in adulthood (Knowles, 1980). These assumptions then inform different strategies, ways of teaching, or ways of understanding learning. For example, adults are assumed to be more self-directed;

that is, their goals and aspirations reflect their self-concept, and they take personal responsibility to learn in order to meet these goals (Knowles, 1980; Merriam & Baumgartner, 2020). Some strategies rising from this assumption include having students participate in planning course progressions, making personal learning goals explicit, and providing choice in how to demonstrate learning. Instead of situating andragogy in direct opposition to pedagogy, many now understand the two as a spectrum encompassing different learning strategies and descriptions of learners of all ages (Merriam & Baumgartner, 2020).

More broadly, adult education as a field expands on these ideas, introducing alternative ways to think about adult learning. At its core, adult education promotes teaching strategies, centered on mutuality and respect, that enable students to be partners. As I learned about theories and frameworks in adult education, I applied them to my classes. For instance, transformative learning theory traces the process of critically reflecting on experiences to form new understandings or embrace new roles (Mezirow, 1997). I built opportunities for critical reflection into my class, incorporating group activities where the different levels of students could work together to solve problems or see situations in new ways. We explicitly acknowledged that learning takes place outside formal education institutions and even occurs unintentionally, and I encouraged students to draw on these experiences. One way to further bolster developing self-concept is to reflect on life experience and clearly articulate what was learned. In this way, I attempted to create a space that encouraged and fostered all types of learning and development, including, but not limited to, the course curricula.

By embracing adult education, my classroom became a place for sharing and exploring. It was as if creating an environment where students could be adult learners had a domino effect. Starting small with some group activities led to students designing their own group activities. Given the space, the students ran with it. Students escaped to the classroom. As teachers we often talked about how you could physically observe students' gait change as they walked through the doors of the school. Students brought proposals for classroom activities, art, and discussions. In so doing, the students were able to further their own educational goals through the program, even if the goals were not fully aligned. For example, I had a number of students working on business plans. I think misalignment between official education programs or curricula and student goals is common. Adult learning theories understand this and make room for both to coexist.

We were open to supporting students beyond the curriculum and prescribed courses. There were days when lesson plans were put aside to debrief news or personal experiences. I spent breaks gathering information students requested from the internet; most of the time, it did not pertain to their class. It was templates for planning their futures, information on social services in the area they planned on living, or even simply random wonderings normally

148   *Nicole Patrie*

answered with a quick search on our phones. Teachers are some of the only plain-clothed (non-uniformed) people in the prisons in which I worked—a sort of visible sign of not being "part" of the institution. Through these supportive actions we demonstrated a connection to the outside. By treating people as people, not as prisoners, we were able to create an environment whereby the students' whole selves were recognized, honored, and reclaimed. It was common to hear students say almost forgot they were in prison when they were in class.

Developing Alternative Practices

Through the alternative practices described below, I attempted to further center students' needs and whole selves. Adult education is not only for what occurs outside formal education; it should also inform the practices and policies of the program itself. Each alternative to more typical postsecondary practices is taken in turn. I outline the challenge that caused me to reject current practices, the alternatives I tried or implemented, and finally, how the program or I pushed the carceral and education systems to adapt their practices.

Experiential Knowledge

Challenge

Student transcripts are a form of academically sanctioned knowledge. They demonstrate the courses a student has taken and the grades they received. But in many ways, they are not a good representation of what students have done; that is, people learn outside the confines of formal education. As a result, past school achievement is rarely a good indication of their current ability. Formal learning builds upon the prior experiences of adult students. Students were surprised at their own abilities despite histories of school failure. They did not connect their turbulent life experience with increased knowledge or ability. However, when they were not in school, they were still learning; for example, adaptability and critical thinking are indispensable skills to develop.

Alternative Practice

I looked at transcripts to plan for graduation rather than decide what course to place a new student in. Students showed me how they thought through problems by talking about their process. As teachers, we needed to be open to alternative ways of demonstrating learning. Common algorithms and for solving problems, writing essays, and structuring arguments often appeared, but so did more creative formats. These alternative methods were often more eloquent. In teaching early math, many students had anxiety about fractions and long division. We succeeded by foregoing traditional algorithms to draw on their experiences (recipes, drug dealing, carpentry). This openness to alternative methods made the classroom a more welcoming place. In more than one instance, students who completed schooling outside Canada taught the entire class different notation systems for basic arithmetic.

Pushing Back/Pushing Forward

Eventually, all the teachers in the prison education program worked with students to place them in appropriate classes. However, education systems are predicated on credentials and step-by-step achievement in a particular order: Grades 10, 11, 12. We worked with the college and provincial education system to apply retroactive credits for students (earning credit in the courses they "skipped" to meet graduation requirements). We pushed back on the college's desire to use mandatory placement tests to assess students. I think we were able to avoid mandatory placement testing because of its cost; there was an associated per-test fee structure, and the education program or college would need to pay. We advocated for students to not have to take the placement test when they left prison and registered in the college as outside students. Ultimately, we did use a (free) placement test; however, it served as a starting point for discussions.

Universal Accommodations

Challenge

In prison, the need for universal accommodation policies was obvious; it was impossible to only accommodate students with documented conditions. Even when students have access to documentation, limiting the availability of accommodations perpetuates inequality in higher education (Lorenz & Facknitz, 2023). In prison, such restrictions are amplified due to even less resources; we did not have access to educational psychologists and doctors who could approve accommodations for documented disabilities. Similarly, many students had previously been streamed into lower academic courses in high school—was this because of a disability, structural barriers like racism and classism, both, or more?

Alternative Practice

We permitted anything that would help students succeed and learn, so long as it was approved by security. Students worked at their pace—some finished quickly and others took longer. Students resubmitted work. I modified assignments to emphasize specific sentences or words to help students decode. Differentiated instruction was made easier in small classes where students

150   *Nicole Patrie*

were studying different courses. They wrote final exams only when they felt prepared. We did all we could to reduce test anxiety. Although it was not always possible to use a familiar and physically comfortable environment for test writing, I offered calming music (of the students' choice) to help drown out institutional noises.

Pushing Back/Pushing Forward

The only situations we could not offer universal accommodations were during official GED, provincial, and apprenticeship tests; if we ignored their strict guidelines, we could lose the ability to offer these credentials. However, with appropriate scaffolding, practice, and earlier support, students were able to experience success even in these rigid situations. More broadly, universal accommodations, available to anyone who needs them, should be the standard in all situations. All people are worthy of access to education.

Trauma-Informed Practices

Challenge

Many students have histories of trauma, before the traumatic experience of being imprisoned (Daniels, 2021). Additionally, my classes usually had high numbers of Indigenous people. As a result of Canada's ongoing history of cultural (and real) genocide, many of my students were dealing with intergenerational trauma. They were survivors of residential schools or 60s scoop practices or had caregivers and family members who were survivors.[4] I observed trauma responses often in my classroom, especially when I was starting a new class with new students. Some students could not have their back to the door or became anxious when someone stood behind them. Some were hyperaware of their course materials and what they wrote down, preferring to keep their reflections oral (and therefore unsearchable by prison staff).

Alternative Practice

I used a semicircular layout in the class, and we kept the door open when possible. I learned to read body language, practiced de-escalation, and adjusted as necessary. Students bring their life experience to class with them, including their trauma, and I was aware of the different manifestations of trauma in my classroom.[5] Recognizing when students were uncomfortable or triggered before situations escalated helped me to avoid larger trauma responses. Students occasionally received bad news during class time, such as losing custody of their children, death of family members, or additional charges, and were not usually able to leave class. In these situations, we gave students space to process the bad news. The day someone loses custody of their children is not always a good day to work on their resume or read a novel. Some students wanted to continue their work, others wanted to talk, and others wanted to be silent.

Pushing Back/Pushing Forward

Trauma-informed practice acknowledges everyone is affected by trauma. While being trauma-informed was a constant for my work in prison education, it was not always the case on the larger college campus. I was invited to give presentations to teachers outside prisons about trauma-informed teaching and how they could create a safer learning environment for students through these practices.

Struggling against the Systems

Off-campus students are often neglected by educational institutions, such as when a college assumed students are local and can commute for events or support. Our students were no different. Most campus supports and events were not open to them, and, as staff, we could not commute to attend lunch-time events or professional development. We often joked about being forgotten or afterthoughts. This meant a lot of the alternatives above went unnoticed and unchallenged—if they could be contained within the prison. Unfortunately, that was not always the case. Our biggest administrative barrier was the various data management systems (i.e., the college registrar and government student data). On a number of occasions, data management limited our ability to do (or at least document) what the students needed.

Convincing systems to change is difficult. People who owed fees or were banned from the college campus were barred from attending class in prison. Students who skipped prerequisites needed retroactive credits, and course start/end dates needed flexibility beyond the semester system. Until we removed these barriers, we found ways to work around them. I registered students only upon completion, permitted banned students to attend classes (while we attempted to temporarily or permanently remove the ban). Until retroactive credits were sorted, students challenged final exams and we submitted grades for the prerequisite courses. We initially dealt with barriers on a case-by-case basis, slowly expanding to "prison students" by demonstrating that the barrier was previously removed without consequence. The goal was pushing to remove the barrier for all students, improving access both inside and outside prison.

Driving everything was the concept of "do what's best for students." While this does not seem radical, it was. The struggles enabled me to see the education system for what it is—a bureaucratic, self-perpetuating business—and to see it for what it can be—a place for learning and emancipation. The latter demands an environment of non-punitive education, where everyone is welcome.

152 *Nicole Patrie*

In contrast, we could not work around barriers in the prison system. Counts, drug dogs, and lockdowns happened regularly, throwing students back into their prisoner identity and disrupting the classroom rhythm. After I built a solid reputation among the prison staff, I could advocate for students; for example, we occasionally got permission to offer standardized exams to students in segregation. Unfortunately, many times our hands were tied. It was a prison first, and we had to stockpile goodwill for when it truly mattered. I adjusted my teaching in order to avoid miniscule conflict: there were no feet on desks, no students moving around, no photocopying artwork. I navigated internal conflict; to be in prison with these students, these were the rules I had to follow, even if I did not fully agree. Does this mean I was ultimately part of the system? Maybe; I am not entirely sure.

Once I built a reputation with prison staff, they were more likely to respond favorably when I asked for exceptions or special treatment. The program itself had existed for decades and had a track record of being dependable, reliable, security-aware, and student-centered. Maintaining this reputation was crucial in order to continue to enjoy relatively easy access to students; I was constantly aware of the fleeting nature of access. It can disappear at any time with one misstep. For this reason, while I use examples of sidestepping barriers in the education system, I did not dare sidestep barriers in the carceral system. Even with my reputation, my ability to enter the prisons could be rescinded at any point.

Conclusion

Doing what is best for students demands empathy for students' complex lives and a deep desire for their success. A willingness to bend a little goes a long way. Students cannot explore and express agency if they are bound by monolithic structures, although there is not much to do about the monolithic prison in which they live. As prison educators, we can and should push against both carceral and educational systems. In my experience, I was able to push the educational system and implement workarounds more openly and directly. We challenged the college's procedures for accessing and assessing education and implemented non-punitive education practices inside the prison school. Pushing the carceral system was done more strategically. We challenged the officers' perceptions of prisoners by sharing student achievements. Where possible, we used our reputation to increase access to education within the prison by occasionally requesting special treatment, expanding to different units, offering pilot programs, and building a library.

Ultimately, prison education, like adult education, is about opening and enabling access to education. Through prison education, we can challenge these structures, showing that people in prison are deserving and capable of education and advocating for their access inside and outside by pushing the carceral and education systems forward.

Notes

1 In Canada, the correctional system is split in two: provincial and federal. Provincial institutions cover anyone who is remanded (awaiting trial) or who has a sentence of less than 2 years, while federal institutions cover sentences over 2 years.
2 While the goal is full employment in meaningful work, many people leaving prison find themselves experiencing unemployment and underemployment (employment in low skilled, low paying, or part time work). A recent study by Statistics Canada and the Correctional Service of Canada found that the average reported income for people who were employed was $14,000; under half of the Canadian average. Furthermore, less than half of the sample reported any income at all. (Babchishin et al., 2021).
3 There are typically 8 separate criminogenic needs, including: "pro-criminal attitudes, antisocial personality, pro-criminal associates, education, employment, family and marital relationships, substance abuse, and leisure/recreation"(Andrews & Bonta, 2010, p. 46). In identifying which needs were addressed in each course we offered, one example would be that a GED course directly addresses education and employment, and indirectly addresses pro-criminal attitudes, antisocial personality, and pro-criminal associates (by engaging in class activities, modelling and developing healthy relationships with peers/mentors/teachers, and overcoming challenges).
4 In Canada, settler-colonialism has had a tremendous impact on the incarceration of Indigenous Peoples. The practice of forcibly removing children from their families to attend Residential Schools continued from before Canada became a country in 1887 to the late 1990s. These government funded schools subjected children to deplorable treatment, in the name of "civilizing" them. (Truth and Reconciliation Commission of Canada, 2015). The 60s scoop refers to the disproportionate number of Indigenous children apprehended into foster care and forced adoption (Indigenous Foundations, 2009). Even today, Indigenous children are overrepresented in the foster care system, just as Indigenous people are overrepresented in the criminal justice system.
5 See Davidson (2017) for a guide on trauma-informed practices in post-secondary education, including a description of some common trauma responses.

References

Andrews, D. A., & Bonta, J. (2010). Rehabilitating criminal justice policy and practice. *Psychology, Public Policy, and Law*, 16(1), 39–55. https://doi.org/10.1037/a0018362
Babchishin, K. M., Keown, L.-A., & Mularczyk, K. P. (2021). *Economic outcomes of Canadian federal offenders* (No. 2021-R002; p. 37). Research Division, Public Safety Canada.
Daniels, E. (2021). *Building a trauma-responsive educational practice*. Routledge.
Davidson, S. (2017). Trauma-informed practices for postsecondary education: A guide. *Education Northwest*. https://educationnorthwest.org/sites/default/files/resources/trauma-informed-practices-postsecondary.pdf

154   *Nicole Patrie*

Indigenous Foundations. (2009). *Sixties Scoop.* https://indigenousfoundations.arts. ubc.ca/sixties_scoop/

Knowles, M. S. (1980). *The modern practice of adult education: From pedagogy to andragogy* (Rev. and Updated). Association Press ; Follett Pub. Co.

Lorenz, D., & Facknitz, H. S. (2023). Challenging academic ableism by cripping crisis learning. In *Reading Sociology: Decolonizing Canada* (4th ed.). Oxford University Press.

Merriam, S. B., & Baumgartner, L. (2020). *Learning in adulthood: A comprehensive guide* (4th ed.). Jossey-Bass.

Mezirow, J. (1997). Transformative learning: Theory to practice. *New Directions for Adult and Continuing Education, 1997*(74), 5–12. https://doi.org/10.1002/ace.7401

Truth and Reconciliation Commission of Canada. (2015). *What we have learned: Principles of truth and reconciliation.* https://publications.gc.ca/collections/collection_ 2015/trc/IR4-6-2015-eng.pdf

16 Excursion and Return

Exploring Transformative Texts, Great Questions, and the Human Experience in the Prison Classroom

Dale Brown

To seek one's own in the alien, to become at home in it, is the basic movement of spirit, whose being is only return to itself from what is other.

(Gadamer, 1960/2013, p. 15)

...which is better—cheap happiness or lofty suffering? Well, which is better?

(Dostoevsky, 1864/1993, p. 128)

I began working on Western Michigan University's college-in-prison project as a graduate student in 2017, forging relationships at and between Western Michigan University (WMU) and the Michigan Department of Corrections (MDOC). During the pilot phase of WMU's program from 2018 to 2020, we offered semester-long, non-credit classes in philosophy, educational foundations, and sociology at a medium-security State prison. Starting in the 2023–2024 academic year, after years small victories and temporary setbacks, WMU's college-in-prison project—Higher Education for the Justice-Involved—will transition into its next phase: a formal academic program which provides college credit toward credentials in the liberal arts.

In building a prison education program, I've come to see that prison-university partnerships are meaningful because they can open a space for harm mitigation. But more than this, they can open a space for humanization. Apart from their (important) role in facilitating instrumental outcomes such as reductions in recidivism and processes of abolition, prison-university partnerships can facilitate the movement of spirit; that is, a movement away from alienation and toward a broader horizon of understanding, a greater sense of belonging or being at home in the world. This chapter gives a grounded account of how this movement toward a more humanizing experience might come about in the context of the WMU/MDOC prison-university partnership.

Based on in-depth conversations, I first relate accounts from formerly incarcerated individuals that detail some of their experiences with the humanizing and transformative potential of higher education in prison—and, in many cases, the lack of opportunity thereof. Second, I explore some ways

DOI: 10.4324/9781003394426-19

156   *Dale Brown*

in which the prison context might bear on the philosophical foundations of higher education (in prison). Finally, I reflect on how experiences of currently and formerly incarcerated individuals (and my own, teaching and learning inside) inform and complicate the work of building a college-in-prison program which aims to offer a shared intellectual experience by addressing the perplexities of human existence via dialogical, relational, intersectional, and textually rich engagement with the liberal arts and humanities.

Time: Easy or Hard; Dead or Alive

In *Wilderness and Razor Wire* (2000), Ken Lamberton makes a distinction between two ways a person may choose to spend (or do) their time in prison: the easy way or the hard way. On the one hand, they may do what he calls easy time:

> In the same way that the prison environment deprives us of touch, we, in turn, deprive ourselves of being wholly human. It is a common reaction to doing time—easy time, it's called. But it's also a coward's way of dealing with prison. In my mind, turning away from emotion, and the reasons behind the emotion, is what is weak. Many people hide in prison. Its very nature isolates and insulates; it constructs barriers deeper that walls and fences. It makes it easy to slip inside your own comfortable and private cocoon. Easy time. No remorse, no depression, no pain.
>
> (p. 101)

On the other hand, an incarcerated person may do what Lamberton calls hard time. Incarcerated himself when he wrote the book, Lamberton chose to do hard time, describing it as consciously "nurturing emotional ties to the outside, to family and friends" (p. 101). And he goes on to say:

> Hard time doesn't depend solely on prison; it depends on relationships. Prison only concentrates and enhances the inevitable pain all relationships cause (and prolongs this pain because prison, at its best, suspends rather than heals), the pain (or grief) of separation, failure, broken promises, broken trust.
>
> (p. 108)

"It takes courage to face the pain," Lamberton writes, "to expose yourself to the consequences of your actions and accept them, particularly the consequences that affect your victims, your family, your children" (p. 177). While Lamberton focuses on the relational aspects of hard time and easy time, others speak compellingly of the wide-ranging nature of the distinction.

Over a series of in-depth phone conversations from fall 2021 to spring 2023, Jamie (a white male in his 50s) related his experiences of being incarcerated, of time, of powerlessness, of emotional surrender. The conversations were recorded with his permission as a part my dissertation project under WMU IRB 20-02-04. Jamie confirmed, as we might expect, that "emotions, soul-searching, admissions of difficulty, vulnerability, openness to someone who loves you on the outside [of the prison] are all viewed negatively." That individuals tend to adopt a sort of "willful ignorance toward any kind of emotional depth." That, in stark terms, you will likely be "thought of as a little bitch if you complain and show your feelings" while in prison. That incarceration, essentially, is a machine coughing up battered, bruised, and broken bodies. Jamie's experiences—and his choice to engage in hard time—forced a change in his worldview, moving him away from one that is analytic and toward one that is (at least quasi) spiritual.

Another formerly incarcerated person, Daniel (a Native American male in his 70s), called my attention to another, related distinction: dead time or alive time. At the end of an Zoom interview conducted under the same dissertation project mentioned above, he said: "I love being able to share my opinion on the [lack of] educational opportunities [in prison] and tell people exactly how dead the time is for those men and women." Despite the incredible hunger incarcerated people have for the opportunity for self-improvement, "they don't have much to reach for." Daniel is recently returned after serving more than 30 years in both the state and federal prison systems. During his incarceration, he participated in several higher education in prison programs—taking over 40 college-level classes while incarcerated—and has earned a Business Administration degree in Computer Programming and Data Processing from a community college. Despite his college education, he still had trouble adjusting to the technological advances that took place during his incarceration, from which he was almost completely shielded. In his view, Corrections has:

> kind of given up helping prisoners to improve themselves. I just came home from 30 years of incarceration. And I didn't know how to use a telephone. I didn't know how to turn the computer on. I didn't know how to get on the internet. [My] kids had to show me how to use these things. How can you expect a man or a woman to come out and be successful and they don't know that?

Elsewhere, I've described DeadTime as a deteriorative force that operates over time—the experience of the process of dehumanization (Brown, 2022). It is that which stunts one's ability to see oneself as more than one is now, and what one might possibly become in the future. This is so much worse than warehousing. This is the destruction of the possibility of a future self who is equipped to understand, expand, and transform the nature of his or her own reality more fully.

Conversations with Jamie, Daniel, and other currently and formerly incarcerated people (including those with whom I've had the pleasure of

158 *Dale Brown*

speaking outside of my dissertation research) have helped me keep in mind many important things about the intersection between higher education and incarceration. I'll highlight two that are relevant for my purposes in this chapter. The first point is that the context (and the setting) matters. Higher education in prison operates at the intersection of two very large, bureaucratic institutions, each with its own aims and purposes. Keeping this front of mind matters for the ways in which we attempt to promote both humanization and justice in the prison setting. Becoming wholly human, cultivating a sense of belonging in the world, being fully alive: these are the ontological foundations of humanization. They are the opposite of DeadTime.

The second point to highlight is that higher education is not a panacea. There are myriad ways to engage in hard time, and higher education doesn't necessarily have to be one of them. Daniel helped me keep this in mind. "In many prison settings," he said, "you can pursue your own education for self-fulfillment...you can create opportunity...to gather books, order books, and do your own study and research." In his case, he used a lot of his time to study the Bible and to study his Native American heritage. Other ways do help. But higher education, I argue, can offer something different, perhaps something more. Before I get to that, however, I'll turn next to the ways in which the context and setting of college-in-prison programs call for—perhaps even necessitate—a different framing of some of the traditional aims of higher education.

Foundations of Higher Education (in Prison)

The philosophical foundations of higher education in prison are, in my estimation, scarcely explicitly attended to in the context of prison-university partnerships. A deeper understanding of *why* we do the work that we do can help us answer important questions. What are the aims and purposes of higher education in prison? In what ways, if any, should those aims differ from the aims and purposes of "traditional" institutions of higher education? How much do higher education and rehabilitation as a form of punishment, or abolition as a form of revolution, have in common?

There are two common justifications given for higher education in prison: rehabilitation (which is a form of punishment) and abolition (which is a form of revolution). In this section, I argue that neither rehabilitation nor abolition should be the *main* justification for engaging in higher education in prison. In the context of prison-university partnerships, both rehabilitation and abolition miss the point of higher education. Carceral higher education should not (primarily) be about punishment. Similarly, carceral higher education should not (primarily) be about abolition. We'll look at each of these briefly in turn before examining humanization, which I do take to be the main point of higher education.

Higher Education as Punishment

Because it occurs under the purview of state and federal departments of correction, higher education in prison is typically and perhaps intuitively viewed narrowly within the context of punishment. In this way, it has been limited to the logic of punishment, the end goal of which is typically to reduce crime (Bedau, 1978; Hoskins, 2013) or, similarly, to reduce recidivism (Castro 2018; Davis et al., 2013). Thus, considering higher education in carceral settings (jails, prisons, detention centers, etc.) almost naturally brings up questions about how the purposes and types of punishment bear on these goals. But there is a sleight of hand involved here. As alluded to above, the goals of punishment are not the same as the goals of higher education. In particular, rehabilitation seems to strike most people as a natural fit to contextualize carceral higher education (CEA, 2023; Davis et al., 2013). Even among scholars of higher education in prison there exists a long history of casting it as a treatment or intervention model of rehabilitation or reform (Castro & Gould, 2018). Rehabilitation theories of punishment attempt to form a person who has committed a crime into the type of person who is less likely to commit crimes in the future.

Despite attempts to justify carceral higher education in terms of rehabilitation, there are at least two main reasons why such attempts fail. First, limiting the discussion to punishment-related concepts such as reform or rehabilitation limits students' educational possibilities (Hoskins, 2013). Rehabilitative theories do not respect individuals' moral agency. And while the failure to respect a person's agency may or may not be a problem for punishment in itself, it certainly poses a problem for higher education (Brighouse, 2006). Education in the name of punishment is often cashed out in terms of intervention, character education, treatment programs, behavioral modification, and so on (Castro & Gould, 2018 Karpowitz, 2017). Learning under this model is heavily, if not entirely, inward facing, guided by a "what works" frame concerned only with improving individual choice-making (Pollack, 2014). As a result, Pollack argues, alternative ways of constructing and understanding oneself and one's experience are at best not possible and at worst unthinkable and thus unspeakable.

Second, and relatedly, to justify education in terms of rehabilitation or reform is to adopt a deficit-based approach, focusing only on a person's negative qualities which, through education, must be made "better." According to Paris and Alim (2014), deficit pedagogies are those that "are filtered through the lens of contempt and pity" (p. 86). The focus is less on potentialities and opportunities than it is on "fixing" what's wrong within the individual. Our focus ought to be on students qua human beings, not students as criminals, inmates, offenders, or felons. Terms such as those in the latter set are offensive in part because they overstate the fluidity and fickleness of human character (Ariely, 2008; Kahneman, 2011; Miller, 2017), and because they often represent racially driven stereotypes (Alexander, 2012). Despite an incessant

160   *Dale Brown*

media-driven narrative which depicts incarcerated people as "monsters" and the like, human beings simply aren't all bad (or all good) all, or even most, of the time (Davis, 2003; Miller, 2017; Sered, 2019). Decades of psychological studies reveal the startling fact that our propensity to do good or bad is sometimes altered by, to provide only food-related examples, the smell of cookies in the air or the extent to which we are hungry (Miller, 2017).

Any rehabilitative benefits stemming from one's punishment via college in prison are the mere byproducts of the intrinsic benefits afforded by quality higher education. To be sure, a mere benefit is still a benefit and should be regarded accordingly. Departments of corrections allow institutions of higher education to operate in their facilities-based sometimes solely on the correlation between education and reductions in recidivism. It behooves even the most idealistic of us in higher education to at least nod at this benefit (and the host of other instrumental benefits) as we seek to instantiate our college-in-prison programs. But while higher education may contribute to an incarcerated person's rehabilitation or reform, such concepts do not provide the right lens through which to view higher education in prison. The question is neither whether punishment has a claim on education nor whether education has a claim on punishment. Punishment and higher education have different objectives that "cannot, in fact, be reconciled" (Karpowitz, 2017, p. 97; see also Castro, 2018, Castro & Gould, 2018). After all, it is paradoxical to say that we educate anyone as punishment, irrespective of citizenship status. A university has no business in the business of punishment. Let's examine one more commonly cited justification for college-in-prison programming: prison abolition.

Higher Education as Abolition

Heppard (2019) argues that the higher education in prison classroom is a space of resistance with radical, revolutionary potential, which calls for a specific type of curriculum: the liberal arts curriculum. Such a curriculum should be humanities-based as it allows for incarcerated students to participate in their own liberation—via the development of their human capacities—which is a prerequisite for revolutionary change. And the specific revolutionary change that Heppard seeks to bring about is the abolition of prisons. Drawing on Arendt's *On Revolution* (1963), Heppard describes the revolutionary two-step this way:

> Revolution first requires a negative freedom, or freedom-from, what might be described as liberation. Before establishing one's own freedom, one must find a way to get free from whatever condition of slavery or oppression in which they find themselves. Yet, even then, not all successful liberatory efforts are revolutionary. Sometimes you find your way out of the frying pan and into the proverbial fire. Therefore,

Excursion and Return 161

the second type of revolutionary freedom entails the establishment of a new system, a positive freedom or freedom-for. Consequently, by creating a new way of living and being in the world, a revolutionary framework is one that ultimately aims at the wholesale dismantling of current systems, particularly oppressive systems such as the carceral system.

(p. 3)

While I do not take issue with the revolutionary two-step espoused by Arendt and endorsed by Heppard, I do take issue with its application to carceral higher education, especially with respect to step two. Even if we buy into (which I do) the value of step one—liberation from oppression via a humanities-based curriculum (and we will continue to explore this in the next section)—further aiming toward revolution might be asking too much. And focusing narrowly on prison abolition even more so.

I'm focused here on the acts of teaching taken to improve the lives of the students and the idea of education as the practice of freedom, about which hooks (1994) writes:

The classroom, with all its limitations, remains a location of possibility. In that field of possibility, we have the opportunity to labor for freedom, to demand of ourselves and our comrades, an openness of mind and heart that allows us to face reality even as we collectively imagine ways to move beyond boundaries, to transgress.

(p. 207)

We can seek a humanizing curriculum and pedagogical approach that engages in education as the practice of freedom without committing to the project of prison abolition—or any revolutionary project, for that matter. For carceral higher education does not require a necessarily revolutionary outlook. Humanization is open to but does not require revolution. The positive freedom in the revolutionary two-step, the "possibility" for hooks, is better captured by a notion of humanization which seeks to pursue with others the understanding, expanding, and transforming of reality to improve the level of fit we have in the world. In this sense, it might be more productive to think of revolution as humanization at scale rather than revolution as abolition.

In terms of higher education, then, we can make a basic distinction between aims and purposes that are intrinsically valuable and those that are merely instrumentally valuable. Some things can be both intrinsically and instrumentally valuable. With respect to punishment and abolition, higher education is used (primarily) instrumentally to achieve those ends. Again, we are prompted to ask: What is the point of higher education? And what is the point of higher education *in prison*? Of course, the point of higher education

162 *Dale Brown*

is itself a point of contention (see, e.g., Allen, 2016; Brighouse, 2006; Gutman, 1999; and Nussbaum, 2010). For my purposes here, let's assume the following four main justifications for higher education: fostering cognition, cultivating character, preparing for economic contribution, and developing citizens (Brown, 2021). These are important, no doubt. But with these aims, too, higher education is used (primarily) instrumentally. Given the context of the prison setting (as discussed in the first section of this chapter), these aims must be framed differently to fully serve the incarcerated student population. Here's my stance: Carceral higher education should *primarily* be about humanization, the process of understanding, expanding, and transforming—with others—the nature of one's reality. A key feature of humanization as the primary intrinsic aim of higher education is that it holds both within and without the prison setting.

WMU's Higher Education for the Justice-Involved

From 2018 to 2020, WMU's Higher Education for the Justice-Involved (HEJI) program offered semester-long, non-credit classes in philosophy, educational foundations, and sociology at a medium-security State prison. After a Covid-imposed hiatus, HEJI is slated to commence its formal, credit- and credential-conferring programming in Fall 2023. Operating out of WMU's Center for the Humanities, HEJI will continue to provide dialogical, relational, textually rich humanities-based higher education.

Engaging the works of, for example, Ralph Waldo Emerson, W.E.B. Du Bois, Paulo Freire, and Hans Georg Gadamer, HEJI has adopted a guiding conception of humanities-rich education that is dialogical, relational, and textually rich—one that is set off by the ideas that have persisted into our modern academic disciplines. As Emerson explains in "The American Scholar," (2000) colleges "have their indispensable office, — to teach elements. *But they can only highly serve us, when they aim not to drill, but to create; when they gather from far every ray of various genius to their hospitable halls, and, by the concentrated fires, set the hearts of their youth on flame*" (my emphasis).

In short, what might get ignited in the hearts of students (and teachers) through the study of influential humanities texts is a desire for perpetual self-formation: the never-ending process of humanization. We assume that all students benefit when they grapple with the enduring questions (e.g., What does it mean to be human? What is freedom? Who am I? What is love? Can we justify suffering?) and themes (e.g., justice, truth, resilience, identity) of human existence. These are the types of questions and themes with which we are invited to engage via robust engagement with the humanities. In seeking understanding, we ask questions of things, of books, of people, and so on. But things, books, and people can also ask questions of us; they can put us into question right back. Humanistic inquiry is not an alternative to professional or technical modes of education; it is the very foundation on which they stand.

Excursion and Return 163

The complexity of this endeavor is not lost on us. For context, I turn to interviews conducted as a part of my dissertation project. Laron, a currently incarcerated former participant of HEJI's pilot program, formulated it this way when I asked him to reflect on the critical thinking course in which he participated. He said "It is both a blessing and a curse to be more aware." What he learned, in other words, was hard to unlearn. Laron said he became more selective of the people with whom he would engage in conversation. He found himself calling out erroneous arguments made by news anchors on television. His "bullshit meter," as he called it, increased greatly in sensitivity. Recall Lamberton's distinction between easy time and hard time. Raising one's consciousness, one's awareness of oneself in the world, might not be so easy to undo. In *Notes from Underground* (1993), Dostoevsky seems to wrestle with something similar. With some force, he asks the reader: "...which is better—cheap happiness or lofty suffering? Well, which is better?" (p. 128). Still, Laron saw participating in the courses as a way to prove something to himself, to the instructors, and to his family. "There is a sense of pride you get from taking college courses," he said.

Conclusion

One question that often arises with carceral higher education is this: why should we provide a college-level education to individuals who have been convicted of committing some crime? The question, I take it, is about what incarcerated individuals deserve. Let me suggest, however, that society's general approach for a long time, if in transition, isn't what *people* deserve in this situation as much as about what *criminals* deserve as a punishment for a crime. If asked, *why do criminals deserve an education?* I always answer this way: Because though designated by the system as "criminals," they are people, and people deserve to be treated as human beings no matter the circumstance.

As Daniel reminded me, vocational education, religious study, adult basic education, counseling, and so on *do* help to cultivate individuals' humanity. And these should be pursued simultaneously where possible. But a humanities-rich higher education can offer something different, perhaps something *more*. It helps an active, truth-seeking soul cast themself out in self-evolving circles in perpetuity (Emerson, 1837/2000). It helps us overcome limit situations in the way that we perceive our world (Freire, 1970/2014). It helps us expand the horizon of our understanding (Gadamer, 1960/2013). It helps us realize that the goal is "to know the end and aim of that life which meat nourishes" rather than to earn the meat alone (Du Bois, 1903/1994). The structure that a humanistic education captures so well is that of excursion and return: an initial puzzlement as we encounter something alien to us, and—in the process of understanding it, of making the strange familiar to us—a return with a broader view of the situation, of ourselves, and of others.

164 *Dale Brown*

"To seek one's own in the alien," explains the German philosopher Hans Georg Gadamer (1960/2013), "to become at home in it, is the basic movement of spirit, whose being is only return to itself from what is other" (p. 15). WMU's partnership with the Michigan Department of Corrections extends higher education's humanizing potential into the community, allowing us to live the University's motto more fully, "so that all may learn." It is clear to us that the study of the humanities can benefit anyone—incarcerated or otherwise.

References

About us. (2023, June 12). Welcome to CEA National | CEA National. https://ceanational.org/about-us/.

Alexander, M. (2012). The new JIM crow: Mass incarceration in the age of colorblindness. The New Press.

Allen, D. (2016). Education and equality. University of Chicago Press.

Ariely, D. (2008). Predictably irrational: The hidden forces that shape our decisions. Harper Perennial.

Bedau, H. A. (1978). Retribution and the theory of punishment. Journal of Philosophy, 75, 601–20.

Brighouse, H. (2006). On education. Routledge.

Brown, D. (2021). The promise of higher education in prison: Humanization. Philosophy of Education, 77(3), 85–98.

Brown, D. (2022). Setting students' hearts on flame: How a humanizing higher education rooted in the humanities can be beneficial for justice-involved people. Philosophy of Education, 78(2), 77–91.

Castro, E. L. (2018). Racism, the language of reduced recidivism, and higher education in prison: Toward an anti-racist praxis. Critical Education, 9(17), 1–14.

Castro, E. L., & Gould, M. R. (2018). What is higher education in prison? Introduction to radical departures: Ruminations on the purposes of higher education in prison. Critical Education, 9(10), 1–15.

Davis, A. Y. (2003). Are prisons obsolete? Seven Stories Press.

Davis, L. M., Bozick, R., Steele, J., Saunders, J., & Miles, J. (2013). Evaluating the effectiveness of correctional education: A meta-analysis of programs that provide education to incarcerated adults. RAND Corporation. DOI:10.7249/rr266

Dostoevsky, F. (1864/1993). Notes from underground. Vintage Classics.

Du Bois, W. E. B. (1903/1994). The souls of black folk. Dover Publications.

Emerson, R. W. (1837/2000). The essential writings of Ralph Waldo Emerson. Modern Library.

Freire, P. (1970/2014). Pedagogy of the oppressed: 30th anniversary edition. Bloomsbury Publishing USA.

Gadamer, H. (1960/2013). Truth and method. A&C Black.

Gutman, A. (1999). Democratic education. Princeton University Press.

Heppard, J. (2019). The art of liberating humanity. Critical Education, 10(3), 1–10. doi:10.14288/ce.v10i3.186302

hooks, b. (1994). Teaching to transgress: Education as the practice of freedom. Routledge.

Hoskins, Z. (2013). Punishment, contempt, and the prospect of moral reform. Criminal Justice Ethics, 32(1), 1–18. doi:10.1080/0731129X.2013.777250

Kahneman, D. (2011). Thinking, fast and slow. Penguin Books.

Karpowitz, D. (2017) College In prison: Reading In an age of mass Incarceration. Rutgers University Press.

Lamberton, K. (2000). Wilderness and razor wire. Mercury House.

Miller, C. (2017). The character gap: How good are we? Oxford University Press.

Nussbaum, M. (2010). Not for profit: Why democracy needs the humanities. Princeton University Press.

Paris, D., & Alim, H. S. (2014). What are we seeking to sustain through culturally sustaining pedagogy? A loving critique forward. Harvard Educational Review, 84(1), 85–100. doi:10.17763/haer.84.1.982l873k2ht16m77

Pollack, S. (2014). Rattling assumptions and building bridges: Community-engaged education and action in a women's prison. In G. Balfour & E. Comack (Eds.) Criminalizing women: Gender and (in)justice in neo-liberal times (pp. 290–302). Fernwood Press.

Sered, D. (2019). Until we reckon. The New Press.

Section IV

Changemaking and Coalition Building

17 The Poem. The Painting. Us

Kyes Stevens

The act of creating is simultaneously the act of becoming.

Just as words, charcoal and paint become something new in the hands and the mind wielding them, so does the process create the person. The connectedness of the two, the twining together, the breath and soul of the person are fused into what is created.

Art in all its forms becomes. It moves through stages and iterations. It rolls around in the conscious or unconscious mind. We cannot know all the intricate roots in the mind and soul. We cannot drop a pin in the moment a creative idea or project begins because microscopic tendrils planted years ago informed and placed the stones in a foundation sequence that eventually gives rise to a manifestation outside the body. Time and space influence how those things inside a person can come into creative being outside the person.

Everything is process.

The poem.

The painting.

Us.

**

People in prisons in Alabama can't access enough to feed the mind. Libraries are growing more slim as Securus PEDs (Personal Education Devices) become more prominent. Not everyone can access those, not everyone can pay to get to certain content, and because they are basically the size of post-card, they exclude people whose physical health does not allow them to see words or images the size of an ant.

Even before the PEDs, opportunities were slim. In the 2000s, when I started classes at new facilities, the Alabama Prison Arts + Education Project was the only program with classes that were literally open to everyone. I worked in facilities that had no GED, no Adult Basic Education (ABE), no trade school. There was church, though.

How do you teach when you are stepping into what is basically a wasteland of access to meaningful materials for learning (other than the resources that people inside are able to get through friends and loved ones)? What approaches encourage students to channel the ingenuity they demonstrate inside for survival into aesthetic development? My goal has always been to

DOI: 10.4324/9781003394426-21

teach in a way that requires the least in order to demonstrate that fancy art supplies are not required to create on fundamental levels. The spirit of us, of APAEP, has always been: What can you do with a pen or a pencil and something to receive the graphite or pigment?

I aimed to create a framework for creating that could utilize what people could access inside. There have been some exceptions to this, of course. People wanted other options than graphite and charcoal, and so as we secured funding, we have offered some additional art making materials. But an unintended impact of teaching a watercolor class is a silent message that says: unless you are in the class, you cannot do this. It becomes one more thing that the majority of people inside cannot access. It is one more way to say: you do not belong. It is a balance that I am not sure we've completely figured out. But you can teach in a way that allows people to see the space around them, to encourage wild imagination, and within the desolate surroundings, to find the inspiration that can infuse their creativity.

The head and heart energy you enter the classroom with sets the tone for it all. I want the spaces of our program to be based in, *hello, welcome, let's learn to do something together*. I want the spaces to be community and human warmth and sincerity that offers a place to begin. The process is starting, taking the risk, and then movement.

**

We all start somewhere. For me, teaching inside was not something I specifically sought when I returned home to Alabama from New York. I was certain I did not want to work with higher education because graduate school showed with impressive precision how exclusive and unwelcoming higher education is to stunning portions of our people in this country. And even though I am from a generationally nerdy family (understand that as generational privilege), I also spent my formative years in working-class neighborhoods and rural America,

The Alabama Prison Arts + Education Project was initially conceived in 2001 when Kyes Stevens began teaching at the Talladega Federal Prison through a fellowship from the National Endowment for the Arts (NEA). APAEP grew from one poet teaching in one prison to a community of hundreds of writers, artists, and scholars teaching in prisons across Alabama. The first phase of what is now APAEP was called The Alabama Prison Arts Initiative, which was first funded by the NEA in 2003. In 2004, APAEP took its current name when it became a full-time program of Auburn University. Course offerings have grown from poetry to a wide variety of courses in the arts and humanities, social sciences, and STEM, and currently include a BS degree in Interdisciplinary

The Poem. The Painting. Us 171

where I did not see clearly until my adult life the inequity in who gets access to fully be present and explore the world through education, art, travel, etc. I would soon eat my words about higher education.

A phone call offering a chance to teach poetry through a fellowship with the National Endowment for the Arts at the Talladega Federal Correctional Institution was my entry. The work chose me, though certainly my life to that point created a pathway. I

Studies from AU made possible by the US Department of Education's Second Chance Pell Experimental Sites Initiative.

APAEP resides in the Office of the Provost at Auburn University, within the administrative leadership of the Office of the Associate Provost for Academic Effectiveness. Over the 22 years of programming, many funding agencies, foundations, partnerships, and individual donors have made possible the programming of APAEP. Over 6000 people have participated in classes and programming. It is a stunningly remarkable community.

stepped into those early classes not so far removed from my MFA program. I entered teaching inside thinking about my experience at Sarah Lawrence College, where grades were not the focus of learning. Curiosity and engagement were the focus. My entire engagement with learning flourished. Never was there a suggestion of why you should not try something—the starting point was *why not try*. Who cares if your angle and approach are unorthodox (as determined by systems of higher education)? Innovation and discovery emerge from not being afraid to seek answers and connect disparate dots.

The early classes at Talladega, and then stepping into Tutwiler Prison for Women with the Alabama Department of Corrections, showed me the way.

I was shown because I listened to the people inside.

Also important to note is that I was stepping into all this as a poet, historian, and photographer. On so many levels, my life was and continues to be about seeing. I had to pay attention to some other hard truths. In 2001, there was only one nonprofit working inside the Alabama Department of Corrections (ADOC) that was not a faith-based program. Aid to Inmate Mothers was a strong presence at Tutwiler, but there was a sea of nothing for the men's facilities. I had intended to build the program as a nonprofit but soon discovered that funding agencies were not interested in supporting administrative salaries—they wanted to support the work. (Yes, this still exists, and the disconnect is stunning). I was working at Auburn University and running the program on the side when a remarkable moment opened up for me to slide in the backdoor and run APAEP as my full-time job at. Knowing that Auburn's institutional support would allow me to pay my student loans, have a place to live, and provide for my animal rescue habit, I took the open door. My goal was to build a program. In order to cultivate all that I dreamed it to be, I needed a place to land. I needed a community. My family

172 *Kyes Stevens*

has been associated with Auburn University for generations, including a beloved grandfather who built the pre-med program. People at the university knew me through my family. Auburn University became that very complicated community.

And just as I wanted to have endless poetry classes inside, I also wanted to make our classes spaces where people could be and shape *their* communities. This truth still resonates with all that is the Alabama Prison Arts + Education Project. Over these past 22 years, my role has been to find the beautiful souls who can step into and lead classes from a place of humanness, to find fiscal resources to support paying those teachers and providing the materials needed for courses, and, as we grew, finding the resources to support other administrative positions with our program at Auburn University.

The community I seek to build is one that dismantles hierarchical notions of success, as it is so commonly applied to our world, which seeks always to create a divide between people. That divide is destroying us. Learning and creating allow us to become not just individuals but also communities. This joint endeavor of growth and community-building is how we envision and embark upon the new pathways to fix so many of the deeply rooted problems of this country.

* *

I am weary of the exceptionalism applied to people inside prisons. Art is good for people who are incarcerated because… education is good for people who are incarcerated because… the tropes of justification to invest in people inside are nearly always linked to recidivism and the ways that whatever programming is going to help someone when they get out. Most often it is not centered in a human being wanting to learn and create and invest in themselves simply… because.

That utilitarian logic is dangerous. It is deeply hurtful to people inside and to people out here. In many ways, it supports the rampant suggestions that people who are incarcerated are somehow less-than.[1] The basis of the work all these years has been to make space and open opportunity, to meet people where they are, to learn, to listen, and to build spaces for creative and intellectual engagement that meet their needs.

In the early years, everything in the world of arts and education as it relates to prisons guided me to situate the value of arts and education as it impacts recidivism, or makes safer prisons, or saves the state money. It took me longer than I would like to admit to gain the insight that investing in that justification makes the programs part of the system of oppression, of hierarchy, of distinction. We don't have to be distinctive. We can simply be. We can build spaces to fill needs and be happy in that.

That people inside must wait years to get a GED is absurd. That there are rules in Alabama dictating who, based on their sentence or conviction, can even access educational programming as provided by the state is so blindly short-sighted. For a while, we were the only non-faith-based program that

The Poem. The Painting. Us 173

people sentenced to Life Without Parole could access. We create a different world when we spend less time building the parameters for who qualifies for education, or access to arts, or who deserves to learn to read.

We practitioners also do not have to be the translators of motivation or impact. Are we not silencing the people we serve when we do that? Let the people who take the classes determine their language. My heart delights when people say they have signed up for a class because they love poetry, or that they want to learn to draw, or that they want to write their story. We, as artists and educators inside, don't need to derail their motivation by our own agendas.[2]

Elmore Correctional is a medium security men's facility about 30 minutes north of Montgomery. It used to be one of our more stable places to offer classes.[3] Classes tended to be made up of returning participants and some new folks. There was a gentleman who took every single literature, history, or STEM (Science, Technology, Engineering, Math) class we offered. One semester, he showed up in a drawing class, and when I said something like, "it is great to see you here," his reply was, "these are my people and this is the only thing here that helps me maintain my humanness, but I can't draw." Everyone laughed. We hear the "I can't draw" all the time—yet those folks still come to class, because they want to learn, they've always wanted to learn, or they are literally bored out of their minds because there is nothing else for them to do. And everyone can learn to draw. The artist teaching the class, Barb Bondy, frequently opened up first days of classes with the practice of mark-making (all the lines, marks, patterns, and textures of drawing—it can be neat, or messy and expressive), challenging students to see more than the straight, neat line, and to understand that there are more expressive lines in the world than straight, neat ones. Scribbling, drawing with the other hand, intentionally weaving unmeasured lines into expressive brilliance. There is always lots of laughter with the experimentation—holding a pencil with two fingers from just the end, gripping a charcoal pencil with the full hand, and marking flat to the page. There were some practice assignments given for people to work on during the week, and when students returned the following week, the man who was somewhat reluctantly in the class, brought back astonishing pieces. By the end of the course, through the study of perspective, light, shadowing, and composition, he and everyone else were stunned by what were very obviously innate abilities in him that he did not know were there.

If there is no opportunity, how do you become? How do you cultivate your sight and expression?

From our first poetry and art classes onward, people wanted their creative work to be seen by others. The first printed collection of student writing was released in early 2003, and every 2 years we publish another anthology of creative writing and art. In 2005, our traveling exhibition "Art on the Inside" launched and has traveled across the country. So many opportunities have developed from people's work being seen—for the individual but also for the program. It was a way to present the work to the public and start having

174 *Kyes Stevens*

public dialogues about opportunity and the lack thereof. People are kind and people are unkind. One of our earliest anthologies, which are openly available, was brought to a parole hearing to use against a person up for parole. The essay, which included memories of fishing with a loved one became the catalyst to imply to the parole board that the person should not be paroled—and he was not. That something meant to acknowledge and highlight the work of writers and artists inside could be used against them dealt me a devastating blow. It still hurts. I doubt that it will ever stop. From then on, we talked candidly with people in classes about that experience and warned that they should consider unintended consequences when submitting work. Artists and writers think about intent all the time. It is part of the work. It means something different when you are inside.

From the very early days of APAEP, I have strategized and offered suggestions to people all over the country about building programming inside. *See people and invest in people.* We do not actually need to overcomplicate this. Seeing and investing cannot only be directed to people who live in prisons. The *de facto* community of the prison is much larger than that. One key to our success is working to treat everyone the same. I build relationships with everyone inside. The officers, the wardens, the maintenance crew, people in our classes, people who are not in our classes. I started developing reading libraries in all the prisons we work with because we wanted to be supportive of all the people inside—we know that many people inside a prison will not sign up for classes. You can be a resource in other ways. COVID-19 certainly reinforced that.[4] These libraries were made up of largely donated books. The hardback books we could often not place inside, so we took those boxes of books to the facilities and put a sign on them right where people clocked in and out. *Please Help Yourself. Thank you for supporting our program.* If you are centered on art and education for everyone, you must do your best to honor that for all the people. It is expensive to buy books—even if you are not incarcerated.

I do believe that to do this work well, intentions and actions matter greatly. All of them.

I have certainly not always done that well. There are moments when I have apologized, and we've moved on. There are moments when moving on is harder because the harm is greater. Offering community education classes for 15 years prior to starting our degree program significantly influenced how APAEP and Auburn stepped into credit programming in 2017, through Second Chance Pell. We had all those years of relationships with people inside and those who work for the DOC. And no different than many other programs around the country, we wanted students in the college program to have so many more opportunities than what the DOC systems could accommodate.

I had an absolute blast teaching our student success class for people entering the college program. The root question: how in the hell can you be a college student in a prison that is not even remotely set up to support learning? There are many layers, but part of it was taking the application of learning to write poetry and bringing it to college inside of prison.

The Poem. The Painting. Us   175

Learning to see, and then considering deeply what is seen, and seeking an answer to *why*.

Once you learn to see, you cannot unsee.

It is a blessing and a curse.

With our first cohort of college students, I did a really poor job talking about white privilege. Relating the whole story is not needed, but the truth is, when you have white people from places of absolute poverty in Alabama, stepping into those complexities requires incredible intention, and it can't be the place where personal frustration with systems emerges. My personal feelings and opinions took over, and it harmed some students. I did exactly what I try to train teachers not to do. My relationship with one student changed for the worse, and I cannot measure my regret.

What I can do is always work to do better.

In January 2002, I first stepped into the Tutwiler Prison for Women to teach a poetry class. Our classroom was a double-wide trailer out on the yard. For me to get to that point, I walked through five iron gates. The ones there are old, the prison finished in the 1940s. Named after one of the great human rights advocates of early Alabama[5], Tutwiler was awful. As is protocol in most prisons, I was searched, my class supplies were searched, and then I was escorted to the trailer. I had to stay inside the yellow lines in the middle of the hallway, and if there were women dressed in prison whites on the hall, the officer would yell, "On the wall!" The women stopped where they were with their noses against the cinder blocks. I walked past two doors without windows, where someone with a mostly steady hand had written in magic marker, Death Row #1 and Death Row #2.

That trailer was something. Decrepit. There was black mold on the ceiling because the roof leaked, so much so that there was a hole in the middle of the floor. An officer might have been in the classroom the first couple times, then they were out on the yard, and then it got to the point of the ADOC giving me a radio and directions to hit the panic button if I needed help. (That was not the help I needed then, nor the help I need now.) That trailer stunk, having no dependable heat or air,[6] but when we got out there to that space, it became the place of our community—it became the place for words to come alive and transcend. The words of that space are in my bones.

* *

In so many ways, I created the Alabama Prison Arts + Education Project like I would create a poem or a painting or find the light and location for a photograph. The root, my root, is seeing, to radically challenge my own sight to this world, most especially here in Alabama. I had to learn to cultivate the goodness that came from people in my community, and to move beyond what has generationally damaged my own people. This process of becoming is centered in seeing the world, my world, and imagining what can be, what could be. To create, we learn, we read, we study, we put ourselves in communities who challenge us to push. My life has been balanced between communities on the outside and communities on the inside.

176 *Kyes Stevens*

To build the poem, you begin, you get all words you can on the page, the ideas, the disparate dots, the questions, the images, the images, the images. And then you set to work on the puzzle of finding how all the pieces fit, what pieces belong to something else entirely. Over and over, reading and cutting, developing, growing the poem. My practice is to boil it down so that a truth might rise. That someone might be able to see, even for a moment, what a single leaf dangling on a spider web on an Alabama October blue sky red dirt road might suggest about hope.

This becoming, this process in being and creating, is as essential to life as breath. We must, must create the community spaces for people to cultivate their own poems, their own visions, their own self.

Notes

1 The language of less-than, here in the deep south for sure, is certainly rooted in Christianity's call to help the least of these. The concept of supporting those who are mostly individuals impacted by abject poverty and lack of access to meaningful education, art, mental health care, employment, housing, etc. is not just a Christian concept, but the language of least and less, no matter a speaker's intention, suggests that people inside are just that. It is a clear demonstration how hierarchical structures are applied to facets of society and living. But the sisters and brothers inside are not less than. They are not the least. They are human beings—and as deserving to be on this planet and thrive just as much as me and you.
2 Much can be said about the agendas of people who step into prisons to do this work, especially when they are tethered to higher education systems and tenure requirements that demand research and publication. This is not the place for that discussion, but it does deserve critical inquiry on the harm caused to people inside by researchers' motivations and the career-building that takes place off of suffering.
3 This is not an essay about the decaying Alabama Department of Corrections and the unbelievable decline in spaces and support for programming. But a fact is fact, it is harder for us to get into facilities to offer programming.
4 In March of 2020, just before the nationwide shutdown due to **COVID-19**, we halted our programming inside recognizing that we were potential carriers of something no one understood. Health care inside the ADOC combined with living conditions means that a serious outbreak would mean the deaths of many. That happened. Our entire team shifted immediately to build programming opportunities for people inside. Within 6 weeks of our pause on programming, we produced our first general education newsletter called The Warbler. Working with the ADOC, this was sent electronically to every prison in the state, and copies were distributed. After several months, when the realities of COVID were becoming painfully clear, we made The Warbler available to any arts/education/prison education in the country/world. Our incredible team still puts those newsletters together weekly and distributes them globally. Issue #164 was just released.
5 This is a travesty—that a place so horrid could be named after a remarkable woman who worked for such goodness in this state. https://encyclopediaofalabama.org/article/julia-s-tutwiler/
6 There is still no air conditioning in Alabama's prisons, except in medical housing areas, education, and administration. And yes, people have signed up for classes in the summer just to get out of the dorms.

18 Building Bridges Through Prison-University Partnerships

Emma Hughes

When I moved back to California from England in 2007 to begin a job as an assistant professor at California State University, Fresno, California prisons were in the midst of rampant overcrowding. Although the California Department of Corrections (CDC) had added "and Rehabilitation" (CDCR) to its name in 2005, in reality the opportunities for incarcerated individuals to engage in constructive and productive activities were severely limited. Even where the desire and resources to offer such programs existed, many of the common areas like gyms that would have been used for such purpose had been converted into makeshift dorms with bunkbeds stacked three high, resulting in there being no space for such activities. As I write this now, in 2023, the landscape is very different. Policy changes, a US Supreme Court ruling that reduced overcrowding, and growing support for rehabilitative endeavors have resulted in rapidly expanding opportunities for delivery of innovative programming, often by community-based organizations (CBOs) and non-profit organizations, including universities. This chapter will tell the story of how Fresno State has created partnerships with prisons within the largely rural and agrarian Central Valley of California. I will consider the impact of such partnerships on the residents of the prisons, on the culture of the prisons, on the university, as well as on the broader community. In so doing, I hope to illustrate the multi-directional and circular nature of such endeavors, and the benefits that can be reaped by all involved.

Despite the overcrowding and the at first quite slow swing of the sentencing policy pendulum from retribution to rehabilitation in the early 2000s, San Quentin was the California prison that was known for its varied and interesting array of programming opportunities, from yoga, to horticulture, to marathon running. The oldest prison in California, nestled in a prime location on the San Francisco Bay, San Quentin's engaging programming over the years has in many ways reflected the community in which it is based. Drawing on volunteers and community-based organizations from the surrounding metropolitan areas of San Francisco, Berkeley, and Oakland, San Quentin has been able to bring the outside community in, allowing socially minded individuals to offer rehabilitative and educational opportunities to the incarcerated men inside, supplemented by and in conjunction with the numerous

DOI: 10.4324/9781003394426-22

178   *Emma Hughes*

self-help programs developed by the incarcerated men as well (Irwin, 2009). As explained by one of the outside volunteers when I undertook research on the role of the voluntary sector in prisons in 2014: "Men know that...if you're a lifer or have a long terminate sentence, the place to...try to get into, because of the programs is San Quentin" (Hughes, 2016, p. 47).

Indeed, the presence of volunteers had been apparent upon a trip I made to San Quentin in 2012 to visit the Prison University Project (now Mount Tamalpais College), which at the time offered the only in-person associate degree program in a California prison, with most of the instructors volunteering their time. Walking out toward the main gate on a misty Sunday in December as dusk turned to dark, accompanied by the college instructors who had completed their afternoon classes, I was surprised to see a gathering of individuals on the other side of the gate. Visiting hours were over, so these were not the family members and friends of the incarcerated men coming for visits. No, I realized, this was a visual representation of what I had heard. This was the evening shift of volunteers and staff from community-based organizations waiting to come inside. The Bay Area coming into San Quentin.

For those prisons in the more rural Central Valley, where cities like Fresno and Bakersfield are still some distance from the closest prisons, there has not traditionally been such a plethora of volunteers. But as the possibilities for creating new partnerships, and for building new bridges between the enclosed world of prisons and the community outside, opened up, Fresno State began to develop a presence inside. In telling the story of this development, I will first look at Fresno State's engagement with a federal prison and will consider the impact that the opening up of a prison to outside visitors may have. Second, I will explore the impact of a support program for formerly incarcerated students at Fresno State, examining the ways the program can help to make the university itself more open and accessible and how this feeds back into connections with prisons. Next, I will share an example of Fresno State collaborating with a CBO to help expand programming in prisons. I will then discuss an art exhibition that Fresno State held in partnership with a prison. Finally, I will report on the new bachelor's degree completion program that Fresno State is delivering in two prisons. While these programs and initiatives are a reflection of the changing landscape, I also hope to demonstrate how these programs and initiatives serve to further shape and reform the landscape.

Opening Up Prisons

Although Fresno State faculty had embarked upon various prison-related initiatives over the years, including the extensive involvement undertaken at Central California Women's Facility (CCWF) by Criminology Professor Dr. Barbara Owen, this grew more pronounced as opportunities for engagement opened up. From my perspective as a then relatively new assistant professor in the Department of Criminology, the first opportunity

Building Bridges Through Prison-University Partnerships 179

for such engagement came through the Federal Bureau of Prisons (BOP), not CDCR. Federal Correctional Institution, Mendota (FCI Mendota) had opened in 2012 and was within a 1-hour drive of the Fresno State campus. Unlike the overcrowded CDCR facilities, FCI Mendota was not even close to capacity, and staff and managers seemed particularly interested in engaging the local community in their reentry efforts, drawing on the BOP's more structured protocol for working with and training volunteers, for whom FCI Mendota holds an annual Volunteer Banquet. FCI Mendota reached out to the Criminology Department in late 2012, and this began a series of regular interactions that only came to a halt with the arrival of COVID-19. Fresno State students and faculty from the Criminology Department would regularly assist with the mock job fairs that the prison held for the men preparing for release, in an effort overseen by the prison's education department and the Reentry Affairs Coordinator.

The mock job fairs involve the men in the prison's reentry program interviewing for imagined jobs in order to practice their interview skills and receive constructive feedback on their performance and resume within a supportive environment. The community volunteers play the role of the prospective employers, representing a business or agency chosen by the prison staff and following an interview script that asks challenging questions such as about gaps in employment history. The interviewees have the chance to test out responses to the questions they may face post-release and gain confidence as a result.

As much as these events were designed as a learning experience for the incarcerated men, it was certainly so for the Fresno State students as well. On the one hand, outside students who are typically working on their own interview preparedness could learn from watching and assessing others' performance in this regard. However, for many of these Criminology students, it was also their first visit to a prison. Students regularly reported to me that the visit shattered stereotypes and preconceived notions that they held about incarcerated individuals, perceptions which had frequently overlooked their humanity. The mock interviews allowed the outside students to interact on a human level, and in relatable ways, with those who, in one case, they had previously imagined as one-eyed monsters. "They miss their families!" was a common remark from Fresno State students who had not previously engaged in this level of interaction with and understanding of the incarcerated population, despite their field of study and likely future career paths. I found it disappointing that recognition of the reality of missing families had not previously been perceived by all of the university students, but I appreciated the opportunity for them to gain this level of understanding. In fact, in the research I undertook with community volunteers in prisons, in which I explored their motivations and experiences, a common refrain from volunteers was that: "All of those stereotypical myths were blown to smithereens" (Hughes, 2016, p. 41), and as one pointed out, "volunteers' hearts change [too]" (Hughes, 2016, p. 48).

180   *Emma Hughes*

It is such findings that have convinced me of the circular and reciprocal benefits of such endeavors. The learning travels in multiple directions, and speaks to the value of breaking down barriers and building bridges between a prison and the outside community. Such efforts can help to reduce the "othering," and "us versus them" divisions which do not bode well for individuals' success upon release due to the negative stigma that may interfere with their efforts to procure jobs, housing, and generally reintegrate into society. Furthermore, with outsiders coming into prisons, it provides a valuable opportunity for increased transparency and accountability within the facilities, and enhanced understanding of what happens behind closed doors. As Nelson Mandela (2013) famously pointed out: "It is said that no one truly knows a nation until one has been inside its jails" (p. 200).

The incarcerated participants benefit from increased opportunities for productive endeavor and a culture more supportive of learning, but there are also profound consequences for their self-perception through interaction with the outside visitors. Formerly incarcerated research participants in the voluntary sector study reported feeling humanized, validated, and recognized for their new and positive identities related to the program undertaking (Hughes, 2016). As one participant pointed out: "I'm not the worst thing that I ever did...I learned all that...because of the volunteers, because they were there to affirm me" (Hughes, 2016, p. 38). And crucially, they did not feel forgotten. Ultimately, participants frequently reported a desire to give back (see also Maruna, 2001), and this can help generate a self-supporting cycle whereby the inside participants seek ways to contribute to their inside communities, and further nourish a culture of purposeful endeavor (Hughes, 2016).

Project Rebound: Opening Up Universities

Parallel to the opening up of opportunities within prisons, I want to address a significant development within the California State University (CSU), of which Fresno State is a part. The CSU is the largest public university system in the United States, comprising 23 separate university campuses, with a total enrollment of approximately 460,000 students (California State University, n.d.). In the late 1960s, Dr. John Irwin, who went on to become a renowned criminologist, created Project Rebound, a support program for formerly incarcerated students at San Francisco State. Irwin had been incarcerated in California in the 1950s. He wanted to help others turn their lives around through education in the way that he had been able to do. Irwin passed away in 2010, but others had been continuing the legacy of Project Rebound since his retirement.

For many years, the Project Rebound staff at San Francisco State had no choice but to turn down requests for assistance from individuals paroling in California but to an area outside of the university's region. In an effort to expand the program's reach beyond the San Francisco Bay Area, in 2015, Jason Bell, leading Project Rebound, and Dr. Leslie Wong, then president of

Building Bridges Through Prison-University Partnerships 181

the campus, sought to expand the program throughout the CSU. With the support of the CSU Chancellor's Office, each CSU campus was invited to participate in this undertaking. I was grateful to be selected by the then Fresno State president to represent our campus in this regard.

The first step of the expansion was realized in 2016. With 3 years of funding from a philanthropic organization, the Opportunity Institute, Project Rebound was able to expand to eight additional campuses, including Fresno State. In 2019, the CSU Project Rebound Consortium became a line item in the California state budget under the general CSU budget, and this provided for ongoing funding for the growth and maintenance of the program. Project Rebound now exists at 15 CSU campuses with expansion to additional campuses forthcoming, fulfilling the vision for a network throughout the state.

Project Rebound conducts outreach in correctional facilities and in the community to help encourage and assist prospective students to apply for higher education and then provides wraparound support services for those who are accepted to the university and enroll. The CSU application has never asked a question about conviction or the arrest history of its applicants. However, students who have been incarcerated still often struggle with self-limiting perceptions of suitability for university study, concerns about whether they would fit in, and concern that a conviction history might preclude their chance to enroll (Hughes, 2022). This is where the outreach work conducted by Project Rebound staff, almost all of whom have histories of incarceration, and by Project Rebound students, who have all been formerly incarcerated, is pivotal, and allows Project Rebound to hold true to one of its founding principles of "each one, teach one." As one student explained, without the personalized and focused model of outreach, in this case a university tour by Jennifer Leahy, the Program Director: "I wouldn't be where I am today, I wouldn't – I would have never imagined myself on that campus" (Hughes, 2022).

Project Rebound students at multiple CSU campuses, including Fresno State, further embody that "each one, teach one" principle when engaging in mentoring programs for incarcerated youth, including participating in initiatives designed to encourage their college enrollment. With such efforts, Project Rebound can help to increase accessibility to a university campus through breaking down stereotypes and preconceived ideas about who a university is for, and opening up horizons of possibility for those who may have, for whatever reason, ruled themselves out from such an endeavor. Additionally, the networks that Fresno State has developed as a result of such outreach and mentoring activities represent a significant milestone in the university's engagement in correctional and reentry facilities. For example, Project Rebound staff often provide speeches at graduation events put on by prison education departments, reflective of an increased willingness of CDCR wardens to permit formerly incarcerated individuals back into their prisons as program facilitators and as prominent participants in educational events. Crucially, the Project Rebound staff and student presence can create

182 *Emma Hughes*

a "buzz" within a facility, as I have consistently heard from prison administrators, staff, and most significantly, from incarcerated individuals, because their presence shows what is possible for those still incarcerated.

On campus, Project Rebound students regularly volunteer to give presentations to classes in departments ranging from public health, to social work, to criminology. The sharing of their lived experiences offers vital insight to those who are studying and will potentially be working in fields where understanding the realities of incarceration and reentry are crucial. The Project Rebound students report growth in self-confidence, pride in owning their story, and greater comfort in public speaking. The academic success of the students, including as recipients of Dean's Medals, and in 2022 the undergraduate President's Medal (the highest academic honor bestowed on campus), has helped to raise the profile of the program along with the extensive efforts of program staff. The achievements of Project Rebound students have generated positive news coverage in mainstream media, on television, and in print, highlighting the students' powerful journeys and the role that education has played, further raising the program's profile and providing a valuable perspective to the community at large. And for the Project Rebound students overall, their involvement with Project Rebound helps them to feel that they truly "belong" on campus (Hughes, 2022).

Expansion of Programs in CDCR Prisons

As previously noted, San Quentin has long benefitted from a tremendous number of volunteers and staff from community-based organizations that provide unique and varied programming. This concentrated presence of outside groups in prisons that are conveniently situated for such purposes highlighted the relative lack of such presence in other more rural facilities. In seeking to address the disparities that this entailed, CDCR began the Innovative Programming Grants (IPG) initiative in 2015, designed to fund the expansion of programs provided by volunteers, CBOs, and non-profit organizations to less-served CDCR facilities. A parallel initiative, the California Reentry and Enrichment (CARE) Grants, started in 2020.

The Insight Garden Program (IGP), which began in San Quentin, sought and received funds to expand to other prisons, including prisons in the Central Valley. This horticultural program that promotes healing and enhanced self-awareness (Insight Garden Program, 2023), recruits volunteers as well as paid staff to facilitate and implement the 12-month curriculum and to oversee the design, creation, and/or maintenance of a garden within the prison. CDCR Captain Doug Snell, a graduate of Fresno State's Criminology Department and now adjunct faculty member, at the time was based at Avenal State Prison, one of the prisons to which IGP was expanding. Captain Snell forged a connection between IPG and the campus so that IGP could seek program facilitators and volunteers from within the university community. This proved to be a successful strategy for a program seeking volunteers and

Building Bridges Through Prison-University Partnerships   183

staff in a region to which it was new. Students, staff, and faculty from at least three different colleges within the university, including the College of Health and Human Services, the College of Social Sciences, and the Jordan College of Agricultural Sciences and Technology, have played a significant role in IGP's course delivery at prisons in the Central Valley, with Project Rebound staff and students keenly involved.

The university's involvement with IGP and the prisons constitutes a multi-way exchange in terms of the benefits that are gained. The garden brings joy to the space, including for the incarcerated participants that tend it and staff and others that pass by (see, for example, Insight Garden Program, 2023). The reference to the joy that it brings is common, echoing the responses that I found in my research on the voluntary sector in prisons (Hughes, 2016). The engagement with IGP has also provided opportunity for professors to take campus student groups on prison visits to see the program at work. Such arrangements, like the mock job fairs mentioned earlier, help to reduce the risk of a prison tour turning into one where the residents feel like dehumanized exhibits in a zoo, and can instead lead to meaningful and substantive exchange. Inside participants and outside students discuss the garden and horticultural practice, and visitors learn from those who are inside about the care for the plants. Such exchanges aim to center the humanity of all involved, and may potentially contribute to the reduction of an "us versus them" mentality.

When one of the program facilitators is formerly incarcerated, and in some cases was housed in the very same prison where the program is operating, this can be particularly impactful for participants inside the prison, as alluded to earlier. This is conveyed through an interview with an incarcerated program participant as part of a local ABC television news story about IGP (ABC30 Action News, 2019). The story focuses on Arnold Trevino, Project Rebound's Outreach Coordinator, who earned his Bachelor and Master of Social Work (MSW) degrees at Fresno State as a Project Rebound student. Arnold Trevino is also a former lifer who served part of his sentence at Avenal. He began work as a facilitator for IGP while pursuing his MSW and, upon graduation, received the Dean's Medal for outstanding graduate student in his college. Avenal's Warden at the time, Rosemary Ndoh, invited Arnold Trevino to wear his graduation regalia and medal to the IGP class that took place after the graduation, to visually demonstrate what can be achieved. The potential for offering hope, and the potential significance of this for encouraging successful outcomes in post-release lives cannot be ignored (see, for example, Burnett & Maruna, 2004).

Insider Art Exhibition

Captain Snell also enabled other connections between Fresno State and Avenal State Prison. He introduced me to some of the self-help groups that were flourishing at the prison and in particular to a self-help art group.

184   *Emma Hughes*

This self-taught group of men met and continues to meet in the gym on their yard, setting up a makeshift art studio at designated times, sometimes accompanied by music groups practicing at the other end of the gym. An impressive mural adorns an outside wall of the gym, painted by some of the artists running the self-help group, and reflective of Warden Ndoh's support for enhancing the prison environment for those living and working within the facility (Ndoh, 2018; Snell, 2018).

The use of the gym for such purposes marked a significant change from the improvised dorm it had been in previous years, filled with bunkbeds as was not uncommon during the peak of overcrowding throughout the CDCR prison system. This continued until the US Supreme Court ruled in *Brown v Plata* (2011) that California was violating the 8th Amendment prohibition against "cruel and unusual punishment" due to the unacceptable levels of health care provision stemming from the extreme overcrowding. The ruling required CDCR's population to be no more than 137.5% of design capacity and this provided the impetus for significant legislation that resulted in a substantial reduction of the prison population. The consequence of this on a practical level was the return of spaces like gyms to their original purposes of recreation and rehabilitation. More constructive activities could take place, allowing the expansion of programs like IGP, as well as the growth of self-help groups.

Although the artwork at Avenal was at times exhibited within the prison, Captain Snell expressed a desire to showcase the work to the outside community. This sparked a series of conversations that led to a collaboration between Avenal State Prison, the Fresno State Department of Art & Design within the College of Arts and Humanities, the Fresno State Center for Creativity & the Arts, and the Criminology Department within the College of Social Sciences. This culminated in *Insider Art*, an exhibition of over 120 works of art from Avenal State Prison at the campus' gallery in downtown Fresno in April 2018. The work covered a variety of media, ranging from acrylic painting to beadwork and soap sculpture, as well as video recordings of bands playing and of actors performing a series of skits as part of the Actors' Gang program. In preparation for the opening, we held a panel on campus and open to the public about the role of the arts in prisons. The opening night occurred in conjunction with the monthly Fresno ArtHop and there was a line out the door ahead of the start. Multiple local TV news programs had covered the run-up to the exhibition and one news station filmed at the opening. The first night audience included students, faculty, administrators and staff from both the university and the prison, local community members, and, crucially, family members and loved ones of the artists. The brother of one of the artists was one of the speakers during the opening ceremony.

An underlying goal for the exhibition was to draw connections between the enclosed world of the prison and the outside community and to help marginalized and silenced voices be heard. This was accomplished not just through artistic expression, but through video displays with attached headsets that presented recorded interviews with some of the artists talking about their engagement with art and the place that it holds in their lives. To approximate a dialogue, we invited exhibition visitors to leave reflections in a comment book, which was then shared with the artists. Visitors left extraordinarily positive and encouraging comments and praised the work and the talent they saw on display, with some expressing surprise at the latter. Like with the student visits to mock job fairs and gardening programs, the focus was upon the recognition of shared humanity and acknowledging positive accomplishment. One visitor commented: "You inspire us all! Please keep making your beautiful art." Another wrote: "Thank you for teaching those of us on the outside how to be free."

The exhibition remained open for a series of weekends, with Project Rebound students serving as docents. More family members of the artists attended during these viewings, at times having traveled significant distance. Some of them reported that they had never previously been to a university venue. The Project Rebound students, true to the "each one, teach one" mantra, shared their personal stories and talked of the "prison to college pipeline," seeking to break down perceptions of barriers connected to access of higher education.

The curator, Dr. Cindy Urrutia, and I co-edited an exhibition catalog for publication (Hughes & Urrutia, 2018), featuring all of the works of art and essays from contributors including Warden Ndoh, Captain Snell, and two of the incarcerated artists. One of the artists, Joseph Frye (2018), helped run the art group until his subsequent release. His essay speaks of the service the group aims to provide through offering classes, enhancing the physical environment, and "finding creative ways of including the outside community" such as through donating artwork for charities to sell. He notes: "We are making amends, moving towards redemption, and finding a reprieve from the prisons of our minds" (p. 22).

A Bachelor's Degree Program Inside

Arguably, all of the engagement detailed above helped pave the way for Fresno State's most significant undertaking in the carceral setting: a Bachelor's Degree completion program offered at CCWF and Valley State Prison for men (VSP). The program started on a pilot basis in Spring 2021, following an approach from CDCR's Director of Rehabilitative Programming, Dr. Brant Choate, and Superintendent of Correctional Education, Shannon Swain, in Fall 2019. After some COVID-19-related delays, this state-funded program is now officially running with a specially created major, an interdisciplinary BA in Social Science, that was approved in Summer 2022. The university admissions and matriculation process began in Fall 2022. There are 27 students enrolled in each prison, with the cohort operating in a dynamic fashion so that as students parole new students join in. At any given time, the cohort consists of a combination of matriculated students and those who are

186 *Emma Hughes*

going through the application process. The students already hold Associate Degrees from community colleges that have been approved by the state since 2014 to offer incarcerated students opportunities to earn their Associate Degrees through the California College Promise Grant fee waiver.

Faculty travel from Fresno State to the prisons and teach their courses as additional assignments through the campus' Division of Continuing and Global Education. It is not unusual to hear faculty proclaim at the end of a term that it was one of their favorite all-time teaching experiences. They regularly praise the achievements and dedication of the students, appreciate the robust and insightful classroom discussion, and report the value of the learning experience for themselves: all experiences to which I, too, can attest. In that vein, I would like to acknowledge and thank the Fresno State students at VSP for their valuable feedback on a draft of this chapter.

We anticipate the first members of the CCWF and VSP cohorts to graduate in the summer of 2024. In the meantime, Project Rebound offers assistance to those who parole before graduating in order to connect them to the CSU campus closest to where they will be living so that they can complete their degree. The network of Project Rebound programs is ideal for such purpose and works alongside the growing number of CSU campuses offering Bachelor's Degrees in prison. California State University, Los Angeles, began this endeavor in 2016, followed by Sacramento State, Fresno State, and San Diego State, with California Polytechnic University, Humboldt, joining soon. In addition, Pitzer College and the University of California, Irvine, offer degrees as well. This rich and evolving tapestry of Bachelor's Degree programs in prisons is not something that I could have imagined when I moved back to California in 2007 and when Petersilia (2007) noted that 50% of men and women had no rehabilitation or work assignment for the duration of their sentence, and the prisons were overflowing.

In reflecting on the shifts that have happened, I want to highlight again the vital and critical role that universities, specifically students, faculty, staff, and administrators, can play in expanding and creating opportunities for constructive, purposeful programming in prison. Universities can offer second chances in prison and post-release and can showcase the power of education for enabling personal transformation. Through encouraging university enrollment amongst system-impacted individuals both inside and outside prison walls, and through recognizing and helping to publicize stories of success and accomplishment, universities can help to challenge divisive stigma and negative stereotypes that all too-often serve to undermine efforts toward successful reintegration. Universities are educators; they can lead by example, break down barriers, and generate cultures of learning. In so doing, they can offer up hope and validation to those who are seeking to change their lives, and provide learning experiences to everyone involved.

However, for such initiatives to thrive, there must be proactive supporters and initiators amongst CDCR headquarters' leadership, prison administration, and staff, who seek out and/or support such programs. Without this,

Building Bridges Through Prison-University Partnerships 187

the programs are vulnerable and subject to change with shifts in policy winds and administration. Moreover, the CDCR grant funding that sustains so many of these programs is limited, and awarded on 3-year cycles that can undermine stability and threaten long-term planning and expansion. This makes the need for champions of such initiatives amongst the gatekeepers in prisons, as well as in the university community, all the more imperative. Without them, the partnerships and collaborations would not function.

Countless people have played a part in the delivery and success of the initiatives and partnerships described herein. A few I have named, many more I have not, but their contributions are no less important. I hope that the groundwork that has collectively been laid, and the circular and self-reinforcing energy generated through the programs' benefits and impact, will help to sustain and fuel such initiatives through any challenges that may lie ahead.

As I write these final words, a collaborative effort is underway in the form of the CSU Project Rebound Outreach Program (CSU PROP) at VSP and CCWF. Project Rebound staff and alumni, joined by other CSU faculty, staff, and administrators, under the guidance of Dr. Jacqueline Mimms, are in the midst of a pre-college orientation program consisting of a five-session series of workshops. The facilitators advise participants about what college education entails, offer strategies for academic success, and encourage educational enrolment. This certificate program is funded via IPG and CARE grants, and has been offered multiple times in five Central California prisons since 2019. In addition to the mentoring that so many of the Fresno State-enrolled students already provide within their prison, several Fresno State students at both VSP and CCWF serve as official facilitators for the CSU PROP workshops. And at VSP, which serves as a hub for incarcerated youth in the prison system, the inside facilitators specifically seek to encourage youth at this prison to consider engaging in education. The university is on the inside. Fresno State students are on the inside. They are fostering cultures of learning, expanding horizons, and building bridges.

References

ABC30 Action News. (2019, October 18). *25 Years to life changed: Former prisoner working to help inmates succeed.* https://abc30.com/localish-all-good-prison-avenal-state/5606220/

Burnett, R., & Maruna, S. (2004). So 'prison works', does it? The criminal careers of 130 men released from prison under Home Secretary, Michael Howard. *Howard Journal of Criminal Justice, 43*(4), 390–404.

California State University. (n.d.). *About the CSU.* Retrieved July 2, 2023, from https://www.calstate.edu/csu-system/about-the-csu/Pages/default.aspx

Frye, J. (2018). Art is powerful. In E. Hughes & C. Urrutia (Eds.), *Insider art: Exploring the arts within prison environment: A collection of work from Avenal State Prison* (pp. 21–23). The Press at California State University, Fresno.

Hughes, E. (2016). Non-profit and voluntary sector programs in prisons and jails: Perspectives from England and the United States. In L. Abrams, E. Hughes,

M. Inderbitzin & R. Meek (Eds.), *The voluntary sector in prisons: Encouraging personal and institutional change* (pp. 21–51). Palgrave Macmillan.

Hughes, E. (2022, November 16–19). 'I felt I belonged here': Experiences of a university support program for formerly incarcerated students [Conference presentation]. American Society of Criminology Annual Meeting, Atlanta, GA, United States.

Hughes, E., & Urrutia, C. (Eds.). (2018). *Insider art: Exploring the arts within prison environment: A collection of work from Avenal State Prison.* The Press at California State University, Fresno.

Insight Garden Program. (2023). *Insight Garden Program transforms incarcerated folks' lives through connection to nature.* https://insightgardenprogram.org

Irwin, J. (2009). *Lifers: Seeking redemption in prison.* Routledge.

Mandela, N. (2013). *Long walk to freedom: The autobiography of Nelson Mandela.* Little, Brown and Company.

Maruna, S. (2001). *Making good: How ex-convicts reform and rebuild their lives.* American Psychological Association.

Ndoh, R. (2018). Space. In E. Hughes & C. Urrutia (Eds.), *Insider art: Exploring the arts within prison environment; A collection of work from Avenal State Prison* (pp. 17–19). The Press at California State University, Fresno.

Petersilia, J. (2007, August 27). Review of the California Expert Panel on Adult Offender and Recidivism Reduction Programming: Summary of findings from the Programming Review Subcommittee: Testimony before the Senate Budget and Fiscal Review Subcommittee No. 4 on State Administration, General Government, Judicial and Transportation. https://bpb-us-e2.wpmucdn.com/sites.uci.edu/dist/0/1149/files/2013/06/Petersilia-Machado-Testimony-with-Appendix-1.pdf

Snell, D. (2018). Reflections from Avenal and the transformative power of art. In E. Hughes & C. Urrutia (Eds.), *Insider art: Exploring the arts within prison environment: A collection of work from Avenal State Prison* (pp. 13–14). The Press at California State University, Fresno.

19 Arts Research in Carceral Settings
Prison Arts Collective

Brian L. Heisterkamp, Bryant Joachim Jackson-Green, Ginny Emiko Oshiro, and Annie Buckley

Introduction

Prison Arts Collective (PAC) is dedicated to expanding access to the transformative power of the arts to people experiencing incarceration[1]. It began with one class in one prison in 2013 and has grown significantly over the past decade, spanning six state universities and fourteen state prisons, facilitating weekly arts classes to over 7000 people incarcerated in California State prisons. Classes are led by collaborative teaching teams that include university faculty, students, and currently and formerly incarcerated artists. PAC classes aim to help participants reconnect with their identities as artists, writers, and musicians, rather than solely focusing on their circumstances as incarcerated individuals. The initial classes in the first couple of years were conducted as part of service learning and internship classes developed and taught by Annie Buckley, then teaching at California State University, San Bernardino. These began without formal research measures but, in collaboration with Brian Heisterkamp and other colleagues from across the University, Buckley and colleagues recognized the need for research and evaluation to assess the effectiveness of the arts programming. This led to collaboration with experts in traditional research methods, and the formalizing of pre- and post-surveys, as well as additional tools to measure wellness.

Conducting research in a prison setting presents numerous challenges, including issues of consent, access, data collection, and ethics. However, with the necessary approvals and protocols in place, PAC's research project collects data from multiple prisons and universities to evaluate the outcomes of their arts programming and ensure its effectiveness in meeting the needs of participants. This chapter discusses the historical development of PAC, some of the challenges of conducting research in this setting, and the specific nature of our research and evaluation focus.

Overview and History of the Prison Arts Collective

The classes began in 2013 at a California State men's prison in Chino as an 8-week pilot, led by graduate and undergraduate students enrolled in Buckley's internship class at CSUSB. Since that time, PAC has continued to expand

DOI: 10.4324/9781003394426-23

190   *Brian L. Heisterkamp et al.*

based on student, faculty, and institutional requests and eventually gained support from numerous state and federal grants and contracts. In the first round of classes, there were no pre- or post-surveys, but Buckley and the student teachers met with participants before and during classes to learn about their experience, learning needs, and interests and designed and taught the classes with these in mind. Because student teachers worked in pairs and taught their classes simultaneously in one large space, classes were relatively small, which allowed for individual attention and adapting teaching to students' needs. The feedback during and after was overwhelmingly positive and one thing that stands out even today was how often participants noted that they felt "human," "relaxed," and "positive" in the classes. None of this was officially recorded but rather implemented in program design.

A year or so into the work, Buckley received an email from a colleague noting that the project required for Institutional Review Board (IRB) status to continue. This process was unfamiliar to Buckley, a professor of visual studies, and she reached out to colleagues, including Heisterkamp and Dr. Annika Anderson from Sociology and Director of Project Rebound at CSUSB. In gaining an understanding of the governing body in the university for research, Buckley was not initially convinced the classes constituted research but proceeded for the benefit of the program. In the process, she gained deeper understanding about research protocols and why PAC programming did constitute a form of research, in that they would, at times, share the results at conferences and in exhibitions and publications. The research team initially included Dr. Annika Anderson, who formalized the pre- and post-surveys and added an additional tool to measure wellness. Over time, additional colleagues joined the research team from disciplines including Psychology, Art Education, Communication, and Criminal Justice. In 2020, during the height of the global pandemic, the current research team came together with Heisterkamp as a lead researcher alongside Jackson-Green, Oshiro, and Buckley, to organize and energize the process and spearhead the ongoing logistical steps of maintaining a large multi-site study as well as the data analysis and interpretation.

Barriers and Challenges

CDCR offers a variety of educational and rehabilitative programs at its institutions. Educational programs provide academic and vocational training programs to help people experiencing incarceration acquire knowledge and skills that can improve their employability and increase their chances of successful reintegration into society. Recreational programs provide opportunities for physical activity, creative expression, and social interaction, among other benefits. These programs focus on promoting general well-being and mental health and are typically structured as group activities or events. PAC fits within the recreational programming offered by CDCR.

After enrolling individuals in PAC programming, a challenge we face both in terms of programming and conducting evaluation research is consistency

Arts Research in Carceral Settings   191

in participation for reasons beyond the control of the participants themselves. Participants can be transferred to other CDCR institutions, be unavailable due to lockdowns, or be unavailable due to other circumstances. Consequently, participants may not be present for all elements of our programming. Or, they may not be present during sessions when our survey instrument is administered, a clear challenge to data collection.

Our primary goal in conducting research in the prison setting is to evaluate the effectiveness of our arts programming. We aim to ensure that we are attaining the outcomes attached to our funding and that we are meeting the needs of our participants. An expanded goal as the research team has evolved is to look at the impact of the arts on wellness for individuals and communities experiencing incarceration. While conducting evaluation research in a prison setting is important for assessing the outcomes of our programming, it does not happen without significant challenges (Lucic-Catic, 2011). For clear reasons, protections are in place at many levels to prevent harm to those who are incarcerated. People who are incarcerated may feel coerced to participate in research because they are under the control of the state (Roberts & Indermaur, 2008). Additionally, they may have less access to information that could help them make an informed decision about their own research participation.

There are a number of concerns associated with conducting this evaluation research including access, data collection, and ethics. While we had access to people in prisons where we were conducting our programming, we also needed additional permissions to conduct our research. In order to obtain access to conduct our evaluation research, we needed the approval of the IRB and the CDCR Office of Research. The IRB ensures the protection and welfare of human participants involved in research studies. The board conducts an ethical review to ensure participants are providing their informed consent, are protecting the rights of participants, and are complying with federal oversight laws. In our case, once we received IRB approval, we needed the additional approval of the CDCR Office of Research, which oversees all research conducted at CDCR facilities. In practice, this involved submitting modification to these boards each time we added a university partner or CDCR facility because they need to approve any change in data collection processes. Changes to the questionnaires including adding questions or changing wording also needed the approval of each board before implementation. Adding and removing members of the research team also involves multiple levels of approval. Perhaps more than many other research sites, conducting research in the prison setting involves significant administrative hurdles.

Data collection is challenging for several reasons. We collect our data through a survey instrument that includes both closed-response items and open-ended questions. Closed-response items provide fixed choices such as "agree" or "disagree" while open-ended questions enable participants to provide longer responses in their own words. Surveys are available in both

192   *Brian L. Heisterkamp et al.*

English and Spanish and are intended to be completed individually. We have observed on some occasions that participants complete them in dyads or small groups in some instances when participants are not able to read the survey themselves. Data is gathered at 14 sites across the state, which is a logistical concern related to the need to maintain the confidentiality of participant data and properly train individuals who are collecting the data on confidentiality and data security measures. In the future, we hope to conduct interviews or focus groups to both address the literacy concern and obtain more qualitative information from our participants. This request to conduct interviews would need to be included in our proposal to the IRB boards for an amendment to the study, with details on how we will conduct interviews, and approved before interviews could take place, a lengthy process that can take months.

Ethical considerations associated with conducting our evaluation research include ensuring that we receive the informed consent of our participants, ensuring that their privacy is protected, and that we allow them to consider the risks and benefits of their participation. We sought and received approval from a number of partners including universities, correctional institutions, and the state-level IRB in order to ensure our compliance with these ethical considerations. From an informed consent perspective, and because participation in programming is highly valued within correctional institutions, we needed to be sure that participants knew that their participation in our evaluation research was not tied to their participation in our programming. So, participants were assured that they could continue to participate in our programming even if they did not participate in our evaluation research.

The COVID pandemic, which closed all CDCR institutions to in-person programming for over a year followed by nearly two shorter of and on closures, necessitated our move to a correspondence format. The teaching teams quickly needed to develop programming packets that could be mailed to program participants who could complete those packets and then return them to us by mail. These packets included activities that participants could complete at their own pace. Some of the activities included writing prompts, ideas for drawings, and instructions for art making projects. Each packet also included opportunities for reflection and forms to provide us with feedback regarding our correspondence packets. As many of us experienced, this distance removed the interpersonal interactions that enabled us to explore the transformative power of the arts. The shift to a correspondence format also reduced the number of survey responses we received for our evaluation research.

Our Current Research Activities

PAC's current research project collects data across 14 prisons in partnership with four California State University campuses. Participating campuses have a designated PAC chapter or partnership and a related agreement or subcontract. Each campus and region has a lead faculty member or teaching artist who undergoes Collaborative Institutional Training Initiative (CITI) training and training regarding PAC's programming and research program. Each lead and anyone distributing and collecting surveys with participant data are added to the PAC IRB application.

The PAC research project combines pre- and post-surveys with administrative data from California Department of Corrections and Rehabilitation (CDCR). When PAC programs begin a new teaching session (Spring, Fall, or Summer semesters), the lead facilitators give an introduction of the research project, often using a script or talking points provided by the research team. If participants choose to engage, they fill out mandatory consent forms, a pre-survey questionnaire, and the Warwick-Edinburgh Mental Wellbeing Scale (WEMWBS). The pre- and post-surveys assess participant perceptions of how they improve over time as artists and program facilitators. The WEMWBS assists researchers in identifying any changes in mental wellness during the program session.

Because PAC's model values and centers reflection, transformation (for participants and the program), and integrated learning, PAC's survey instruments reflect these goals. The pre-survey is a combination of Likert scale questions and open-ended questions. The five-point Likert scale questions ask participants to signify if statements related to their creativity, art experience, learning style, leadership, cooperation, effort, and communication are "not at all" like them or "like" them (with 1 being "false" and 5 being "true"). The open-ended questions allow participants to provide responses in their own words regarding their experience with art, interest in the course, and experience with teaching.

The WEMWBS is a validated survey instrument and was an intentional tool used by PAC researchers to get a more holistic view of arts programming in prison (Stewart-Brown et al., 2011). While measuring the improvement of art technique is of interest, it is covered by the PAC pre- and post-surveys. In addition to technique, PAC equally prioritizes understanding the impact of arts programming on the wellness of its participants. Further, given that PAC programs are designed to provide participants with translatable skills that can be used daily, the research team utilizes a measurement tool well-suited to evaluate integrated development in participants. WEMWBS emphasizes experiences and feelings associated with mental well-being and focuses on positive aspects of well-being. Additionally, WEMWBS includes questions related to many PAC goals and outcomes, such as connection to others, self-efficacy, and problem-solving.

At the close of each course session, PAC facilitators distribute post-surveys and the WEMWBS survey. The post-survey utilizes both open-ended questions and redistributes the five-point Likert scale questionnaire provided at the initiative of the course. The PAC post-survey is both evaluative of the PAC program and of the participants' perceptions of technique improvement

194 *Brian L. Heisterkamp et al.*

and gaining creativity and understanding through the arts. The WEMWBS survey is once again employed to assist researchers in identifying any changes in participants' mental well-being.

Aside from the questionnaire data we collect from our participants, the research team has requested administrative data from CDCR including variables on prison admissions and sentencing (i.e., admission date, age, commitment offense group, sentence type and length of stay) and in-custody data (gender, ethnicity, and rule violation reports) to help determine the impact of PAC programming on the correctional population. For obvious reasons related to confidentiality, this data is difficult to obtain from CDCR. We needed to submit a variety of forms, sign contracts, and complete livescan fingerprinting. We have been working for over two years to obtain this data and as of this writing are waiting to receive this valuable piece needed for our evaluation research.

Collaborations and Input

Our research involves collaborations with several groups including our university partners, CDCR facilities, and the participants themselves. The teaching staff for PAC programs are located across California. In addition to PAC headquarters at San Diego State University, PAC chapters are also located at California State Polytechnic University, Humboldt, and the California State University, Sacramento, and a research partnership with San Bernardino. Faculty at each of these universities help design and deliver PAC programming at 14 different CDCR facilities. While the chapter model expands PAC's teaching capacity and the diversity of arts instruction PAC can offer, it also broadens the perspectives PAC draws from when considering updates to program practices and research. Since instructors administer the data collection process directly, they are best positioned to suggest changes in process and procedure that might not be obvious to researchers who are not engaged, face-to-face in data collection process. In addition, substantive feedback on survey questions and methodology from instructors has helped our surveys develop from a simple questionnaire to a larger data collection apparatus that supports grant applications, informs internal PAC goals, demonstrates the efficacy of arts programming, and suggests areas for improvement.

Hearing directly from participants is essential to the mission, vision, and values of PAC. PAC engages with evaluation to be reflexive and responsive to participant feedback and assessment to better articulate the power of arts-based prison programming to a broader audience. Empirical investigation and assessment of PAC programs is helpful to the program and its participants; however, the contribution is to the field and the community more broadly. Research done by Larry Brewster (2010a, 2010b, 2014, 2015) determined the value and efficacy of art-based prison programs with great impact in correctional science and public policy. Brewster's work has contributed to the advancement and validation of arts-programs in prison and

PAC seeks to expand this work through its contributions regarding personal perceptions of well-being and administrative records regarding institutional and post-release behavior. The PAC research project outcomes will be shared with the public to guide the successful implementation of policy which supports the wide-spread adoption of community-based arts programs in prison, and shift stereotypes and stigmas regarding the possibility of redemption for currently incarcerated people.

Participant feedback about their experiences with PAC programming deeply informs PAC program priorities. In the pre-surveys issued before any programming has taken place, we make a point of asking about participants' experiences with art and the goals they have coming into the class. Responses varied from those expressing an interest in practices and developing technical, artistic capacities "to gain the skills to be able to teach others to express themselves and how they're feeling" to education for "a deeper appreciation for different techniques and [learning] art history." In addition, seeking collaborative and team-building skills are a common theme in participant goal setting. As one participant put it, they sought "to gain experience not only in "art" but also in participating in group projects." This feedback informs the kinds of lessons instructors delivered during the semester. In the post-surveys we ask for feedback on the quality of instruction, whether learning goals were met, and suggestions for future courses. Here, participants might express interest in different art mediums than have been offered that semester, make suggestions about program delivery (especially during the Covid-19 pandemic), or offer reflections about the benefits of participating in arts programming.

Additionally, one of PAC's unique programs is an arts facilitator training designed to train participants to become arts teachers themselves in their home facilities. The facilitator training lasts for 60 hours and is followed by a 3-month apprenticeship. Upon completion, students become teachers and cultivate a creative community in the prison through teaching weekly arts classes. Currently PAC has 50 peer facilitators that have graduated and are teaching classes in 8 prisons, creating a pipeline of participants to instructors that further supports our teaching partnerships.

Finally, research collaborations with stakeholders across campuses and regions have been essential to PAC's growth and development over the last decade. PAC research involves collaborations with faculty and graduate students at San Diego State University, California State University, San Bernardino, and the University of California, Irvine. Individual team members bring a variety of disciplinary expertise to PAC projects from communication studies to art, criminology, law, and social-ecological perspectives. PAC aims to take an interdisciplinary approach to research evaluation, an approach that is particularly important in designing educational programming (Carr, Loucks & Blöschl, 2018). While the research focus until now has been on qualitative and quantitative assessments of the wellness impact of arts programming on participants in CDCR, future research approaches we aspire

196 *Brian L. Heisterkamp et al.*

to implement include community-based and collaborative research designs, research on arts programming's potential impact on criminogenic outcomes, and diversity and inclusion considerations in access to arts programming in correctional settings.

Conclusion

PAC has undergone significant growth and expansion over the past decade, evolving into a statewide program that brings arts programming to incarcerated individuals across California. What initially began as an effort to provide real-world learning experiences for undergraduate students and expand access to arts opportunities in the community has transformed into a transformative program that helps incarcerated individuals reconnect with their identities as artists, writers, and musicians.

PAC's classes have received overwhelmingly positive feedback, with participants noting feelings of relaxation, positivity, and a sense of humanity. For example, program participants overwhelmingly report increased technical abilities and a more robust understanding of art and art history. PAC continues to find that program participants report developing a positive identity and often apply implicit lessons to their lives. A student from a PAC class at California Institution for Men said, "Because of this program, I can call myself an artist." Another participant from Pelican Bay State Prison offered, "I learned how to be patient. I learned that different people learn at different speeds." Lastly, PAC continues to find that practicing art creates a common bond between incarcerated participants themselves and the community more broadly. As one student from Chuckawalla State Prison remarked, "I learned that there is still a great deal of people who see the good in everyone, and that prisoners are more than their crimes, people with the same hopes, dreams, fears, and feelings."

To ensure the effectiveness of their programming, PAC has embraced evaluation research, collaborating with experts in traditional research fields and implementing surveys and evaluation tools to measure wellness and program effectiveness. Conducting research in a prison setting poses challenges related to consent, access, data collection, and ethics, but PAC has navigated these hurdles with the necessary approvals and protocols in place.

Looking toward future directions, PAC continues to expand its reach and refine its research and evaluation efforts. The program now spans six state universities and 14 state prisons, with designated chapters at each campus and partnerships with correctional institutions. PAC's current research project collects data from multiple prisons, combining pre- and post-surveys with administrative data from the California Department of Corrections and Rehabilitation (CDCR). The surveys assess participants' perceptions of their artistic growth and mental well-being, while also incorporating open-ended questions for participants to provide qualitative feedback. PAC values reflection, transformation, and integrated learning, and their survey

Arts Research in Carceral Settings 197

instruments reflect these goals. As the program moves forward, there is a goal to conduct interviews or focus groups to gather more in-depth qualitative information from participants. Despite challenges related to consistency in participation and data collection, PAC remains committed to evaluating the outcomes of their arts programming, ensuring it meets the needs of participants, and upholding ethical considerations throughout their research endeavors.

Note

1 Prison Arts Collective (PAC) is supported by the California Arts Council, California Department of Corrections and Rehabilitation, and the National Endowment for the Arts.

Works Cited

Brewster, L. (2010a). The California arts-in-corrections music programme: A qualitative study. International Journal of Community Music, 3(1), 33–46.

Brewster, L. (2010b). A qualitative study of the California arts-in-corrections program. San Francisco, CA: University of San Francisco.

Brewster, L. (2014). The impact of prison arts programs on inmate attitudes and behavior: A quantitative evaluation. Justice Policy Journal, 11(2), 1–28.

Brewster, L. (2015). Prison fine arts and community college programs: A partnership to advance inmates' life skills. New Directions for Community Colleges, 2015(170), 89–99.

Carr, G., Loucks, D. P., & Blöschl, G. (2018). Gaining insight into interdisciplinary research and education programmes: A framework for evaluation. Research Policy, 47(1), 35–48.

Lucic-Catic, M. (2011). Challenges in conducting prison research. Criminal Justice Issues Journal of Criminal Justice and Security, 11(5–6), 59–73.

Roberts, L., & Indermaur, D. (2008). The ethics of research with prisoners. Current Issues in Criminal Justice, 19(3), 309–326. https://doi.org/10.1080/10345329.2008.12036436

Stewart-Brown, S., Platt, S., Tennant, A., Maheswaran, H., Parkinson, J., Weich, S., Tennant, R., Taggart, F., & Clarke, A. (2011). The Warwick-Edinburgh Mental Well-being Scale (WEMWBS): A valid and reliable tool for measuring Mental Well-being in diverse populations and projects. Journal of Epidemiology & Community Health, 65(Suppl 2), A38–A39. https://doi.org/10.1136/jech.2011.143586.86

20 Reimagining Our Futures

The Beginning, Middle, and End of the Digital Higher Education Journey for Incarcerated Learners

Helen Farley and Stephen Seymour

Introduction

Prisons throughout Australia have implemented tertiary education programs for incarcerated individuals, encompassing vocational education, pre-tertiary initiatives, and importantly, higher education (Barrow et al., 2019). The engagement of prisoners in education serves multiple purposes, including keeping them occupied and away from trouble (Rocheleau, 2013), facilitating the establishment of vocational pathways that enhance post-release employment opportunities (Rosmilawati & Darmawan, 2020), fostering prosocial behavior among participants (Farley & Pike, 2016), and directly reducing recidivism rates (Davis et al., 2013).

Despite a prevailing bias against higher education in correctional spaces in Australia, the University of Southern Queensland (UniSQ), located in the rural Darling Downs and committed to social justice, had long provided higher education materials in physical form to prisons across Australia. However, as with most other higher education institutions globally, UniSQ underwent a transition to online offerings, which posed significant challenges to providing higher education to prisoners (Farley & Seymour, 2022; Farley & Willems, 2017). The security priorities and strict practices ingrained in prisons created a learning environment that did not readily support the same level of "flexible delivery" that digital university learning designers typically assumed (Farley & Hopkins, 2018).

The Making the Connection project, led by the University of Southern Queensland (UniSQ) and funded by the Australian government, provided access to digital higher education through providing servers networked into existing computer labs and laptops that could be used in-cell, preloaded with course materials and requiring no access to the internet (Farley et al., 2016). The project built on a number of other prison technology projects led by the university since 2011 (Farley & Seymour, 2022). The processes and technologies developed as part of the Making the Connection project have since been incorporated into standard operating procedures for incarcerated learners at UniSQ.

DOI: 10.4324/9781003394426-24

Toward a Sustainable Project

The project attracted $AUD4.4 million ($USD2.9 million) from the Australian government through the Higher Education Participation and Partnerships Program in 2013. Once the project team was in place, we set about formulating a project philosophy. According to the funding rules, we had to deploy four programs into 13 prisons. We spent half a day deciding if we were just going to do the project at hand (and "miss the point"; overlooking the opportunity to make lasting change) or if we were going to create a sustainable solution that would continue once there was no more funding and the project personnel had left the university. Unanimously we decided that we wanted the project to be sustainable and to continue to make a difference past the end date. To do this, we had to forecast what resources would be available and what procurement relationships would be in place at the end of the project. This significantly impacted the way we ran the project and was considerably more complicated. At that time, we thought the project would run for 3 years; in fact, we stretched the funding out to nearly 5 years and achieving three times our contracted Key Performance Indicators. Though we committed to working in 13 correctional centers, by the end of the project we were active in 39 correctional centers across four jurisdictions.

Staffing the Project

Wherever possible, we used UniSQ staff who were already in place rather than recruiting specialist project personnel. We wanted to ensure that, at the end of the project, the expertise did not walk out the door. The main challenge with this approach lay in the fact that most people were already busy, without the imposition of additional project duties. Where possible, we "bought out" people's time but suitable support was not always available. This was made more difficult by the senior leadership team at the university being unreliable in their support for the project. Though they enjoyed the funding and prestige that came from the many awards the project and project team won, some seemed to harbor prejudice against incarcerated learners. There were three Vice Chancellors at the university during the time of the project. One was very supportive and called Making the Connection the "jewel in the crown" of UniSQ. Another made decisions that rendered programs unavailable, excluded the project team from key meetings, and restricted access to staff. This made it easier for people who did not want to support the project to find a way around doing so.

Though the Making the Connection project did employ personnel to direct various aspects of the project, the overwhelming majority of the work was done by staff already employed by the university. Teaching academics modified course materials for the offline environment, and the Information and Communication Technology (ICT) personnel adapted the learning

200 *Helen Farley and Stephen Seymour*

management system for use on the servers and laptops. It would have been easier to buy in the expertise. It was a constant struggle to bring already overworked people onboard and to make sure they met the strict project deadlines necessary to get technologies in place for the beginning of each semester. Where possible, we took academics and senior leaders into the prisons to meet with the incarcerated learners and the prison staff who supported them so that they could see the impact of their work as a means to foster engagement and drive motivation.

When the project finished midway through 2018, even as the project personnel went onto other roles at other workplaces, most of the project expertise remained with the university. They continue to modify course materials, meet deadlines, and continue with the processes necessary to ensure the provision of higher education to incarcerated learners across Australia. Accommodating incarcerated learners has become everyone's concern, and initiatives to do this better now come from every corner of the university.

Using Existing Business Units

To make the project sustainable, we made sure that any business units that would look after aspects of the incarcerated student experience once the project finished did so from the very start. So those who worked with student enrollment also looked after the incarcerated student enrollments, and the library staff also looked after the reference materials needed by learners in the prisons. It seemed hard to justify at the beginning of the project when student numbers were low, but the value soon became evident as numbers increased. Some of these staff were enthusiastic about the challenges of dealing with incarcerated learners. They developed systems and processes, and made suggestions to the project team. Others had to be pushed and/or alternatively cajoled to participate. It was difficult to bring the ICT personnel onboard, probably because they already had a high and persistent workload. They had also been involved in a number of projects in the past, which did not continue. They wanted to be sure that the project persisted before they would invest heavily in it.

As the project progressed, the ICT division saw that the project was designed to be sustainable. They supported the project and modified the learning management system to meet the requirements of the carceral environment. They continue to do this and are proactive in their planning to accommodate software and hardware updates.

Leveraging Procurement Relationships

At the beginning of the project, an options analysis was conducted to determine which device would be most suitable for deployment in prisons to prisoners. A large number of tablets and laptops were considered. Tablets were quickly eliminated because of the large range of operating systems that

Reimagining Our Futures 201

were available and the amount of screen area that was lost through the use of virtual keyboards. We also wanted to ensure that the digital skills that incarcerated learners developed using these devices were transferable to the technologies they would encounter in the workplace or study once released. For these reasons, we decided that it was preferable to use laptop computers. UniSQ had a relationship with a large technology provider who supplied all of their desktop and laptop computers. We were frustrated because these laptops were considerably more expensive than other models we could have purchased locally. Again, because we wanted the project to be sustainable, we bought laptops through the existing provider, and under their warranty conditions. Though it was uncertain at the beginning of the project whether this was the right approach, it soon became evident it was. We had estimated the lifespan of the computers would be 2 years in the carceral environment; it turned out it was almost 5 years.

UniSQ continues to procure laptops from their technology provider. There is just one hardware procurement relationship for UniSQ to maintain, and importantly ICT support staff only have to understand one type of computer and how software performs on that platform. This is also useful for those learners returning to study with UniSQ once released, as they will already be familiar with the hardware.

Making the Case

To overcome a lack of consistent support from leadership across the university, we had to find out how much money tuition from incarcerated learners brought into the program. Up until this time, there were few restrictions on which courses incarcerated learners could enroll in at the university. As a consequence, they were enrolled in around 192 courses in 2017. In most cases, there were only one or two learners in each of these courses, and teaching academics had to make ad hoc changes to the courses for these learners. These were both inefficient and the quality of learning for incarcerated learners was highly variable. It also meant that incarcerated learners were enrolling in programs they could not complete while they were in prison due to the practical nature of the courses or the requirement for lab work.

We also looked at how long incarcerated learners stayed with us while they were incarcerated. People are in prison for an average of 3 years in Australia (Statista, 2023), compared to the United States of America, where the average sentence length is 12 years (Council on Criminal Justice, 2022). Due to the relatively short sentence lengths for prisoners in Australia, we found that learners were only with us for about three consecutive semesters while they were in prison. We were not making special allowances for them for the entirety of their degree. And nearly all were studying halftime, so only about 20 per cent of their study was done while they were in prison. This puts the cost to the university in perspective. In addition, we found that incarcerated learners had a better retention rate than their non-incarcerated peers.

For these learners, retention rates sat at around 77 per cent, compared to 69 for non-incarcerated learners. We found that tuition from incarcerated learners brought in millions of dollars to the university every year, and to grow this number made good economic sense.

Whole programs were adapted to the offline environment. In the first instance, the programs adapted were: the Tertiary Preparation Program, the Diploma of Business Administration, the Diploma of Science (in Environment and Sustainability), and the Diploma of Arts in Community Welfare and Development (Farley & Seymour, 2022). These programs were made up of 59 courses, a much more manageable number. This would constitute a significant cost saving for the university. And incarcerated learners would be able to complete those programs if they were in prison long enough. If they were not in prison long enough to complete the program into which they were enrolled, they could complete them when they were released from custody or use those courses as credit against another program. As time has passed, the programs that incarcerated learners can enroll in has changed but the same principles apply. Incarcerated learners can only enroll in a limited number of programs and courses, but they are able to complete programs while incarcerated (if they are in there long enough). A wider range of courses are available so that learners can use these as a credit against other qualifications once released.

Over time, UniSQ is slowly teaching out those incarcerated learners who have enrolled in courses and programs outside of those now offered. New enrollments of students who are incarcerated are only taken into the prescribed programs. Information around those programs is widely and reliably disseminated to corrections education personnel and prospective learners. Career guidance resources are also provided to help guide learner choices.

Relationships Are Key

The project employed two specialist engagement leaders: A project engagement leader and an Indigenous engagement leader. It was soon recognized that managing stakeholders internal and external to the university was key. Internal stakeholders included academics, senior leadership, business unit staff, reference groups, and so on. External to the university, stakeholders included NGOs supporting prisoners and their families, correctional jurisdictions including all levels of leadership from commissioners to frontline staff. Of course, the ultimate external stakeholders were the incarcerated students themselves and both engagement leaders would travel to prisons to talk to staff and prospective (and current) learners about the project.

Stakeholders were also invited to the university to talk with academics and senior leaders. Sometimes, this engagement took the form of professional development for frontline corrections staff. To cement these relationships, we would often present at conferences or publish with corrections staff. Stakeholders were kept informed with an up-to-date website, website blog, and newsletters. UniSQ project staff were well regarded by jurisdictions, evidenced by the fact they were elected to senior positions within the Australasian Corrections Education Association, the peak body for corrections education in Australia.

Our Indigenous Engagement Leader

Aboriginal and Torres Strait Islander Australians are overrepresented in Australian prisons. Making up just 3 per cent of the general population, they make up some 28 per cent of the prison population (Australian Bureau of Statistics, 2023). A particular focus of the Making the Connection project was encouraging Aboriginal and Torres Strait Islander prisoners into higher education. These prisoners had been failed by colonialist structures and were wary of our attempts to encourage them into higher education. Our Indigenous engagement leader, a Larrakia elder from the Northern Territory, would slowly build relationships with Indigenous prisoners over several months, guiding them through any study they needed to do, before encouraging them into enrolling with the project (Lee et al., 2017). He was also welcomed by the staff within prisons as he had previously served as a corrections officer and was generally welcomed as "one of us." Without a doubt, the relatively large number of enrolments of Indigenous learners the project attracted was in no small way due to his efforts.

Connecting with Custodial

When we went into prisons, we were very respectful of the existing relationships. We didn't come in as the "experts" which is what many academics do (Reiter, 2014). Instead, we listened and learned what we could from those staff and people in prison who were living the reality. These were the people who regularly contended with the difficulties imposed by a problematic architecture, rules, and regulations drafted in a central office far away, and the thorny encounters and emotional outpourings precipitated by inhabiting a dangerous emotional and physical space. The greatest skill I learned through this time was to sit and listen without comment, to make a space where not only frustrations and anguish but also hope and purpose could be expressed and heard without judgment (Hamm, 2018). Once heard, that person would put aside their cynicism and work with us toward a solution. Many challenges which at first flush seemed insurmountable, melted away when we worked together toward a common purpose, fears and anxieties put to one side, and often lubricated with a laugh.

In the jurisdictions we dealt with, each prison would have a separate education team that worked with learners and guided them toward various educational offerings. These education officers were responsible for discerning literacy levels, balancing sentence length with program length, and completing all of the administrivia required by external educational institutions.

They were responsible for dealing with the corrections officers and ensuring that all of the security checks were completed satisfactorily. At first, we left the negotiations that enabled technologies to be brought onto prison sites to these education teams.

One day, I was walking along a covered walkway with an education officer when a corrections officer passed by, muttering a derogatory comment under his breath. When I questioned the education officer, she spoke of the fractious relationship between the custodial side of the business and the education team. I began to question these education officers at many prison sites, and they reported similar challenges in their relationship with corrections officers. A dive into the literature revealed this is a common problem in jurisdictions globally (Walters, 1995; Williams, 1983). We could see that what we were asking of education teams made those relationships more complex, yet those people believed in what they were doing and the transformative power of education, so they willingly took that on.

To alleviate these pressures and to try and circumvent some of the barriers put before us in the name of "security," we started engaging directly with corrections officers. We would invite them to a meeting, bring the technologies we were using, and discuss the project. They could pick up the laptops, peer into them, and ask us any question that came to mind. What we quickly found was that the corrections officers were poorly briefed about the project, probably because of the difficult relationship with the education teams. They carried lots of assumptions that were not true. For example, they believed scientific calculators could be used to make phone calls. Importantly, they believed that incarcerated learners were entitled to subsidized education that other people could not access, and this just "wasn't fair." We were able to tell them that they were—or any other Australian citizen—eligible for the same education as the incarcerated learners and at the same cost. In Australia, incarcerated learners have the same access to the Higher Education Contribution Scheme (HECS), where loans are repaid post-graduation when a certain income level is reached as other students (Ostini & Farley, 2022). This was a deliberate decision we had made to help us work around the objections put forward by victims' rights groups. The corrections officers were satisfied with this and worked with us, rather than against us, to deploy the project in their prison. They became advocates for our programs.

Offering higher education in our prisons meant that we had to set up exam centers in the prisons at the end of the semester. Usually, custodial officers would supervise exams and had to be registered as invigilators at the university. All of a sudden, we found that we could not secure invigilators at a number of prisons. We were perplexed as we thought we had made strong connections with officers through our demonstrations and presentations. Upon closer investigation, we found that the corrections officers had enrolled in university programs and were therefore ineligible to act as invigilators. We were surprised and delighted that the officers had enrolled with us. Indeed, this was an unexpected but welcome consequence of our direct engagement with them. Working with the prisons, we could find enough invigilators and the problem was resolved.

Conclusion

The fruits of the Making the Connection project are still being realized around Australia, and indeed in Aotearoa New Zealand. The initial decision of the project team to make the initiative sustainable sometimes made for a very uncomfortable and challenging journey. But the costs associated with the commitment to sustainability and our belief in the transformative power of education paid dividends. As project personnel prepared to finish up, we drafted an Incarcerated Student Strategy that was adopted by the UniSQ in 2018. It lays the groundwork for the continued support of incarcerated learners. Through the COVID-19 pandemic, the in-cell technologies developed by the project were a boon for those learners locked down in prisons around the country, as they continued to work through their courses and programs. As learners are released from custody, they are reconnecting with UniSQ to continue their studies and contribute to a lively community of learners with lived experience. For UniSQ, the numbers of incarcerated learners continues to grow, attracting around 500 course enrollments each semester, three semesters a year. But for those learners who have studied either directly with the project or with those technologies and processes developed as part of the project, it is everything as they reimagine a new future for themselves and for their families. To those people we say "thank you," for showing us the power of a dream and for making it come true come what may.

References

Australian Bureau of Statistics (2023). Prisoners in Australia. Retrieved from: https://www.abs.gov.au/statistics/people/crime-and-justice/prisoners-australia/latest-release#key-statistics

Barrow, L., Ambler, T., Bailey, M., & McKinnon, A. (2019). Incarcerated students, the technological divide and the challenges in tertiary education delivery. *International Journal of Bias, Identity and Diversities in Education (IJBIDE)*, 4(1), 17–34. https://doi.org/10.4018/ijbide.2019010102

Council on Criminal Justice (2022). New Analysis Shows U.S. Imposes Long Prison Sentences More Frequently than Other Nations. Retrieved from: https://counciloncj.org/new-analysis-shows-u-s-imposes-long-prison-sentences-more-frequently-than-other-nations/

Davis, L., Bozick, R., Steele, J., Saunders, J., & Miles, J. (2013). Evaluating the Effectiveness of Correctional Education: A Meta-Analysis of Programs That Provide Education to Incarcerated Adults. https://doi.org/10.7249/rr266

Farley, H., Dove, S., Seymour, S., Lee, C., Macdonald, J., Abraham, C., & Eastment, T. (2016). *Making the connection: Improving Access to Higher Education for Low Socio-Economic Status Students with ICT Limitations*. Paper presented at the ASCILITE 2016: 33rd International Conference on Innovation, Practice and Research in the Use of Educational Technologies in Tertiary Education – Show me the learning, Adelaide, Australia: https://2016conference.ascilite.org/wp-content/uploads/ASCILITE-2016-full-proceedings-Updated-1512.pdf

Farley, H., & Hopkins, S. (2018). Moving forward together: Supporting educators to support incarcerated students in Australian prison-based higher education. *Advancing Corrections: Journal of the International Corrections and Prisons Association, 6*, 145–152.

Farley, H., & Pike, A. (2016). Engaging prisoners in education: Reducing risk and recidivism. *Advancing Corrections, 1*(1), 65–73.

Farley, H., & Seymour, S. (2022). Higher education for all: Prisoners, social justice, and digital technology. *Histories and Philosophies of Carceral Education*, 163–187. https://doi.org/10.1007/978-3-030-86830-7_8

Farley, H., & Willems, J. (2017). Digital equity: Diversity, inclusion and access for incarcerated students in a digital age. In *Proceedings of Me, Us, IT! ASCILITE2017: 34th International Conference on Innovation, Practice and Research in the Use of Educational Technologies in Tertiary Education* (pp. 68–72). University of Southern Queensland.

Hamm, M. S. (2018). Using prison ethnography in terrorism research. *Doing Ethnography in Criminology*, 195–202. https://doi.org/10.1007/978-3-319-96316-7_16

Lee, C., Farley, H., Cox, J., & Seymour, S. (2017). Tackling indigenous incarceration through promoting engagement with higher education. *Indigenous Pathways, Transitions and Participation in Higher Education*, 169–188. https://doi.org/10.1007/978-981-10-4062-7_11

Ostini, J., & Farley, H. (2022). Beyond idealism to the realities of incarcerated higher education: What we know about the provision of higher education in prisons. *Histories and Philosophies of Carceral Education*, 11–30. https://doi.org/10.1007/978-3-030-86830-7_2

Reiter, K. (2014). Making windows in walls: Strategies for prison research. *Qualitative Inquiry, 20*(4), 417–428. https://doi.org/10.1177/1077800413515831

Rocheleau, A. M. (2013). An empirical exploration of the "pains of imprisonment" and the level of prison misconduct and violence. *Criminal Justice Review, 38*(3), 354–374. https://doi.org/10.1177/0734016813494764

Rosmilawati, I., & Darmawan, D. (2020, June). The Benefit of Prison Education: Inmate Students' Self Reflection. In *International Conference on Science and Education and Technology (ISET 201)*, (pp. 592–595). Atlantis Press. https://doi.org/10.2991/assehr.k.200620.120

Statista (2023) Median aggregate sentence length for sentenced prisoners in Australia from 2005 to 2019, by gender (in months)*. Retrieved from: https://www.statista.com/statistics/648383/australia-median-prison-sentence-length-by-gender/#:~:text=In%202019%2C%20the%20average%20aggregate,Australia%20was%20around%2039%20months.

Walters, S. (1995). The custody orientation of correctional officers: An international comparison. *International Journal of Comparative and Applied Criminal Justice, 19*(1), 61–71. https://doi.org/10.1080/01924036.1995.9678537

Williams, T. A. (1983). Custody and conflict: An organizational study of prison Officers' roles and attitudes. *Australian & New Zealand Journal of Criminology, 16*(1), 44–55. https://doi.org/10.1177/000486588301600105

21 Structuring the Conduit

Expanding Prison-University Partnerships Through the Readers' Circle

Keziah Poole and Rowan A. Bayne

Beginning the Readers' Circle (*Keziah Poole*)

The obstacles that one can face while teaching in a prison classroom are multiple: difficulty establishing partnerships with new facilities, approval of new courses and syllabi, securing clearance for instructors and TAs, limited contact with students, and monitoring of interactions and materials that pass between students and teaching staff. For those coming from a university teaching background, the restrictions attached to the correctional classroom can be felt as a form of "culture shock" (Wright, 2005, p. 21), wherein instructors are forced to rethink their pedagogical practices in adherence with environmental logics that may run counter to their teaching philosophy. Pedagogical impulses toward service, community, and freedom of expression must be curbed and reevaluated in the face of surveillance, correction, and control.

The Readers' Circle is a direct product of this tension. In Spring 2021, as a graduate student in Comparative Literature at the University of Southern California, I began teaching Creative Writing via Zoom to students in a Los Angeles reentry facility. From the start, I was blown away by their enthusiasm for my course. What I quickly realized, however, was that their interest in writing far preceded and exceeded what we were able to cover in the classroom. One student kept a notebook with him at all times, from which he would occasionally ask to share a relevant poem. Another student wrote stories for his children that he said he hoped to one day publish. A student who joined the workshop a few weeks late, after hearing that there was a USC professor teaching a writing class, had finished a screenplay while incarcerated and was already busy lining up pitch-talks with production companies from his facility. Every week, I was asked for individual feedback which—against all of my pedagogical instincts—I felt obliged to refuse. I was unable to review the work within our scheduled sessions, and, teaching virtually, I could not take it with me. Logistics aside, I didn't even know if I would be allowed to look over writing that the students hadn't been assigned directly.

DOI: 10.4324/9781003394426-25

Hoping to give my students a different answer, I approached the co-directors of USC's Prison Education Project (PEP), Nik De Dominic and Kate Levin, with a simple request: Might there be a way to formalize the exchange of non-curricular writing between instructor and student, so as to support the work of incarcerated authors who were already writing, without upsetting our relationships with the partner facility? USC-PEP has offered writing instruction through classes taught by faculty and students in California Department of Corrections and Rehabilitation (CDCR) facilities since 2017, and in Spring 2023 introduced its first fully accredited, co-curricular writing program at the California Institute for Women. In talking through my conundrum, it quickly became apparent that mine was not an isolated problem. What I had imagined simply as a shared email account for which we could seek approval at one facility thus rapidly expanded into a national prison writing program. We recruited a handful of student and faculty editors from PEP's volunteer pool and began offering typing, editing, and feedback services to students experiencing incarceration who were finishing USC-PEP's various writing classes. Within a year, the Readers' Circle had built a community of over 400 volunteer editors providing regular feedback to writers in custody. As word spread—not only through our classes, but between the writers we were serving and amongst fellow prison education advocates—we also found ourselves engaging authors far beyond the scope of our course offerings: At the time of writing, we now work across 28 states with over 200 writers, many of whom live in restricted housing or in remote facilities where there is minimal access to educational programming.

The exponential growth of the Readers' Circle in its first year of operation demonstrates what prison educators have long known: that carceral facilities are filled to the brim with talented writers who need and deserve a creative outlet beyond the limited programming that is available to them. As writers and instructors, we also know that being able to share your work and to forge community with other writers can have a profound impact, not only on your craft but also on your sense of self. Yet, for many authors in custody, not being able to write (or to share one's writing) is a functional reality of their incarceration. It is for this reason that the Readers' Circle was conceived: to encourage and facilitate the writing that *is already happening* in facilities across the country and to build community around this work. Providing individualized, remote feedback to authors in custody from across the United States, however, poses its own unique set of problems. In this chapter, we will outline the many ways in which a writer-to-writer model succeeds in circumventing the tensions found in a traditional prison-university partnership. Drawing on the challenges we face as we continue to grow the Readers' Circle, we will also explore the logistical and strategic limitations inherent to running such a program. Finally, we will suggest opportunities for replicating the writer-to-writer model as

Structuring the Conduit 209

we expand the Readers' Circle community while making an argument for greater administrative investment from universities toward dismantling creative injustice.

Writing Without Definite End(s): Challenges and Opportunities
(*Keziah Poole and Rowan Bayne*)

The Readers' Circle differs from more traditionally academic prison-university partnership models both in its practical functioning and its core purpose. We are, first and foremost, facilitators of writing as a means of creative expression. Indeed, exchanges between volunteer editors and incarcerated writers need not have any end beyond such expression and its acknowledgment by a reader. This is important in the face of the overwhelming correctional logics of self-improvement and redemption that carceral settings impose. Such logics show up, for instance, in statements prepared for parole board hearings, where narratives of "insight" and repentance bear the weight of delivering potential freedom (Bower et al., 2019); these logics subtend any approach to "correctional education" that emphasizes "needed education and career training" with the explicit aim of reducing recidivism (California Department of Corrections and Rehabilitation, 2023). While some writers in our network seek feedback on documents with such material implications, this is neither the norm nor a prerequisite. And the reader on the other end is frequently not someone acting in a capacity to grant the kinds of accreditation or vocational knowledge that other valuable programs provide: our diverse community of volunteer editors includes acclaimed creative writers, first-year undergraduates, campus staff members, alumni, graduate students, and faculty, but in their feedback editors are encouraged to respond as engaged readers rather than as experts, authorities, or gatekeepers. That is, editors are encouraged to respond as fellow writers.

Our writer-to-writer model is firmly embedded in the university and in carceral facilities, then, without requiring formal relationships among them. We deliver no curriculum and use no classroom spaces; we do not offer credit, formal training, or a venue for publication. Our exchanges therefore bypass some of the barriers to entry that exist in other prison education contexts: for the writer in solitary confinement, on a life sentence without parole and thus ineligible for programming at their facility; for the writer in a facility where no partnership with a higher education program exists or is likely to exist (given the facility's distance from campuses or another reason). We offer a means for such writers to write, to be read, and to develop their writing.

Though the merits of a peer-editing and feedback program may seem evident to professional writers and writing pedagogues, prison facilities can be less convinced of the necessity for creative exchange between incarcerated individuals and the broader community. Accordingly, the Readers' Circle has no trouble attracting submissions and placing them with willing editors—but we must contend daily with the logistical barriers levied against incarcerated writers. For example, in order to submit work for editing, writers must first find a way to contact us: either via mail, using the electronic mailing system in operation at their facility, or through a friend or family member. There are many who do not have access to these resources, and while we happily provide (real or electronic) stamps for those who cannot afford them, some facilities do not allow us to purchase pre-paid stamps for writers (or else severely limit them). It took one author several months to submit a book manuscript through his facility's "email" system, because the interface would only allow us to attach one prepaid "stamp" to each of our replies (and every message was limited to—a comparatively generous—6000 characters). Another author, who attempted to mail us her manuscript using the stamps and envelopes we provided, had her writing promptly delivered back to her cell without them, which she took to be a clear message that her activities as a writer were not welcome.

Many authors cite fears of censorship when sending us their work, as mail has been known to go missing and electronic messages are not infrequently withheld for ambiguous reasons. This can be devastating for those who have written lengthy manuscripts (often by hand) and have no means of saving or copying the work before submitting it. Many also face the frustration of not receiving their feedback from us in a timely manner, due to limitations placed on incoming mail (which vary from facility to facility) such as no color ink, sticky labels, or double-sided printing. The free Publishing Toolkit that we share with writers, offering basic tips on how to prepare a manuscript and listing outlets that accept submissions from incarcerated authors, has also gone missing on occasion and has been impounded in a handful of facilities on grounds that it informs residents how to enter into "business" while incarcerated.

It is worth noting that while the content and profitability of their published works can be restricted depending on state law, there is nothing legally standing in the way of incarcerated individuals' producing and sharing writing. Nonetheless, the practical barriers discussed above— which only begin to scratch the surface—can make writing an exhausting and defeating process for many. Running a program like the Readers' Circle is not just a matter, then, of providing editorial support to those in custody; it requires an in-depth knowledge (and persistence in the face) of these structural barriers that often silence expression. While it is true that there are remarkable organizations invested in the publishing and elevation of incarcerated voices, few to our knowledge offer the logistical support that these authors require in order to produce and circulate their work in the first place. Over the last 2 years, we have found (as we suspected) that there are many with the will and expertise to provide editorial support to incarcerated writers. However, very few have the knowledge and resources to navigate such projects within the carceral landscape, and those who do often only have the capacity to do

Structuring the Conduit 211

so in support of work that is destined for publication (and some even charge incarcerated authors for the privilege).

Our goal is to make writing possible in settings that often make writing virtually *im*possible—where writers may lack access to quiet, paper, pens, writing surfaces, computers, and printers, not to mention forums for dialogue and interaction around their words. We aim to provide practical and creative support to those without it by encouraging all who have an interest in developing or making a connection through their writing—regardless of their focus or conventional "ability" as a writer. The Readers' Circle therefore plays a strong facilitatory role, and our staff has become an important source of ongoing moral support and care for authors struggling to create in the face of systematic obstruction. We do not publish or "give voice" to writers, but we are committed to providing the essential tools for them to polish and find purpose in their work as they choose to proceed. Above editing, we have come to understand the utmost importance of being a reliable resource and ally in the pursuit of self-advocacy and self-expression through writing in custody. The more we experience the obstacles that are placed between incarcerated writers and their creative goals, the more we realize that this is the crux of what we have to offer as an organization rather than a barrier to our services.

Another way of saying this is that we have been trying to catch up with just how much administrative muscle is required to facilitate creative expression given the obstacles we have mentioned. Whereas our lens heading into the work had been one of prison *education*, one rooted in trauma-informed teaching among other pedagogical considerations, we have found ourselves more squarely in the realm of logistics on a day-to-day basis: not in the classroom but in the mailroom, stamping envelopes; not only in the foreground bringing the university into prisons, but also in the background, several tabs deep in a Google spreadsheet, tracking down a manuscript that has been received, logged, scanned, sent out for typing, sent out again for substantive feedback, and now needs to be circulated for a final round of proofreading before making its way back (we hope) into its author's hands. This realization about the extent of administrative coordination involved is not simply the one that any administrator learns on day one of the job: that there is far more to running a program than one had anticipated. It is also, here, the realization that what the university is positioned to provide in the writer-to-writer partnerships we facilitate *is* centrally administrative. The writers who share work with us are certainly learning, as are our hundreds of on-campus volunteers; there are profound teachings here, mutual education. But this learning is not measurable in the form of a deliverable, even one as fuzzy as a course outcome: because we are investing in the potential of writing for its own sake, and because we aim to give authors the autonomy of setting the terms by choosing what and when to write, our task as prison educators here is, in one sense, to spark an exchange and then step out of the way as it unfolds (or, rather, to step into the background of those many Google spreadsheets).

212 *Keziah Poole and Rowan A. Bayne*

This model of prison-university partnership—more properly a writer-to-writer partnership that the university is poised to facilitate—is therefore less about the knowledge or credentials that higher education can bestow upon learners than it is about the university choosing to leverage resources toward the tedious, essential work of clearing the thickets around carceral communication.

One reorientation for university partners to consider from this is that preparing students (and faculty) to enter the field of prison education may involve significantly more attention to administration than we believe is typical. Our experience running the Readers' Circle suggests that gathering volunteers eager to respond to writing is not the hard part. What can be a tougher sell, under the rubric of prison education, is the benefit of investing significant resources in a primarily facilitatory capacity, one that seems to lack the immediate appeal of offering university students an off-campus experience and offering incarcerated participants an experience that mirrors that of the university classroom. Given this, how might universities invest in long-term, adaptable programming that enacts a belief in everyone's right to creative expression and that can reach those marginalized even by many existing forms of prison education? We believe that the Readers' Circle offers one response. While we may not exactly be teaching, training, or publishing, we hope—as one author captures our ethos in the poem he decided to write for us to share with prospective funders—that we are "structuring the conduit that allows these words to flow" (Williams, 2022).

Looking Ahead (*Keziah Poole and Rowan Bayne*)

We want to end by highlighting three key affordances of the relatively nimble model of a writer-to-writer network run both within and beyond the bounds of a campus. While the Readers' Circle remains relatively new and we are mindful that our assessment comes from our position outside of the carceral facilities from which the writing flows, we believe that we are learning lessons that can speak more broadly to efforts to reconfigure and extend prison-university partnerships. First, by contrast with one-time class offerings for incarcerated students and "plug and play" service-learning opportunities for university-enrolled teaching assistants, the Readers' Circle can facilitate ongoing exchanges across space and time. Some of the first authors to submit work in 2021 remain in regular contact with our program through electronic correspondence, successive submissions, and ongoing work on book-length projects (creative ambitions that, we know all too well, often do not fit neatly within the bounds of a single course or workshop). Second, our program circumvents some hierarchies of merit and value that can attach to efforts within the "correctional education" framework that many formalized prison-university partnerships are compelled by circumstance to adopt: a Readers' Circle writer needn't be going up for parole, be inspired by the course material available in a given semester (here astronomy, there Shakespeare), be deemed eligible to enroll in (or likely to benefit from) a facility's educational offerings, or even be located in a facility where such offerings exist. Third, because those on both ends of the exchange write and read outside of the relative structure of a classroom, we all confront the immense barriers to communication and expression that exist around carceral facilities—a confrontation that creates opportunities for each party. For the university-based volunteer, there is a small window into these barriers, and so a chance to develop skills for continuing to facilitate communication within the strictures (beyond the usual scope of prison-related pedagogical training). For the university as an institution, there is a spur to invest in the administrative infrastructures needed to facilitate this communication over the long term—and thereby to invest in writers who may not be reached by existing programming. And, most importantly, for the writer in custody, there is an opportunity— we hope—to keep writing.

Moving forward, we remain motivated by the ever-growing interest in our program, but we are focused on addressing the administrative needs behind its maintenance and expansion. We have begun experimenting with ways to maintain the writer-to-writer model in different areas of the university community. By embedding editing work within USC classes and workshops in writing, literature, and community engagement, we have been able to fulfill the current editorial requests of our authors, allowing us to begin branching into partnerships with nonprofit publishers and writing advocates to support writers' work beyond our program's range of services. This has given the Readers' Circle a vital sense of community, connecting authors and editors from different regions, disciplines, and organizations in the pursuit of creative justice and learning. Drawing on the diverse knowledge and expertise of our participants, we have been able to extend our services to offer much-needed Spanish-language support for writers in custody, and we have plans to partner more closely with Readers' Circle authors to facilitate writer-to-writer events and workshops within facilities. Yet, the labor that goes into coordinating these projects and providing reliable support to the authors who request our services is something often overlooked in the university context: our hundreds of manuscripts are processed, allocated, tracked, verified, and returned by just three part-time student workers, with varying assistance from the faculty directors and course-based volunteers. As we progress to develop new partnerships and programs, it is clear that we do not need to convince the university community of the value in connecting with writers in custody, so much as of the educational, professional, and social justice opportunities inherent in making this creative exchange possible. As we have seen, an administrative investment in writer-to-writer programming can exponentially increase the opportunity for participation on campus and in facilities. Furthermore, we believe that students and faculty who learn—as we have had to—of the logistical impediments faced by authors in custody at every juncture of

214 *Keziah Poole and Rowan A. Bayne*

the writing process will be uniquely equipped to tackle systemic injustice in their immediate and professional communities. By building engagement around the obstacles posed to prison education programming, the Readers' Circle is not only able to raise awareness of the systemic marginalization of incarcerated voices, but to equip aspiring advocates with the concrete tools necessary to address these creative injustices.

References

Bower, S. M. P. R., Artiano, E. M. W., & Pack, B. (2019). The truth will set you free: Reflections on the rhetoric of Insight, responsibility, and Remorse in rhetoric for the Board of Parole hearings. *Reflections, 19*(1), 79–112.

California Department of Corrections and Rehabilitation. (2023). *Office of Correctional Education.* https://www.cdcr.ca.gov/rehabilitation/oce/

Williams, K. (2022). To the financiers of the Readers' Circle. Unpublished manuscript.

Wright, R. (2005). Going to teach in prisons: Culture shock. *The Journal of Correctional Education, 56*(1), 19–38.

22 An Octopus in the Scaffolding
Ten Years of Prison Arts Collective

Annie Buckley

The Ocean

We are in a stark gym in one of the oldest prisons in California, but you would never know it from the bright energy bubbling throughout the room. It is the day of the culminating performance of our first collaborative workshop. In this workshop series, participants are invited to work together on a creative piece of their own design that can engage multiple media. In the first few days of the workshop, the men in our class are game but relatively confused. What we are asking of them—that they set aside expectations, share their ideas with one another, and collaborate on one project together using their various skills and talents—would be challenging in any classroom but presents unique barriers here in the prison. Within the confines of institutionalized life, the artists in our classes are accustomed to following strict rules and sticking to themselves. By this time, we had been teaching art in this facility for 4 years. Amid the warmth, enthusiasm, creativity, and excitement in our weekly classes, I had noticed that artists tended to stick to themselves. When faced with a new grant opportunity, I thought about how we could challenge our program, and participants, and shift the boundaries in new ways; thus, the collaborative project idea was hatched.

On this final day, the artists are as nervous and excited as any group would be on the day of the final performance. We have brought guests from the outside as well as two art writers. When we enter the gym, we walk through a forest of suspended words, each one handcrafted from cardboard and other found materials. The words trace a journey from struggle to hope and redemption, a transformative narrative that is both unique to each individual in the class and also shared. As the audience settles, another aspect of the performance begins. The artists stand, in their prison blues, holding up signs painted to mirror their requisite clothing, with words that state another aspect of their identity than the one emblazoned on their back: son, father, peer, human. This quiet and striking performance is followed by a song, Redemption, written and performed on guitar by the artists in the class. As it ends, the audience rises in a rollicking applause (Image 22.1 and 22.2).

DOI: 10.4324/9781003394426-26

216 *Annie Buckley*

Image 22.1 "Redemption," a collaborative installation by artists at the California Institution for Men, photo by Ashley Woods, 2017.

Image 22.2 "Redemption," a collaborative performance by artists at the California Institution for Men, photo by Ashley Woods, 2017.

An Octopus in the Scaffolding 217

A week or so before this, one of the students came up to me and asked shyly, "If I tell you something, you won't get mad?" I smiled, a bit nervous, and assured him I would not. "When you first told us about this project, I thought you were crazy!" He said with a big grin. I laughed and reminded him that I understood it was a challenge and was proud of their work together. Creativity can be a sense of madness, a journey into the depths—of ourselves, of emotion, of the world around us—and to do it together, in the tightest of spaces, feels like deep sea diving.

Shoreline

This story, like all stories tracing the past, begins at a place in time located in retrospect, with the imperfect mix of memory and reflection. That is to say, this program did not begin on a particular day but rather evolved into being. In 2013, I was a new teacher at a state university. I was really excited to have the job as it gave me the opportunity to meld my experience as an educator and artist with a goal to expand access to the arts. I didn't set out to start an art program in prisons, let alone what has evolved into Prison Arts Collective (PAC), a large collaborative project engaging students, faculty, staff, and volunteers across the state of California and the world[1]. I set out to bring art to the local community while simultaneously helping my university students—most of whom were the first in their families to go to college and often worked and took care of children or parents—gain the real-world experience, confidence, and connections needed to be successful in their chosen career path of teaching art. While guiding this project into the large statewide program it is today has become my primary creative and educational practice, PAC is not and never has been a singular effort. It is possible with the collective efforts of students, faculty, and staff from universities; artists from local and global communities; staff in the prisons where we teach; and thousands of people experiencing incarceration who take part in and co-facilitate PAC classes across California.

For me, art has always been a means of connecting, processing, and sharing. It is something that has brought me joy, calm, grounding, and adventure. I have been a teacher for nearly three decades and have taught students from kindergarten through graduate school. Throughout, I have seen that art can be fun, meaningful, and life-changing. This is often most true in difficult times. In my first job out of college in the early 90s, I was a bilingual teacher in the Pico Union area of Los Angeles. I was only partway through my first year on the day that the LA riots broke out in response to a jury acquitting four white police officers accused of beating an African American man. Throughout the day, plumes of smoke arose all around us as the city burned. That afternoon, I gazed at the young faces of the few students whose parents had not yet picked them up and knew we needed to change course. I set aside the lessons planned for that day and instead we painted to music.

218 *Annie Buckley*

Unfortunately, communities with significant sociocultural and economic stressors—situations in which the arts could be extremely impactful—are the places where the arts are often cut. Children in poverty consistently lack access to the meaningful stress relief, identity formation, expression, and connection that the arts can provide. Across the country, Black and Latino children earn 30% and 25%, respectively, less art credits than their White peers (U.S. Department of Education, 2018). Students with low socioeconomic status who do have access to the arts have a dropout rate of just 4%, five times lower than their peers in a similar socioeconomic group that did not experience the arts. Students from low-income families who are able take part in the arts are also twice as likely to graduate from college than their peers without access to the arts (Catterall et al., 2012). The arts make a difference in lives and futures. What does the cultivation of art and creative community mean in the context of prisons, objectively the most restrictive places on earth?

In early 2013, I had the opportunity to teach a new course that I had developed for the first time. It was a service-learning course, which means that students are meant to learn while also providing a needed service in the community, with both receiving mutual benefit. My university students would get hands-on experience facilitating arts programming and the community partners that opted to work with us would gain arts workshops. Before the class began, I collaborated with the University's office for community partnerships, reaching out to the local area to see who would be interested in arts courses. We received replies from an after-school program in a public housing project, a housing community for low-income seniors, the county office for youth probation, and a nonprofit that supported young women who were victims of human trafficking. I met with each organization to set up a plan for the workshops, paired students with an organization based on their preferences, and got started.

Shortly afterward, the group that worked with victims of human trafficking pulled out as it proved too difficult to get the girls to the arts classes. In retrospect, and through the lens of remote programming gained during 2020-21 due to the impact of the COVID-19 pandemic, I wished we had created some form of creative journaling with student feedback for the girls. Around the time that the nonprofit pulled out, my department chair transferred a call to me. When I picked up, I heard the booming and friendly voice of a staff member at the local prison. The caller shared that the warden at the prison wanted art classes. I listened carefully, wondering whether the prison could replace the community partner that had just dropped out. After the call, I went down the hall to my classroom, where a handful of students were gathered. I explained the call and asked, "Does anyone want to go with me to visit the men's prison?" All but one signed up to join the visit.

A few weeks later, the students, department chair, and I drove 45 minutes to the prison where we met the coordinator from the call, the warden, and several men who were incarcerated. In a drab conference room in the state prison, the warden, a slender Black woman in command of the prison, shared her enthusiasm about how helpful the arts classes could be for the population. Before we left, she told us, "You don't want to know why these men are here and you are not to ask them." This is a rule for programs working in California prisons, but it has also allowed us, then and since, the opportunity to focus on our students as people: as artists, writers, musicians, and students, simultaneously supporting participants in our classes to evolve and reconnect to such identities rather than focus on their ever-present situational context of being a person who is incarcerated.

On that first day, everything was new. We came with a goal to be responsive to what the prison and our future students wanted to learn. But when we asked the men what kind of art they wanted to study, we were met with blank stares. They were unaccustomed to choices and agency. We waited, cajoled, and asked the question in different ways. Eventually, they opened up. We listened to their thoughts and experiences and went back to campus to design classes with their input in mind. While my university students developed classes reflecting their knowledge and what they heard at the prison, my department chair and I worked together to construct a plan for the classes that allowed for teamwork, collaboration, and safety. Each class would be co-taught by a pair of student teachers, and they all taught at the same time. Participants would have the option to choose which class they took based

Image 22.3 Multidisciplinary arts classes are facilitated by student teachers and faculty from state universities at prisons in California, photo by Peter Merts, 2017.

220 *Annie Buckley*

on their interests. Classes would take place in a space where a correctional officer or staff was present. We didn't know it at the time, but the plan we mapped out that day and in the weeks that followed has become the norm for most of our classes since that time (Image 22.3).

Between the Buoys

On a sunny afternoon, about a year later, I met a small group of students outside the prison. By this time, we had familiarized ourselves with the attendant rituals of entering a prison to teach. We drove from locales across the region, most traveling an hour or more to get here. While still in the parking lot, we turned off our phones and locked them in our cars, waiting for everyone to arrive so we could enter together. Once inside, we signed our names in a large book, looking over one another's shoulders to help, ensuring that we all complete each section of the chart: name, date, time, ID number, badge number, and whether we needed an escort. We showed our pre-approved list of supplies to the officer who counted each item, checking colored pencils and paintbrushes off the list. One of the undergraduate students was familiar with the institution since her mother had been a correctional officer there. Another had been jailed as an adolescent while another student had been with a parent and other relatives in prison.

In contrast to the ebb and flow of the creative practice celebrated in our classes, everything here was measured and methodical. We passed through multiple gates. At each one, an officer looked at our identification, and then looked into our eyes, confirming that we were the person in the photo, that we were on the list, that we were allowed entrance into this most restrictive of spaces. When we reached the last metal gate, we pressed a button and the door opened with a click. We stepped into the bright California sunshine and walked across a vast prison yard. The ground under our feet circled a track where men in prison blues and the occasional white t-shirt allowed for exercise, walked the track, or lifted weights. Others sat on benches, chatting in the morning sun. Once in a while, a cluster gathered to sing or play guitar. Many called out friendly greetings.

We all wore black to avoid being turned away at the gates due to an unanticipated infraction of the complex rules governing what guests can wear to visit the prison. Perhaps a teacher had thought that a pair of charcoal jeans looked black enough to wear, but the officer interpreted them as grey, a color disallowed on the list. Or a green shirt was read at the gate as olive or khaki, similar to what the officers wear, and thus disallowed. Any infraction and we could be sent away, forced to take the hour or more return trip we drove to get here before even getting inside the gate. To avoid all that, most of the time, we wore black. Our shoes were flat and closed-toed, as required, "so that you can run if you need to" an officer explained

An Octopus in the Scaffolding 221

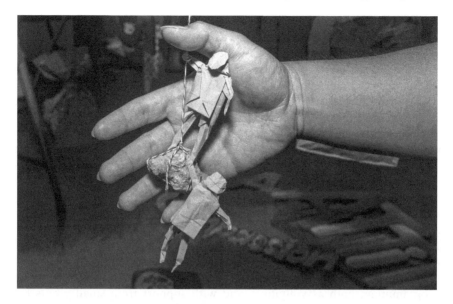

Image 22.4 Origami art created by Lyle, artist participating in PAC programming, photo by Ashley Woods, 2017.

to me once. Despite all the rigor to get to the space, once we arrived in the gym, what unfolded in our classes was the beautiful, messy, creative light of art (Image 22.4).

Into the Waves

We have continued to teach art classes at that first prison since we began. But shortly afterward, both the prison and the student teachers began to request that we expand. First, it was to another yard or facility in the prison. Then, it was to a nearby prison for women. Each time, I aimed to respond to the requests. I was eager to support our students in and out of the prison to expand access to the wild, creative, and connective space of art in this most confining reality. While I sought to be responsive and community engaged, what I had not anticipated was how much the administrative burden of this process would expand as we grew the creative arts programming.

As the student teachers graduated, they requested to continue and I was faced with a new question: How? Initially, they taught as students in internship courses, but now, they would no longer be students. Would they be covered by the same institutional support that allowed us to bring students to the prison? We quickly learned two things that helped in this effort: the

222 *Annie Buckley*

complex process for people to volunteer, which meant lengthy applications both at the prison and at the university, and that there was a grant coming out for bringing arts into prisons. While some of the university graduates decided to embark on the volunteer process, most had other jobs, or needed to get them, and couldn't take that route. In the meantime, I collaborated with students and former students on a lengthy application for the grant to bring arts to prisons, funded by the state.

I quickly learned that, as a faculty member, I couldn't apply directly to the grant but would need to do so in collaboration with the auxiliary that facilitated research grants for the university. I spent a couple frantic weeks gathering information from and with students and former students, writing drafts, talking to the grants officer—who has remained a supporter even after leaving the agency and serves on our advisory board—and writing what ended up being a nearly 100-page narrative with bios and course outlines. It wasn't pretty, but we got it in on time. Not long afterwards, we learned that we didn't get the grant. We continued our program anyway. This same process played again the following year, and yet we found ways to continue programming, both as volunteers and with support from small grants for faculty from the university.

In the meantime, I applied for another grant directly from CDCR to support people serving life sentences at distant prisons with limited access to volunteer programming. In responding to this call, I combined my knowledge of teacher education with what I had learned from teaching in the prisons so far, and imagined a program in which incarcerated students with experienced in art—we had already seen that there were many—whether self-taught or otherwise, would take part in an in-depth training program, and then teach classes to their peers. I wrote it out, submitted the grant to the grants office, and happily, we received it and got our first funding from outside the university to support the program. With it, the growth continued, and I began to learn the implications of expansion from the perspective of imagination and interest versus detailed planning.

That summer, a handful of willing students ventured with me to the desert to lead our first teacher training. It was at least 115 degrees in the shade, and it was the first time the students would assist me instead of teaching their own art classes with my support. It was a long, hot, inspiring adventure with a steep learning curve, and I am grateful to this day to those students who were willing to be on that journey as I figured out with them what was needed, how to guide them in this process, and how this new training would play out in real time. We soon learned that the men doubted that they would ever be able to teach, even if they completed the course. "They'll never let us do that," they said skeptically, but still showed up. We explained that it was part of the grant, and they would be able to teach, but they had not seen it done and so were dubious. We persisted in working with the helpful staff at the prison to come up with a plan for their classes and, after much discussion, planning, and some delays,

Image 22.5 Peer facilitator with PAC installation part of a collaborative artwork, photo by Peter Merts, 2017.

the men graduated and began to teach. By staying positive and consistent, keeping our focus on the goal of expanding access to the connection and creativity of art, we made our way through various stumbles and a sea of doubt. Despite early challenges, many of the men who completed our first facilitator training are still teaching in the prison today and others, upon release, taught with us outside (Image 22.5).

Soon afterward, with support from the university auxiliary and the state agency, we applied again to the grant we had been denied and received further funding to continue the art classes we had started at the local prison and expand to more sites. Here, the real challenge of maintaining the flow of creativity within the structure of bureaucracy was thrown into sharp relief. I had been working as a teacher and an artist all of my adult life and was used to juggling and keeping long hours, but the flow of requirements and new information was so steady as to be nearly unmanageable. In addition to teaching my classes on campus and trying to maintain (if in a limited way) my art and writing, I found myself learning the requirements of human resources when hiring and managing staff, writing and balancing budgets for multiple simultaneous programs, designing and leading training for new student and staff teachers, communicating with colleagues at state prisons and partner state universities about the work that we did and how to collaborate to grow it, and so much more. The levels of procedural and administrative requirements seemed to grow daily (Image 22.6).

224 *Annie Buckley*

Image 22.6 Student teachers lead a workshop for participants at an Arts in Corrections conference, photo by Peter Merts, 2017.

Swimming in Cages

As the fluid, organic, and powerful creative inspiration in our classes inside the prisons continued to deepen and thrive, the structures it took to maintain this programming multiplied. Just as we had learned on the go with the first facilitator training, each new endeavor had new and unforeseen requirements, challenges, and needs. I had to find and hone the skills to write grants, manage budgets, forge partnerships, recruit and hire team members, write procedures, and most of all, identify what exactly it was that we were doing to create this beautiful, thriving art spaces behind bars and communicate that to others with enough clarity and enough space for creativity for them to replicate it in the way that worked best for their communities. I made mistakes. We all did. But working together, we learned, grew, and expanded our patience and empathy in the process.

One of the first things we identified was a model for our classes that included three, and later four, parts that each teacher would include. This gave consistency to our work while also allowing teachers creativity to innovative and be responsive to their students' needs and interests. Of course, art-making or creative practice is one, but that is only part of what we do. Early on, I began to see that the participants in our classes were almost completely unaware of other artists in the world and throughout history. I felt that this

An Octopus in the Scaffolding 225

knowledge could empower their work while also helping them to see that they are part of a larger story. So, art or cultural history is a second part of our model of classes. The third and last for the first few years is reflection. In this way, we ask participants to reflect on their own and others' work. This can be done in writing, in conversation, in pairs or in large groups, with one another or with teachers. Reflection offers participants opportunities to express themselves and their ideas and, at the same time, to widen their perspective about how others see and understand the world. This can be difficult to attain when locked into a space and reflection supported it. The fourth part is the cultivation of a safe space for creative practice. While we had discussed its importance since the early days, it wasn't until several years later that one of our team who is formerly incarcerated asked why it wasn't one of the parts since it is vital. We all agreed and added safe space to the other three parts of the PAC model. For us, safe space is about cultivating belonging and community, imagination, and dreaming. We reach through and around to build connections and community and hope in a space that is not designed to support any of these—the magical aqueous movement of an octopus within the foundational structure of a cage.

Ten years into the story, it is impossible to know if it is still the beginning, the middle, or near the end. I can only hope to continue to collaborate with incredible partners across the state and around the world to find avenues for the magical connection of art within the ever-growing structure of correctional, educational, and legislative institutions, transforming from within (Image 22.7).

Image 22.7 Author with PAC participants and student teachers with a collaborative mandala, photo by Peter Merts, 2016.

Note

1 Prison Arts Collective (PAC) is supported by the California Arts Council, California Department of Corrections and Rehabilitation, and the National Endowment for the Arts.

Works Cited

Catterall, James; Dumais, Susan; Hampton-Thompson, Gillian. The Arts and Achievement in At- Risk Youth: Findings from Four Longitudinal Studies. National Endowment for the Arts, 2012.

U.S. Department of Education. Status and Trends in the Education of Ethnic Groups: Institute of Education Science, 2018.

Index

Note: Page numbers in *italics* refer to figures.

abolitionism 18
abolitionist college course 31
abolitionist practices 32, 36–40
Aboriginal and Torres Strait Islander
    prisoners 203
ACE *see* Adult Continuing Education
activism 61, 63–65, 86
Adams, R. 132
addiction: and incarceration 13; reentry
    journeys 13
add-on (collaborative) drawings 88, 90
ADOC *see* Alabama Department of
    Corrections
Adult Continuing Education (ACE)
    program 95; BoP's Education
    Program 96–97; poetry writing
    classes 96–99
adult education: group activities 147;
    prison students 146; supportive
    actions 147–148; teaching
    strategies 147; transformative
    learning theory 147
aggression, carefully planned 80
Aid to Inmate Mothers 171
Alabama Department of Corrections
    (ADOC) 171
Alabama Prison Arts + Education
    Project (APAEP) 169,
    172; course offerings 170;
    credit programming 174;
    programming 171
Alabama Prison Arts Initiative, The 170
Alejandrez, D. 104, 106, 109
Alim, H. S. 159
alive time 157
*America Made Me a Black Man: A
    Memoir* (Farah) 60

American Prison Writing Archive 67
Anderson, A. 190
andragogy 146, 147
anger 33
antifascism 76
antisocial behavior 24, 140
anxiety 4, 10, 12, 15, 26, 45, 90, 138,
    148, 150, 203
APAEP *see* Alabama Prison Arts +
    Education Project
apathy 31, 97
Arrowood, B. 29
art, education, and activism on death
    row: add-on (collaborative)
    drawings 88, 90; classes and
    exhibitions 88–91; collaborative
    exercises 88, 90; drawing
    exercise 85–86, 88–89, *89*;
    surrogate projects 88, 90
art exhibition 183–185
Art in Prison 90
"Art on the Inside" 173
arts facilitator training 195
arts research *see* Prison Arts Collective
Ashbury, J. 120
Auburn University 170–172
Austin, J. 101
authentic thinking 81
Avenal State Prison 182–184

bachelor's degree program, CCWF and
    VSP 185–187
*Bad Boys: Public School in the Making
    of Black Masculinity* (Ferguson) 5
Bain, B. 59
Baldwin, J. 61
"banking" concept of education 69, 70

228 *Index*

Barrel Fever (Sedaris) 94
Barthes, R. 125
Batchen, G. 125
Beauty in Photography (Adams) 132
Bedford Hills Correctional Facility 117
Bell, J. 180
Belmont University 92
Besteman, C. 31, 32, 36
"big four" risk factors, recidivism 140
Bird and The Fox, The (Coleman) 64
Black Lives Matter 121
Boal, A. 63
Bondy, B. 173
BOP *see* Bureau of Prisons
Boston University Prison Education
    Program 59, 61–62
Braha, J. 59
Brewster, L. 194
Broken Column, The 122
Brown vs. Plata 184
brutality 31, 65, 72, 104
brutal stories: essay, wasted life
    82–84; punk shows 77;
    schooling 77–78; shopping,
    Sacramento 80–81; teaching in
    prison 81–83; warfare through
    language 80
Buckley, A. 189, 190
Bureau of Prisons (BOP) 179
Bureau of Prison's Program (BoP)
    Statement 96
Burn (Lowery) 33
Burnett, A. 27, 29
Butler, J. 108, 109

California Correctional Institution 24
California Department of Corrections
    (CDC) 177
California Department of Corrections
    and Rehabilitation (CDCR) 21,
    25, 177, 179, 181, 208, 222;
    funding 187; IGP 182–183;
    Insider Art exhibition 183–185;
    PAC 190–196; programs in
    182–185
California Reentry and Enrichment
    (CARE) Grants 182
California State University (CSU) 15,
    19, 22, 177, 180, 181, 186, 187,
    189, 192, 194, 195
California State University, Los Angeles
    (CSULA) 21; BA Graduation
    Initiative 23; PPF yard 26;
    Project Rebound 22

California State University, Sacramento
    (CSUS) 13
Canadian correctional facilities:
    administrative barriers 151;
    adult education 146–148;
    education, purpose of 145–146;
    experiential knowledge
    148–149; trauma-informed
    practices 150–151; universal
    accommodations 149–150
CARE Grants *see* California Reentry
    and Enrichment
CBOs *see* community-based
    organizations
CCG *see* Cemanahuac Cultural Group
CCWF *see* Central California Women's
    Facility
CDCR *see* California Department of
    Corrections and Rehabilitation
cell 8
Cemanahuac Cultural Group (CCG)
    108–110
Central California Women's Facility
    (CCWF) 178, 185, 186, 187
child neglect, *suspected* 36
Childs, J.B. 106, 107, 109
Choate, B. 185
CITI *see* Collaborative Institutional
    Training Initiative
Civil Rights movement 107
classes and exhibitions 88–91
classroom: computer lab, access to 7;
    environment 6; interruptions
    7–8; security measures 7
Claudel, C. 119, 121
Clendenning, A. 127
Clotho 119
co-creation 63
Colby College 31, 32
Coleman, W. 59–61, 64, 65
Collaborative Institutional Training
    Initiative (CITI) 193
collective liberation 34
college 4–5
College Ten 110
College Writing class 76, 78, 80, 83–84
Columbus Day Painting 119
Combahee River Collective 71
communication 81–82
community-based in-prison programs 18
community-based organizations
    (CBOs) 177
community-building 172
computer lab, access to 7

Index   229

Cone, G. 93
correctional rehabilitation 18
covid-19 pandemic 92, 101, 112, 117, 179, 185, 218; DOC programs 10; EPI and DOC, collaborative effort 10; prison 9–10
creativity 87, 217
Crenshaw, K. 71
cruelty 31, 60, 65, 184
CSULA *see* California State University, Los Angeles
CSU Project Rebound Consortium 181
CSU Project Rebound Outreach Program (CSU PROP) 187
CSU PROP *see* CSU Project Rebound Outreach Program
CSUS *see* California State University, Sacramento
Cyrano de Bergerac 135

Daguerre, L. 125
dead time 157, 158
death by incarceration 35
Debra K. Johnson Rehabilitation Center 134
dehumanization 5, 6, 8, 10, 60, 68, 72, 87, 96, 106, 157, 183
deindividuation 104
Department of Correction (DOC) 3–7, 10, 11, 174
de Quadros, A. 59–62
Diep, C. 109
digital higher education: business units 200; cases 201–202; connecting with custodial 203–204; engagement leaders 202, 203; procurement 200–201; staffing 199–200; stakeholders 202–203; sustainable project 199
disappearing act: banking model, education 69, 70; collective anger, students 68; course materials, removal of 67; day-to-day survival, prison 68; feminist liberation projects 68, 71, 72; feminist teaching 70; freedom, educational spaces 72–74; liberatory education, denial of 69; punishment culture, school 73; systems of power 70–71; visual map, composing 71
discipline *vs.* intimacy 85
DOC *see* Department of Correction

Dodson, N. 128
Doors of Perception, The 128, *129*
Dostoevsky, F. 163
drawing: class 170, 173; exercise 85–86, 88–89, *89*
dread 24, 139
Du Bois, W. E. B. 162
Dumont, B. 59

each one, teach one principle 181
East Point Peace Academy, Oakland 108
easy time 156
educational journey 22–23
Education Behind the Wall: How and Why We Teach College in Prison 6
education, purpose of 145–146
Elmore Correctional 173
Emerson Prison Initiative (EPI) 3, 4, 6–8, 10, 11
Emerson, R.W. 162
empathy 19, 35, 45, 64, 87, 102, 152, 224
Empowering Song approach: class 62; figured worlds 59–61; formation and synthesis 60; RPJA 62–65; as vehicle for liberation 61
enslavement 72
EPI *see* Emerson Prison Initiative
evaluation research, prison 190–192, 194, 196
exhibitions: add-on drawings and surrogate projects 90; *"Art on the Inside"* 173; *Insider Art* 183–185; *Life after Death and Elsewhere* 90–91, *91*; *Marking Time: Art in the Age of Mass Incarceration* 131; *Windows from Prison* 42
experiential knowledge: alternative practice 148–149; challenge 148; pushing back/pushing forward 149

face-to-face courses 26
Farah, B. J. 60
Farrell, C. 107
fear 12, 24
Federal Correctional Institution-Elkton 94, 95, 97, 98, 102, 103
Federal Correctional Institution, Mendota (FCI Mendota) 179
feminist pedagogy, carceral spaces: banking model, education 69, 70; collective anger, students 68; course materials, removal of 67; day-to-day survival, prison 68;

230   *Index*

feminist teaching 70; freedom, educational spaces 72–74; liberation projects 68, 71, 72; liberatory education, denial of 69; punishment culture, school 73; systems of power 70–71
Ferguson, A.A. 5
figured worlds: Coleman, W. 59–60; de Quadros, A. 60; Morin, K. 61
Fischli, P. 126, 127
Fisch, V. 64
Fisher, J. 130
Fleetwood, N.R. 131, 132
Floyd, G. 63
Foernzler, S. 126, 127
Forgotten Prophets (Martinez) 33
foster care 35
freedom: educational spaces 72–74; revolutionary 160–161
Freedom & Captivity Curriculum Project: abolitionist practices 32, 36–40; circle questions, answering of 35; group discussions 35; incarcerated people, experiences of 35; meetings 32; pilot class 33; radical love 38, 39, 40; short-term goal 40; teaching the curricula 34; website 33
Freedom & Captivity Initiative and Abolition Night 31
Freire, P. 63, 67, 69, 70, 73, 74, 162
Fresno ArtHop 184
Fresno State Center for Creativity & the Arts 184
Fresno State Department of Art & Design 183, 184
Frye, J. 185
fugitivity 72

Gadamer, H.G. 162
Gellman, M. 8
General Educational Diploma (GED) 94, 138
Gentileschi, A. 119, 121
Getting Out By Going In (GOGI) 23
Gibson, C. 29
Gilmore, R.W. 71, 72
GOGI *see* Getting Out By Going In
Goode, R.C. 141
Great League of Peace 106
group cohesion 35
Guenther, L. 86
Guernica 121

Gulag Archipelago, The (Solzhenitsyn) 91
Gumbs, A.P. 72

Haney, C. 104
hard time 156–158
harm reduction 31, 40
Harriet Tubman-ness 72
Hartman, K. 24
HECS *see* Higher Education Contribution Scheme
Heisterkamp, B.L. 189, 190
HEJI program *see* Higher Education for the Justice-Involved
Heppard, J. 160, 161
Higher Education Contribution Scheme (HECS) 204
Higher Education for the Justice-Involved (HEJI) program 155, 162–163
higher education in prison: as abolition 160–162; challenges and barriers 27–28; educational journey 22–23; exam centers 204; graduation ceremony, Lancaster Prison 21, 22; and healing 25; in-person BA degree program 26; justifications for 162; master's degree confirmation ceremony 23; peer support 25; philosophical foundations of 158–162; PPF 23, 24, 26; Project Rebound 22, 23, 27; as punishment 159–160; and reentry support 21–22; rehabilitation 158; rehabilitation and transformation 24–25; school-to-prison pipeline, reversing of 28; transformation and change 25–26
Holidays on Ice (Sedaris) 94
Holland, D. 59
Holy Cross College 123
homelessness 12, 13
Honor Yard 24, 25
hooks, b. 67–69, 73, 161
Hopper, E. 119
human experiences, prison classroom: foundations of higher education 158–162; HEJI program 155, 162–163; time 156–158; WMU/MDOC prison-university partnership 155
humanization 155, 158, 161–162
Humanize the Numbers collaborative photography project 47, 48, 49;

Index 231

approval 42; benefits 48–49; cameras in prison 42, 43, 46, 47, 53; Choices *44*; constraints 43; Creator, The *44*; I am not a number *54*; learning experience 46; Lifers *50*; Loss of identity *54*; mutual trust, building of 45; ownership, image 46; paint over photograph *43*; reflection, students 51; support, MDOC 48; Tired of the Chaos *53*; working relationships 50
humility 45
humor 139, 140
Huxley, A. 128
hypervigilance 25

ID13 Project 95
IGP *see* Insight Garden Program
imposter syndrome 26
Indigenous people 150, 203
inequity 40, 86, 112, 171
inhumanity 59, 102, 104
Innovative Programming Grants (IPG) initiative 182
in-person associate degree program, California prison 178
in-person bachelor's degree program 26
insecurity 12
Insider Art exhibition 183–185
Insight Garden Program (IGP) 182–183
Institutional Review Board (IRB) 190–192
interactive prison cell 104, *105*
IPG initiative *see* Innovative Programming Grants
IRB *see* Institutional Review Board
Irwin, J. 15, 22, 180
isolation 32

Jackson, C. 129, 130
Jackson-Green, B.J. 190
John R. Lewis College 106, 110
Jordan College of Agricultural Sciences and Technology 183
Jordan, J. 68
Judith Beheading Holofernes 121

Kaba, M. 74
Kahlo, F. 120–122
Kallman, M. 140
Kaphar, T. 119
Kent State University 95
Kidder, K. 135, 136

King, E. 31, 36
Kingian nonviolence certification workshops 108, 109
King, J. 132

Lamberton, K. 156
Lancaster State Prison 23
language learning: beginning 136–137; expensive textbooks 135; fears and expectations 137–139; first day 134–135; grammatical errors 138–139; learning to laugh/laughing to learn 139–141; LIFE program 136–138, 141; teaching inside, preparations of 135–136
Leahy, J. 181
Lewis, J.R. 110
liberal arts curriculum 160
liberation 17, 61, 160
liberatory education 69, 74
libraries 169, 174
Life after Death and Elsewhere 90–91, *91*
LIFE program *see* Lipscomb Initiative for Education
life-without-the-possibilityof-parole (LWOP) 21, 24–26
Limits of Prison Education (Austin) 101
Lipscomb Initiative for Education (LIFE) program 136–138, 141
Lipscomb University 136, 141
lived experience 16, 29, 36, 68, 69, 182, 205
Lopez, J. 135
Lorde, A. 68
Love, B. 70, 72
Lowery, Y. 33
low self-esteem 12
LWOP *see* life-without-the-possibilityof-parole

Maine Department of Health and Human Services 36
Making the Connection project: business units 200; custodial officers 203–204; engagement leaders 202–203; focus 203; funds 198, 199; incarcerated learners 201–202; procurement 200–201; sustainable 199; UniSQ staff 199–200
Mandela, N. 180
Marking Time: Art in the Age of Mass Incarceration 131

232 *Index*

Martinez, J. 33
Mary-mount Manhattan's College program 117
Massachusetts Correctional Institution-Concord 6
Master of Social Work (MSW) degree 183
MCI *see* Moreau College Initiative
McIntosh, P. 71
Mcintyre, J. 65
MDOC *see* Michigan Department of Corrections
Michigan Department of Corrections (MDOC) 42, 45, 47, 48, 49, 155
Mimms, J. 187
Mitchell, J. 119, 120, 121
Mohanty, C. 71
Mora, R. 108, 109
Moreau College Initiative (MCI) 123, 126, 130, 132
Morin, K. 59, 61, 62
Mount Tamalpais College 178
movement schedule 5–6
Moyer-Duncan, C. 6
MSW *see* Master of Social Work
Mule Creek State Prison 76
mutual trust, building of 45

National Endowment for the Arts (NEA) 170, 171
Ndoh, R. 183–185
NEA *see* National Endowment for the Arts
neoclassicism 125
Nguyen, T. 28
No Name on the Street (Baldwin) 61
non-punitive learning environments: administrative barriers 151; adult education 146–148; education, purpose of 145–146; experiential knowledge 148–149; individual shortcomings 145; long-remand students 144; trauma-informed practices 150–151; universal accommodations 149–150
nonviolence 106–110
Norfolk prison 59, 60, 61, 63
Notes from Underground 163

Olatushani, N. 92
On Revolution (Arendt) 160
Opportunity Institute, the 181
oppression 32, 61, 62, 68, 70, 71, 74, 79, 80, 160, 161, 172

organized abandonment, the 71
Oshiro, G.E. 190
Owen, B. 178

PAC *see* Prison Arts Collective
Paris, D. 159
Paris, R. 87
Patel, L. 69
PCAP *see* Prison Creative Arts Project
"Peace Warriors" 107–109
Pedagogy of the Oppressed (Freire) 63
PEDs *see* personal education devices
peer support 25
Pell Grant funding 21, 31
Pepper 126
personal education devices (PEDs) 169
personality types, prison 24
Petersilia, J. 186
photographic collaboration *see Humanize the Numbers* collaborative photography project
photographic vision and carceral experience: aspirational quality 132–133; class time 124; conceptual thinking 129; *Doors of Perception, The* 128, 129; MCI 123, 126, 130, 132; *Pepper* 126; portrait photography 131–133; proto-photographic practices 124; still life, photographic genre 125–127, 127, 128; storage room 123–124; wildlife and nature photographs 129–130, 130
Picasso 121
Pine Tree Legal Assistance 36
Pitzer College 186
poetry class 171–172, 175
poetry writing classes 96–99
Pollack, S. 159
Positive Peace 109
positive social identity 26, 27
poverty 39, 59, 86, 90, 112, 175, 218
power of proximity 85
PPF *see* Progressive Programming Facility
Practical Activism Conference 104, 105, 106
PREA *see* Prison Rape Elimination Act
Prism Way, The 29
Prison Arts Collective (PAC) 19; barriers and challenges 190–192; collaborations and

input 194–196; collaborative installation 215, *216*; community partnerships 218; current research 192–194; grants 222–223; historical development 189–190; multidisciplinary arts classes 218–219, *219*; origami art *221*; "Redemption" 215, *216*; reflection 225; students, low socioeconomic status 218; student teachers, workshop *224*, *225*; volunteer process 222; workshop series 215
prison arts programs 101–102
Prison Arts Project 59
Prison BA Graduation Initiative pilot program 21, 23, 24, 26, 28
Prison Creative Arts Project (PCAP) 42, 48
prison creative writing: ACE courses 96–97; feedback and audience 100–101; journal entry *95*, 102–103; poetry writing class 98–99; prison arts programs 101–102; technology, access to 99–100; word choice 96
prison higher education *see* higher education in prison
Prison Rape Elimination Act (PREA) 134
prison-to-school pipeline 104
prison-university partnerships: bachelor's degree program 185–187; CDCR prisons 182–185; *Insider Art* exhibition 183–185; opening up prisons 178–180; Project Rebound 180–182; Readers' Circle 207–214; San Quentin 177, 178
Prison University Project 178
PRLA *see* Project Rebound Los Angeles
Progressive Programming Facility (PPF) 23, 24–26
Project Rebound 18, 19, 183, 186; campuses 181; creation of 180; CSU 22; at CSULA 22, 23; expansion 181; function 16; giving back, importance of 27; outreach work 181; student achievements 182; students as docents, exhibition 185; support to narrative 17; wrap-around services 15, 17
Project Rebound Los Angeles (PRLA) 22, 23, 27, 28
proximity 85–86

psychological abuse 104
punishment and higher education 159–160
punishment theory 18

Quiet Afternoon 126

Race, Prison, Justice Arts (RPJA) 59, 65; activism through arts 63; deep listening and art-making 64; public virtual gallery 64; race and mass incarceration 63
racism 86, 108, 110, 113, 146, 149
radical love 38, 39
Readers' Circle: beginning 207–209; challenges and opportunities 209–212; partnerships and programs 213; "plug and play" service-learning 212
recidivism 20, 27, 101, 109, 140, 155, 159, 160, 172, 198, 209
recreational programs 190
redemption 215, *216*
reentry journeys 13–14, 16; *see also* Project Rebound
rehabilitation: American Justice System 86; as punishment 158, 159; services, prison 18
respect, ethics of 106
revolutionary freedom 160–161
Rich, A. 69
Rivera, E. 109
Riverbend Maximum Security Institution 85, 86, 92
Rodin, A. 119
RPJA *see Race, Prison, Justice Arts*

Sacramento County Jail 78
sadness 33
Salomone, A.M. 135
San Diego State University 194, 195
San Francisco State University 15, 22
San Quentin: rehabilitative and educational opportunities 177; self-help programs 178; volunteers, presence of 178
Santa Cruz Barrios Unidos (SCBU) 104, *105*, 106
Sarah Lawrence College 171
SCBU *see* Santa Cruz Barrios Unidos
school-to-prison pipeline 28, 73
Search for Education, Elevation, and Knowledge (SEEK) 69
Second Chance Pell program 31
Sedaris, D. 94

234 *Index*

SEEK *see* Search for Education, Elevation, and Knowledge
self-actualization 11
self-care 9, 34
self-concept 147
self-corrections 139
self-doubt 39
self-esteem 45
self-formation 162
self-help: classes 25; groups 183–184; programs 178
self-identification 36
self-improvement 40
service-learning course 218
SNCC *see* Student Nonviolent Coordinating Committee, the
Snell, D. 182–185
sober living facility 13
social behavior 140
social debate 86
social inequality 36
social justice 34, 63, 74, 107, 109–112, 198
Soledad Correctional Training Facility 106, 108–110, *111*, 112, 113
solitary confinement 87, 104, 106
Solzhenitsyn, A. 91
Southern Maine Women's Reentry Center 31
Stanford Prison Experiment 104
Steerage, The 124, 125
Stevens, K. 170
Stevenson, B. 85
Stieglitz, A. 124
Strandquist, M. 42
St. Thomas Aquinas College, New York 87, 90, 92
Student Nonviolent Coordinating Committee, the (SNCC) 107
Suffolk County Jail 64
Sullivan Correctional Institution, Fallsberg 92
surrogate projects 88, 90
surveillance *vs.* observation 85
survivalism 78
suspicion *vs.* trust 85
Swain, S. 185
Szarkowski, J. 123, 125

Taconic and Bedford Hills Women's Facilities 117
Talladega Federal Correctional Institution 171
Taylor, B. 63

technology, access to 7, 99–100
Tennessee Prison for Women 134
Through Fences 95, 100, 102
Thumb Correctional Facility 42
time: alive 157; appreciation for 4; dead 157, 158; easy 156; hard 156, 158
transcommunality 106; Barrios Unidos Prison Project 106–109; CCG, work by 109; definition 106; ethics of respect 106; peacemaking class 106, 110, *111*, *112*
Transcommunality: From the Politics of Conversion to the Ethics of Respect 106
Transcommunal Peacemaking and Cooperation 106, 108, 109, 110, 113
transformation: daily routine 8–9; pandemic 9–10
transformation and redemption: academia 14; addiction 13, 16; community-based in-prison programs 18; homelessness 12, 13; PAC 19; Project Rebound 15–18; reentry journeys 13–14, 16; supportive community 17
transformative learning theory 147
transitions: cell 8; classroom 6–8; college 4–5; movement schedule 5–6; prison 4
trauma-informed practices 150–151
Trevino, A. 183
Tubman, H. 72
Tutwiler Prison for Women 171, 175

Underground Scholars 104
unhealed grief 35
UniSQ *see* University of Southern Queensland
universal accommodation policies 149–150
University of California, Santa Cruz (UCSC) 104; College Ten 110; Practical Activism Conference 104, *105*, 106; social justice and community 109–112; Transcommunal Peacemaking course 106, 110, *111*, *112*
University of Massachusetts 107
University of Michigan 42, 46, 51
University of Southern Maine 31
University of Southern Queensland (UniSQ): incarcerated learners 201–202, 205; Making the Connection project 198–205

Index   235

University of Utrecht 109
Urrutia, C. 185
"us *vs.* them" mentality 180, 183

Valley State Prison (VSP) 185–187
Vanderbilt University 86
Varghese, B. 108, 109
Veal, D. 104, 106
Vermont College of Fine Arts 118
violence 24, 29, 31, 33, 39, 73, 77, 83, 84, 87, 106, 107, 109, 112
Volunteer Banquet 179
VSP *see* Valley State Prison

Walters, W. 6
Warwick-Edinburgh Mental Wellbeing Scale (WEMWBS) 193–194
Watkins College of Art 87, 91, 92
Weiss, D. 126, 127
Welcome to the Zo (animated video project) 67
WEMWBS *see* Warwick-Edinburgh Mental Wellbeing Scale
Western Michigan University (WMU) 155, 162–163
Weston, E. 126
Westville Correctional Facility 123

What the Water Gave Me 120
White Australia Policy 60
white privilege 175
white supremacy 60
Wilderness and Razor Wire (Lamberton) 156
William Eggleston's Guide (Szarkowski) 123
Williams, T. 87
Windows from Prison 42
WMU *see* Western Michigan University
Wong, L. 180
Woods, T. 135
writing 78, 80, 83–84; *see also* prison creative writing
writing about art: Bedford Hills class 118; epistolary approach 118; interpretations 121–122; prompts, short writing exercise 119–120; reviewing essay 118–119; still life, describing of 120; three-part formula, essays 119

Yontz, B. 87

Zimbardo, P. 104

www.ingramcontent.com/pod-product-compliance
Lightning Source LLC
Jackson TN
JSHW061650200825
89703JS00008B/34